Emerging Technologies Law

Societal Constructs for Regulating Changing Technologies

Vol. 2

Victoria Sutton

Copyright © 2021 Victoria Sutton

All rights reserved. No part of this publication may be reproduced, stored in a retrieval system or transmitted in any form or by any means, electronic, mechanical or photocopying recording, or otherwise without the prior permission of the publisher.

Published by:
Vargas Publishing
P.O. Box 6801
Lubbock, TX 79493

ISBN: 978-0-9968186-9-8

The trouble with our times is that the future is not what it used to be."

Paul Valéry

We are at the start of what may be emerging as a new discipline of academic study: technology regulation, the study of how technologies are or should be regulated.

Bert-Jaap Koops
Tilburg University
Tilburg Institute for
Law, Technology, and Society
July 2, 2010

Table of Contents

Chapter 4. Administrative Law and Emerging Technologies

Chapter 5. International Law and Emerging Technologies

Chapter 6. Criminal Law and Emerging Technologies

Chapter 7. Tort Law and Emerging Technologies

Chapter 8. Intellectual Property Law and Emerging Technologies

Chapter 9. Banking and Finance Law and Emerging Technologies

Chapter 10. Scientific Evidence and Emerging Technologies

Chapter 11. Space Law

Chapter 12. Law of War and Emerging Technologies

PART 3. THE FIVE HORSEMEN of EMERGING TECHNOLOGIES
Chapter 13. Biotechnology

Chapter 14. Nanotechnology

Chapter 18. Research in Emerging Technologies Law

Prof. Del Marin, Law Librarian

Chapter 19. The Future and Emerging Technologies Law

Chapter 6

Criminal Law and Emerging Technologies

5.1.3 Criminal Law--Basics

Brigham and Women's Hospital in Boston made this statement after one of their physician's was robbed of his laptop:

"During the robbery, the assailants forced the victim to disclose the passcodes and encryption keys to these devices. Possession of the passcodes and encryption keys, along with the devices themselves, could provide an individual the ability to view information stored on the laptop or cell phone. . ."[1]

The types of crimes are evolving with the rapidly changing emerging technologies frontier. As Marc Goodman writes in Future Crimes, "Crime, too, has entered the age of Moore's law, and it has exponential consequences for us all."[2]

5.2.1   Criminal Law—Search and Seizure
History of 4th Amend. Search & Seizure
Expectation of Privacy

The law on the expectation of privacy begins with the Fourth Amendment which reads, "the right of the people to be secure in their persons, houses, papers and effects against unreasonable searches and seizures."

The following line of cases illustrates the development of the search analysis based on a "reasonable expectation of privacy" standard (*Katz*) which followed the early analysis based on a trespassory theory (*Olmstead*). These are cases which focus on emerging technologies which are sense-enhancing and collect information in new, better or enhanced ways, which may or

---

[1] http://www.databreachtoday.com/device-robbers-demand-encryption-keys-a-7573 .
[2] Marc Goodman, Future Crimes 40 (2015).

may not constitute a search using the degree of intrusion test originating in the trespassory theory analysis.

In one of the first cases to address the warrantless gathering of information without a physical trespass, the court in *Olmstead v. United States*[3] (1928), held that overheard conversations did not meet the criteria of trespass. Therefore, the court held, the existence of a search is dependent upon whether there is a physical trespass under local property law. For example, a microphone against the wall is not search; whereas a microphone fed through the wall is a search because it is a physical trespass.

The Supreme Court in the next case moved to a test based upon privacy interests, largely because of changes in technology where trespassory theories of physical invasion were yielding results of its analysis that were clearly affecting privacy where physical intrusions would be clearly unconstitutional without a warrant.

In *Katz v. United States*[4], a listening device against a telephone booth was utilized to enable the FBI to detect illegally transmitted wagering information across state lines, without a search warrant. Here, the technology detected vibrations in the glass of the phone booth, which set the standard for against the wall, rather than through the wall tests. In that case, Justice Harlan articulated the "reasonable expectation of privacy" test and replaced the property concept of search to some degree with a two prong test: (1) expectation of privacy; and (2) that the expectation of privacy be reasonable.

In *United States v. Knotts* (U.S., 1983) , the Court held that a tracking device on a car as long as it was in public, was not a search, because the same information could be acquired through visual surveillance.

Then in *Dow Chemical v. United States (U.S., 1986)*,[5] the court held about the changing technology that "the effect of modern life, with its technological and other advances, serves to eliminate or reduce a person's justified expectation of privacy. . ." Using the Katz analysis: (1) There WAS a subjective expectation of privacy; however (2) It was NOT reasonable, because anyone could have taken those pictures. Also, in Dow, the court determined whether an act is observable by the general public, it is unreasonable to expect privacy in that act.

Then in *California v. Greenwood*[6] (1988), the court found no reasonable expectation of privacy where garbage bags left on the curb before pickup, were readily accessible "to scavengers, snoops and other members of the public."
The continuing criticism of the Katz two-prong test has been that it is a circular argument — the Supreme Court protects only those expectations that are reasonable, while the only expectations that are reasonable are those which the Supreme Court is willing to protect.

Then in *Florida v. Riley*, 488 U.S. 445, 450 (1989), a low flying helicopter which observed marijuana growing in a garage with a partial roof was not a search because it was in the public view, since it was not uncommon for helicopters to fly at this elevation in this area.

---

[3] 277 U.S. 438 (1928).
[4] 389 U.S. 347 (1967).
[5] 476 U.S. 227 (1986).
[6] 486 U.S. 35 (1988).

5.2.2   Criminal Procedure—Search & Seizure
History of 4th Amend. Search & Seizure, Kyllo case, sniffing dog case

CIRCUITS HOLDINGS ON THERMAL IMAGING DEVICES
The Fifth, Eighth, Ninth and the Eleventh Circuits have held that thermal image detection was not a "search" within the meaning of the Fourth Amendment. No Circuit Court has held a conflicting opinion with these Circuits, except for a short period when the Tenth Circuit in United States v. Cusumano, 67 F.3d 1497 (10th Cir. 1995), found thermal imaging a search, but the opinion was vacated. A rehearing en banc resulted in that issue not being decided.
The U.S. Supreme Court decided Kyllo, June 14, 2001 and found that thermal image searches without a warrant violated the Fourth Amendment protection against warrantless search and seizure. The Kyllo court set a new standard that the technology must be in the public use, to fall outside of the reasonable expectation of privacy standard of Katz.

Given the new standard articulated in *Kyllo,* and new biotechnologies and bioinformatics capabilities, how will the court analyze emerging technologies? This standard can lead to absurd results as in the next case where it was acknowledged that a highly trained, sense-enhancing sniffing dog is not "in the public use".

Florida v. Jardines
569 U.S. 1 (2013)

. . . "Where, as here, the Government uses a device that is not in general public use, to explore details of the home that would previously have been unknowable without physical intrusion, the surveillance is a 'search' and is presumptively unreasonable without a warrant." Ibid.
That "firm" and "bright" rule governs this case: The police officers here conducted a search because they used a "device ... not in general public use" (a trained drug-detection dog) to "explore details of the home" (the presence of certain substances) that they would not otherwise have discovered without entering the premises.

And again, the dissent's argument that the device is just a dog cannot change the equation. As Kyllo made clear, the "sense-enhancing" tool at issue may be "crude" or "sophisticated," may be old or new (drug-detection dogs actually go back not "12,000 years" or "centuries," post, at 1420, 1424, 1428, but only a few decades), may be either smaller or bigger than a breadbox; still, "at least where (as here)" the device is not "in general public use," training it on a home violates our "minimal expectation of privacy"—an expectation "that exists, and that is acknowledged to be reasonable." 533 U.S., at 34, 36, 121 S.Ct. 2038.2 That does not mean the device *1420 is off-limits, as the dissent implies, see post, at 1425 – 1426; it just means police officers cannot use it to examine a home without a warrant or exigent circumstance. See Brigham City v. Stuart, 547 U.S. 398, 403–404, 126 S.Ct. 1943, 164 L.Ed.2d 650 (2006) (describing exigencies allowing the warrantless search of a home).

5.2.3   Criminal Procedure---Search & Seizure
GPS case, Cell phone case

The next cases address emerging technologies in communication technologies and new contexts for expectations of privacy.

City of Ontario v. Quon
560 U.S. ___ (2010)
Synopsis

Petitioner Ontario (hereinafter City) acquired alphanumeric pagers able to send and receive text messages. Its contract with its service provider, Arch Wireless, provided for a monthly limit on the number of characters each pager could send or receive, and specified that usage exceeding that number would result in an additional fee. The City issued the pagers to respondent Quon and other officers in its police department (OPD), also a petitioner here. When Quon and others exceeded their monthly character limits for several months running, petitioner Scharf, OPD's chief, sought to determine whether the existing limit was too low, i.e., whether the officers had to pay fees for sending work-related messages or, conversely, whether the overages were for personal messages. After Arch Wireless provided transcripts of Quon's and another employee's August and September 2002 text messages, it was discovered that many of Quon's messages were not work related, and some were sexually explicit. Scharf referred the matter to OPD's internal affairs division. The investigating officer used Quon's work schedule to redact from his transcript any messages he sent while off duty, but the transcript showed that few of his on-duty messages related to police business. Quon was disciplined for violating OPD rules. He and the other respondents—each of whom had exchanged text messages with Quon during August and September—filed this suit, alleging, inter alia, that petitioners violated their Fourth Amendment rights and the federal Stored Communications Act (SCA) by obtaining and reviewing the transcript of Quon's pager messages, and that Arch Wireless violated the SCA by giving the City the transcript. The District Court denied respondents summary judgment on the 2 ONTARIO v. QUON Syllabus constitutional claims, relying on the plurality opinion in O'Connor v. Ortega, 480 U.S. 709, to determine that Quon had a reasonable expectation of privacy in the content of his messages. Whether the audit was nonetheless reasonable, the court concluded, turned on whether Scharf used it for the improper purpose of determining if Quon was using his pager to waste time, or for the legitimate purpose of determining the efficacy of existing character limits to ensure that officers were not paying hidden work-related costs. After the jury concluded that Scharf's intent was legitimate, the court granted petitioners summary judgment on the ground they did not violate the Fourth Amendment.

The Ninth Circuit reversed. Although it agreed that Quon had a reasonable expectation of privacy in his text messages, the appeals court concluded that the search was not reasonable even though it was conducted on a legitimate, work-related rationale. The opinion pointed to a host of means less intrusive than the audit that Scharf could have used. The court further concluded that Arch Wireless had violated the SCA by giving the City the transcript.

Held: Because the search of Quon's text messages was reasonable, petitioners did not violate respondents' Fourth Amendment rights, and the Ninth Circuit erred by concluding otherwise. Pp. 7–17. (a) The Amendment guarantees a person's privacy, dignity, and security against arbitrary and invasive governmental acts, without regard to whether the government actor is investigating crime or performing another function. Skinner v. Railway Labor Executives' Assn., 489 U. S. 602, 613–614. It applies as well when the government acts in its capacity as an employer. Treasury Employees v. Von Raab, 489 U. S. 656, 665. The Members of the O'Connor Court disagreed on the proper analytical framework for Fourth Amendment claims against government employers. A four-Justice plurality concluded that the correct analysis has two steps. First, because "some [government] offices may be so open . . . that no expectation of privacy is reasonable," a court must consider "[t]he operational realities of the workplace" to determine if an employee's constitutional rights are implicated. 480 U. S., at 718. Second, where an employee has a legitimate privacy expectation, an employer's intrusion on that expectation "for noninvestigatory, work-related purposes, as well as for investigations of work-related misconduct, should be judged by the standard of reasonableness under all the circumstances." Id., at 725– 726.

JUSTICE SCALIA, concurring in the judgment, would have dispensed with the "operational realities" inquiry and concluded "that the offices of government employees . . . are [generally] covered by Fourth Amendment protections," id., at 731, but he would also have held "that government searches to retrieve work-related materials or Cite as: 560 U. S. ____ (2010) 3 Syllabus to investigate violations of workplace rules—searches of the sort that are regarded as reasonable and normal in the private-employer context—do not violate the . . . Amendment," id., at 732. Pp. 7–9. (b) Even assuming that Quon had a reasonable expectation of privacy in his text messages, the search was reasonable under both O'Connor approaches, the plurality's and JUSTICE SCALIA's. Pp. 9–17. (1) The Court does not resolve the parties' disagreement over Quon's privacy expectation. Prudence counsels caution before the facts in this case are used to establish far-reaching premises that define the existence, and extent, of privacy expectations of employees using employer-provided communication devices. Rapid changes in the dynamics of communication and information transmission are evident not just in the technology itself but in what society accepts as proper behavior. At present, it is uncertain how workplace norms, and the law's treatment of them, will evolve. Because it is therefore preferable to dispose of this case on narrower grounds, the Court assumes, arguendo, that: (1) Quon had a reasonable privacy expectation; (2) petitioners' review of the transcript constituted a Fourth Amendment search; and (3) the principles applicable to a government employer's search of an employee's physical office apply as well in the electronic sphere. Pp. 9–12. (2) Petitioners' warrantless review of Quon's pager transcript was reasonable under the O'Connor plurality's approach because it was motivated by a legitimate work-related purpose, and because it was not excessive in scope. See 480 U. S., at 726. There were "reasonable grounds for [finding it] necessary for a noninvestigatory work-related purpose," ibid., in that Chief Scharf had ordered the audit to determine whether the City's contractual character limit was sufficient to meet the City's needs. It was also "reasonably related to the objectives of the search," ibid., because both the City and OPD had a legitimate interest in ensuring that employees were not being forced to pay out of their own pockets for work-related expenses, or, on the other hand, that the City was not paying for extensive personal communications. Reviewing the transcripts was an efficient and expedient way to determine whether either of these factors caused Quon's overages. And the review was also not "excessively intrusive." Ibid. Although Quon had exceeded his monthly allotment a number of times, OPD requested transcripts for only August and September 2002 in order to obtain a large enough sample to decide the character limits' efficaciousness, and all the messages that Quon sent while off duty were redacted. And from OPD's perspective, the fact that Quon likely had only a limited privacy expectation lessened the risk that the review would intrude on highly private details of Quon's life. Similarly, because the City had a legitimate reason for the search and it was not excessively intrusive in light of that justification, the search would be "regarded as reasonable and normal in the private employer context" and thereby satisfy the approach of JUSTICE SCALIA's concurrence, id., at 732. Conversely, the Ninth Circuit's "least intrusive" means approach was inconsistent with controlling precedents. See, e.g., Vernonia School Dist. 47J v. Acton, 515 U. S. 646, 663. Pp. 12–16. (c) Whether the other respondents can have a reasonable expectation of privacy in their text messages to Quon need not be resolved. They argue that because the search was unreasonable as to Quon, it was also unreasonable as to them, but they make no corollary argument that the search, if reasonable as to Quon, could nonetheless be unreasonable as to them. Given this litigating position and the Court's conclusion that the search was reasonable as to Quon, these other respondents cannot prevail. Pp. 16–17. 529 F. 3d 892, reversed and remanded.

KENNEDY, J., delivered the opinion of the Court, in which ROBERTS, C. J., and STEVENS, THOMAS, GINSBURG, BREYER, ALITO, and SOTOMAYOR, JJ., joined, and in which SCALIA, J., joined except for Part III–A. STEVENS, J., filed a concurring opinion. SCALIA, J., filed an opinion concurring in part and concurring in the judgment.

OPINION (Excerpt)

Even if Quon had a reasonable expectation of privacy in his text messages, petitioners did not necessarily violate the Fourth Amendment by obtaining and reviewing the transcripts. Although as a general matter, warrantless searches "are per se unreasonable under the Fourth Amendment," there are "a few specifically established and well-delineated exceptions" to that general rule. Katz, supra, at 357. The Court has held that the "'special needs'" of the workplace justify one such exception.

. . . .

Furthermore, and again on the assumption that Quon had a reasonable expectation of privacy in the contents of his messages, the extent of an expectation is relevant to assessing whether the search was too intrusive. See Von 14 ONTARIO v. QUON Opinion of the Court Raab, supra, at 671; cf. Vernonia School Dist. 47J v. Acton, 515 U. S. 646, 654–657 (1995). Even if he could assume some level of privacy would inhere in his messages, it would not have been reasonable for Quon to conclude that his messages were in all circumstances immune from scrutiny. Quon was told that his messages were subject to auditing. As a law enforcement officer, he would or should have known that his actions were likely to come under legal scrutiny, and that this might entail an analysis of his on-the-job communications. Under the circumstances, a reasonable employee would be aware that sound management principles might require the audit of messages to determine whether the pager was being appropriately used. Given that the City issued the pagers to Quon and other SWAT Team members in order to help them more quickly respond to crises—and given that Quon had received no assurances of privacy—Quon could have anticipated that it might be necessary for the City to audit pager messages to assess the SWAT Team's performance in particular emergency situations.. . .

This approach was inconsistent with controlling precedents. This Court has "repeatedly refused to declare that only the 'least intrusive' search practicable can be reasonable under the Fourth Amendment." Vernonia, supra, at 663; see also, e.g., Board of Ed. of Independent School Dist. No. 92 of Pottawatomie Cty. v. Earls, 536 U. S. 822, 837 (2002); Illinois v. Lafayette, 462 U. S. 640, 647 (1983). That rationale "could raise insuperable barriers to the exercise of virtually all search-and-seizure powers," United States v. Martinez-Fuerte, 428 U. S. 543, 557, n. 12 (1976), because "judges engaged in post hoc evaluations of government conduct can almost always imagine some alternative means by which the objectives of the government might have been accomplished," Skinner, 489 U. S., at 629, n. 9 (internal quotation marks and brackets omitted). The analytic errors of the Court of Appeals in this case illustrate the necessity of this principle. Even assuming there were ways that OPD could have performed the search that would have been less intrusive, it does not follow that the search as conducted was unreasonable. Respondents argue that the search was per se unreasonable in light of the Court of Appeals' conclusion that Arch Wireless violated the SCA by giving the City the transcripts of Quon's text messages. The merits of the SCA claim are not before us. But even if the Court of Appeals was correct to conclude that the SCA forbade Arch Wireless from turning over the transcripts, it does not follow that petitioners' actions were unreasonable. Respondents point to no authority for the proposition that the existence of statutory protection renders a search per se unreasonable under the Fourth Amendment. And the precedents counsel otherwise. See Virginia v. Moore, 553 U. S. 164, 168 (2008) (search incident to an arrest that was illegal under state law was reasonable); California v. Greenwood, 486 U. S. 35, 43 (1988) (rejecting argument that if state law forbade police search of individual's garbage the search would violate the Fourth Amendment). Furthermore, respondents do not maintain that any OPD employee either violated the law him- or herself or knew or should have known that Arch Wireless, by turning over the transcript, would have violated the law. The otherwise reasonable search by OPD is not rendered unreasonable by the assumption that Arch Wireless violated the SCA by turning over the transcripts. Because the search was motivated by a legitimate workrelated purpose, and because it was not excessive in scope, the search was reasonable under the approach of the O'Connor plurality. 480 U. S., at 726. For these same reasons—that the employer had a legitimate reason for the search, and that the search was not excessively intrusive in light of that justification—the Court also concludes that the search would be "regarded as reasonable and normal in the private-employer context" and would satisfy the approach of JUSTICE SCALIA's concurrence. Id., at 732. The search was reasonable, and the Court of Appeals erred by holding to the contrary. Petitioners did not violate Quon's Fourth Amendment rights. C Finally, the Court must consider whether the search violated the Fourth Amendment rights of Jerilyn Quon, Florio, and Trujillo, the respondents who sent text mes Cite as: 560 U. S. _____ (2010) 17 Opinion of the Court sages to Jeff Quon. Petitioners and respondents disagree whether a sender of a text message can have a reasonable expectation of privacy in a message he knowingly sends to someone's employer-provided pager. It is not necessary to resolve this question in order to dispose of the case, however. Respondents argue that because "the search was unreasonable as to Sergeant Quon, it was also unreasonable as to his correspondents." Brief for Respondents 60 (some capitalization omitted; boldface deleted). They make no corollary argument that the search, if reasonable as to Quon, could nonetheless be unreasonable as to Quon's correspondents. See id., at 65–66. In light of this litigating position and the Court's conclusion that the search was reasonable as to Jeff Quon, it necessarily follows that these other respondents cannot prevail. * * * Because the search was reasonable, petitioners did not violate respondents' Fourth Amendment rights, and the court below erred by concluding otherwise. The judgment of the Court of Appeals for the Ninth Circuit is reversed, and the case is remanded for further proceedings consistent with this opinion.

It is so ordered

———————————————

United States v. Davis
754 F.3d 1205 (11th Cir. 2013)

As we suggested above, the question whether cell site location information is protected by the Fourth Amendment guarantees against warrantless searches has never been determined by this court or the Supreme Court. Two circuits have considered the question, but not in the context of the use of the evidence in a criminal proceeding. Also, one of those opinions issued before the Supreme Court's decision in *United States v. Jones,* —— U.S. ——, 132 S.Ct. 945, 181 L.Ed.2d 911 (2012), the most relevant Supreme Court precedent.

While Jones is distinguishable from the case before us, it concerned location information obtained by a technology sufficiently similar to that furnished in the cell site location information to make it clearly relevant to our analysis. The present case, like Jones, brings to the fore the existence of two distinct views of the interests protected by the Fourth Amendment's prohibition of unreasonable searches and seizures. The older of the two theories is the view that the Fourth Amendment protects the property rights of the people. This view is sometimes referred to as the "trespass" theory and "our Fourth Amendment jurisprudence was tied to common-law trespass, at least until the latter half of the 20th century." Jones, 132 S.Ct. at 949 (collecting authorities). However, in the twentieth century, a second view gradually developed: that is, that the Fourth Amendment guarantee protects the privacy rights of the people without respect to whether the alleged "search" constituted a trespass against property rights.

. . . .

While the Jones case does instruct our analysis of the controversy before us, it does not conclude it. As discussed at length above, Fourth Amendment jurisprudence has dual underpinnings with respect to the rights protected: the trespass theory and the privacy theory. In Jones, Justice Scalia delivered the decision of the Court in an opinion that analyzed the facts on the basis of the trespass theory. Because the agents had committed a trespass against the effects of Jones when they placed the GPS device on his car, the opinion of the Court did not need to decide whether Jones's reasonable expectation of privacy had been violated because his rights against trespass certainly had.

As the United States rightly points out, in the controversy before us there was no GPS device, no placement, and no physical trespass. Therefore, although Jones clearly removes all doubt as to whether electronically transmitted location information can be protected by the Fourth Amendment, it is not determinative as to whether the information in this case is so protected. The answer to that question is tied up with the emergence of the privacy theory of Fourth Amendment jurisprudence. While Jones is not controlling, we reiterate that it is instructive.

In Jones, Justice Scalia's opinion for the Court speaks on behalf of the author and three other Justices, Chief Justice Roberts, and Justices Kennedy and Thomas. It is, however, a true majority opinion, as Justice Sotomayor, who wrote separately, "join[ed] the majority's opinion." Jones, 132 S.Ct. at 957. However, she did so in a *1215 separate concurrence that thoroughly discussed the possible applicability of the privacy theory to the electronic data search. We note that she fully joined the majority's opinion, and was certainly part of the majority that held that such a search is violative under the trespass theory.

Four other justices concurred in the result in an opinion authored by Justice Alito, which relied altogether on the privacy theory. Justice Alito wrote, "I would analyze the question presented in this case by asking whether respondent's reasonable expectations of privacy were violated by the long-term monitoring of the movements of the vehicle he drove." Id. at 958 (Alito, J., concurring in the result). Justice Alito and the justices who joined him ultimately concurred in the result because they did conclude that "the lengthy monitoring that occurred in this case constituted a search under the Fourth Amendment." Id. at 964. Justice Sotomayor, in her separate concurrence, opined that it was not necessary to answer difficult questions concerning the applicability of the reasonable-expectation-of-privacy test to the Jones facts "because the government's physical intrusion on Jones' jeep supplies a narrower basis for decision." Id. at 957 (Sotomayor, J., concurring). Conspicuously, she also noted that "in cases involving even short-term monitoring, some unique attributes of GPS surveillance relevant to the Katz analysis will require particular attention." Id. at 955. She noted that electronic "monitoring generates a precise, comprehensive record of a person's public movements that reflects a wealth of detail about her familial, political, professional, religious, and sexual associations." Id. (citing People v. Weaver, 12 N.Y.3d 433, 882 N.Y.S.2d 357, 909 N.E.2d 1195, 1199 (2009)).

Even the opinion of the Court authored by Justice Scalia expressly did not reject the applicability of the privacy test. While chiding the concurrence for "mak[ing] Katz the exclusive test," the opinion of the Court expressly noted that "[s]ituations involving merely the transmission of electronic signals without trespass would remain subject to [the] Katz [privacy] analysis." Id. at 953. In light of the confluence of the three opinions in the Supreme Court's decision in Jones, we accept the proposition that the privacy theory is not only alive and well, but available to govern electronic information of search and seizure in the absence of trespass.

Having determined that the privacy theory of Fourth Amendment protection governs this controversy, we conclude that the appellant correctly asserts that the government's warrantless gathering of his cell site location information violated his reasonable expectation of privacy. The government argues that the gathering of cell site location information is factually distinguishable from the GPS data at issue in Jones. We agree that it is distinguishable; however, we believe the distinctions operate against the government's case rather than in favor of it.

Riley v. California
573 U. S. 373 (2014)
Syllabus

First Circuit reversed the denial of the motion to suppress and vacated the relevant convictions.

Held: The police generally may not, without a warrant, search digital information on a cell phone seized from an individual who has been arrested. Pp. 5–28.

(a) A warrantless search is reasonable only if it falls within a specific exception to the Fourth Amendment's warrant requirement. See Kentucky v. King, 563 U. S. ___, ___. The well-established exception at issue here applies when a warrantless search is conducted incident
to a lawful arrest.

Three related precedents govern the extent to which officers may search property found on or near an arrestee. *Chimel v. California*, 395 U. S. 752, requires that a search incident to arrest be limited to the area within the arrestee's immediate control, where it is justified by the interests in officer safety and in preventing evidence destruction.

In *United States v. Robinson*, 414 U. S. 218, the Court applied the Chimel analysis to a search of a cigarette pack found on the arrestee's person. It held that the risks identified in Chimel are present in all custodial arrests, 414 U. S., at 235, even when there is no specific concern about the loss of evidence or the threat to officers in a particular case, id., at 236. The trilogy concludes with Arizona v.Gant, 556 U. S. 332, which permits searches of a car where the arrestee is unsecured and within reaching distance of the passenger compartment, or where it is reasonable to believe that evidence of the crime of arrest might be found in the vehicle, id., at 343. Pp. 5–8.

(b) The Court declines to extend Robinson's categorical rule to searches of data stored on cell phones. Absent more precise guidance from the founding era, the Court generally determines whether to exempt a given type of search from the warrant requirement "by assessing,on the one hand, the degree to which it intrudes upon an individual's privacy and, on the other, the degree to which it is needed for the promotion of legitimate governmental interests." Wyoming v. Houghton, 526 U. S. 295, 300. That balance of interests supported the search incident to arrest exception in Robinson. But a search of digital information on a cell phone does not further the government interests identified in Chimel, and implicates substantially greater individual privacy interests than a brief physical search. Pp. 8–22.

(1) The digital data stored on cell phones does not present either Chimel risk. Pp. 10–15.
(i) Digital data stored on a cell phone cannot itself be used as a weapon to harm an arresting officer or to effectuate the arrestee's escape. Officers may examine

the phone's physical aspects to ensure that it will not be used as a weapon, but the data on the phone can

endanger no one. To the extent that a search of cell phone data might warn officers of an impending danger, e.g., that the arrestee's confederates are headed to the scene, such a concern is better addressed through consideration of case-specific exceptions to the warrant

requirement, such as exigent circumstances.

Carpenter v. United States
585 U.S. ___ (2018)

On writ of certiorari to the united states court of appeals for the sixth circuit
Decided, June 22, 2018

Chief Justice Roberts delivered the opinion of the Court.

This case presents the question whether the Government conducts a search under the Fourth Amendment when it accesses historical cell phone records that provide a comprehensive chronicle of the user's past movements.

I.A

There are 396 million cell phone service accounts in the United States—for a Nation of 326 million people. Cell phones perform their wide and growing variety of functions by connecting to a set of radio antennas called "cell sites." Although cell sites are usually mounted on a tower, they can also be found on light posts, flagpoles, church steeples, or the sides of buildings. Cell sites typically have several directional antennas that divide the covered area into sectors.

Cell phones continuously scan their environment looking for the best signal, which generally comes from the closest cell site. Most modern devices, such as smartphones, tap into the wireless network several times a minute whenever their signal is on, even if the owner is not using one of the phone's features. Each time the phone connects to a cell site, it generates a time-stamped record known as cell-site location information (CSLI). The precision of this information depends on the size of the geographic area covered by the cell site. The greater the concentration of cell sites, the smaller the coverage area. As data usage from cell phones has increased, wireless carriers have installed more cell sites to handle the traffic. That has led to increasingly compact coverage areas, especially in urban areas.

Wireless carriers collect and store CSLI for their own business purposes, including finding weak spots in their network and applying "roaming" charges when another carrier routes data through their cell sites. In addition, wireless carriers often sell aggregated location records to data brokers, without individual identifying information of the sort at issue here. While carriers have long retained CSLI for the start and end of incoming calls, in recent years phone companies have also collected location information from the transmission of text messages and routine data connections. Accordingly, modern cell phones generate increasingly vast amounts of increasingly precise CSLI.

B

In 2011, police officers arrested four men suspected of robbing a series of Radio Shack and (ironically enough) T-Mobile stores in Detroit. One of the men confessed that, over the previous four months, the group (along with a rotating cast of getaway drivers and lookouts) had robbed nine different stores in Michigan and Ohio. The suspect identified 15 accomplices who had participated in the heists and gave the FBI some of their cell phone numbers; the FBI then reviewed his call records to identify additional numbers that he had called around the time of the robberies.

Based on that information, the prosecutors applied for court orders under the Stored Communications Act to obtain cell phone records for petitioner Timothy Carpenter and several other suspects. That statute, as amended in 1994, permits the Government to compel the disclosure of certain telecommunications records when it "offers specific and articulable facts showing that there are reasonable grounds to believe" that the records sought "are relevant and material to an ongoing criminal investigation." 18 U. S. C. §2703(d). Federal Magistrate Judges issued two orders directing Carpenter's wireless carriers—MetroPCS and Sprint— to disclose "cell/site sector [information] for [Carpenter's] telephone[ ] at call origination and at call termination for incoming and outgoing calls" during the four-month period when the string of robberies occurred. App. to Pet. for Cert. 60a, 72a. The first order sought 152 days of cell-site records from MetroPCS, which produced records spanning 127 days. The second order requested seven days of CSLI from Sprint, which produced two days of records covering the period when Carpenter's phone was "roaming" in northeastern Ohio. Altogether the Government obtained 12,898 location points cataloging Carpenter's movements— an average of 101 data points per day.

Carpenter was charged with six counts of robbery and an additional six counts of carrying a firearm during a federal crime of violence. See 18 U. S. C. §§924(c), 1951(a). Prior to trial, Carpenter moved to suppress the cell-site data provided by the wireless carriers. He argued that the Government's seizure of the records violated the Fourth Amendment because they had been obtained without a warrant supported by probable cause. The District Court denied the motion. App. to Pet. for Cert. 38a–39a.

At trial, seven of Carpenter's confederates pegged him as the leader of the operation. In addition, FBI agent Christopher Hess offered expert testimony about the cell-site data. Hess explained that each time a cell phone taps into the wireless network, the carrier logs a time-stamped record of the cell site and particular sector that were used. With this information, Hess produced maps that placed Carpenter's phone near four of the charged robberies. In the Government's view, the location records clinched the case: They confirmed that

Carpenter was "right where the . . . robbery was at the exact time of the robbery." App. 131 (closing argument). Carpenter was convicted on all but one of the firearm counts and sentenced to more than 100 years in prison.

The Court of Appeals for the Sixth Circuit affirmed. 819 F. 3d 880 (2016). The court held that Carpenter lacked a reasonable expectation of privacy in the location information collected by the FBI because he had shared that information with his wireless carriers. Given that cell phone users voluntarily convey cell-site data to their carriers as "a means of establishing communication," the court concluded that the resulting business records are not entitled to Fourth Amendment protection. Id., at 888 (quoting Smith v. Maryland, 442 U. S. 735, 741 (1979)).

We granted certiorari. 582 U. S. ___ (2017).

II. A

The Fourth Amendment protects "[t]he right of the people to be secure in their persons, houses, papers, and effects, against unreasonable searches and seizures." The "basic purpose of this Amendment," our cases have recognized, "is to safeguard the privacy and security of individuals against arbitrary invasions by governmental officials." Camara v. Municipal Court of City and County of San Francisco, 387 U. S. 523, 528 (1967). The Founding generation crafted the Fourth Amendment as a "response to the reviled 'general warrants' and 'writs of assistance' of the colonial era, which allowed British officers to rummage through homes in an unrestrained search for evidence of criminal activity." Riley v. California, 573 U. S. ___, ___ (2014) (slip op., at 27). In fact, as John Adams recalled, the patriot James Otis's 1761 speech condemning writs of assistance was "the first act of opposition to the arbitrary claims of Great Britain" and helped spark the Revolution itself. Id., at ___ – ___ (slip op., at 27–28) (quoting 10 Works of John Adams 248 (C. Adams ed. 1856)).

For much of our history, Fourth Amendment search doctrine was "tied to common-law trespass" and focused on whether the Government "obtains information by physically intruding on a constitutionally protected area." United States v. Jones, 565 U. S. 400, 405, 406, n. 3 (2012). More recently, the Court has recognized that "property rights are not the sole measure of Fourth Amendment violations." Soldal v. Cook County, 506 U. S. 56, 64 (1992). In Katz v. United States, 389 U. S. 347, 351 (1967), we established that "the Fourth Amendment protects people, not places," and expanded our conception of the Amendment to protect certain expectations of privacy as well. When an individual "seeks to preserve something as private," and his expectation of privacy is "one that society is prepared to recognize as reasonable," we have held that official intrusion into that private sphere generally qualifies as a search and requires a warrant supported by probable cause. Smith, 442 U. S., at 740 (internal quotation marks and alterations omitted).

Although no single rubric definitively resolves which expectations of privacy are entitled to protection,[1] the analysis is informed by historical understandings "of what was deemed an unreasonable search and seizure when [the Fourth Amendment] was adopted." Carroll v. United States, 267 U. S. 132, 149 (1925). On this score, our cases have recognized some basic guideposts. First, that the Amendment seeks to secure "the privacies of life" against "arbitrary power." Boyd v. United States, 116 U. S. 616, 630 (1886). Second, and relatedly, that a central aim of the Framers was "to place obstacles in the way of a too permeating police surveillance." United States v. Di Re, 332 U. S. 581, 595 (1948).

We have kept this attention to Founding-era understandings in mind when applying the Fourth Amendment to innovations in surveillance tools. As technology has enhanced the Government's capacity to encroach upon areas normally guarded from inquisitive eyes, this Court has sought to "assure[ ] preservation of that degree of privacy against government that existed when the Fourth Amendment was adopted." Kyllo v. United States, 533 U. S. 27, 34 (2001). For that reason, we rejected in Kyllo a "mechanical interpretation" of the Fourth Amendment and held that use of a thermal imager to detect heat radiating from the side of the defendant's home was a search. Id., at 35. Because any other conclusion would leave homeowners "at the mercy of advancing technology," we determined that the Government—absent a warrant—could not capitalize on such new sense-enhancing technology to explore what was happening within the home. Ibid.

Likewise in Riley, the Court recognized the "immense storage capacity" of modern cell phones in holding that police officers must generally obtain a warrant before searching the contents of a phone. 573 U. S., at ___ (slip op., at 17). We explained that while the general rule allowing warrantless searches incident to arrest "strikes the appropriate balance in the context of physical objects, neither of its rationales has much force with respect to" the vast store of sensitive information on a cell phone. Id., at ___ (slip op., at 9).

B

The case before us involves the Government's acquisition of wireless carrier cell-site records revealing the location of Carpenter's cell phone whenever it made or received calls. This sort of digital data—personal location information maintained by a third party—does not fit neatly under existing precedents. Instead, requests for cell-site records lie at the intersection of two lines of cases, both of which inform our understanding of the privacy interests at stake.

The first set of cases addresses a person's expectation of privacy in his physical location and movements. In United States v. Knotts, 460 U. S. 276 (1983), we considered the Government's use of a "beeper" to aid in tracking a vehicle through traffic. Police officers in that case planted a beeper in a container of chloroform before it was purchased by one of Knotts's co-conspirators. The officers (with intermittent aerial assistance) then followed the automobile carrying the container from Minneapolis to Knotts's cabin in Wisconsin, relying on the beeper's signal to help keep the vehicle in view. The Court concluded that the "augment[ed]" visual surveillance did not constitute a search because "[a] person traveling in an automobile on public thoroughfares has no reasonable expectation of privacy in his movements from one place to another." Id., at 281, 282. Since the movements of the vehicle and its final destination had been "voluntarily conveyed to anyone who wanted to look," Knotts could not assert a privacy interest in the information obtained. Id., at 281.

This Court in Knotts, however, was careful to distinguish between the rudimentary tracking facilitated by the beeper and more sweeping modes of surveillance. The Court emphasized the "limited use which the government made of the signals from this particular beeper" during a discrete "automotive journey." Id., at 284, 285. Significantly, the Court reserved the question whether "different constitutional principles may be applicable" if "twenty-four hour surveillance of any citizen of this country [were] possible." Id., at 283–284.

Three decades later, the Court considered more sophisticated surveillance of the sort envisioned in Knotts and found that different principles did indeed apply. In United States v. Jones, FBI agents installed a GPS tracking device on Jones's vehicle and remotely monitored the vehicle's movements for 28 days. The Court decided the case based on the Government's physical trespass of the vehicle. 565 U. S., at 404–405. At the same time, five Justices agreed that related privacy concerns would be raised by, for example, "surreptitiously activating a stolen vehicle detection system" in Jones's car to track Jones himself, or conducting GPS tracking of his cell phone. Id., at 426, 428 (Alito, J., concurring in judgment); id., at 415 (Sotomayor, J., concurring). Since GPS monitoring of a vehicle tracks "every movement" a person makes in that vehicle, the concurring Justices concluded that "longer term GPS monitoring in investigations of most offenses impinges on expectations of privacy"—regardless whether those movements were disclosed to the public at large. Id., at 430 (opinion of Alito, J.); id., at 415 (opinion of Sotomayor, J.).. . . .

III

The question we confront today is how to apply the Fourth Amendment to a new phenomenon: the ability to chronicle a person's past movements through the record of his cell phone signals. Such tracking partakes of many of the qualities of the GPS monitoring we considered in Jones. Much like GPS tracking of a vehicle, cell phone location information is detailed, encyclopedic, and effortlessly compiled. . . .

A

A person does not surrender all Fourth Amendment protection by venturing into the public sphere. To the contrary, "what [one] seeks to preserve as private, even in an area accessible to the public, may be constitutionally protected." Katz, 389 U. S., at 351–352. A majority of this Court has already recognized that individuals have a reasonable expectation of privacy in the whole of their physical movements. Jones, 565 U. S., at 430 (Alito, J., concurring in judgment); id., at 415 (Sotomayor, J., concurring). Prior to the digital age, law enforcement might have pursued a suspect for a brief stretch, but doing so "for any extended period of time was difficult and costly and therefore rarely undertaken." Id., at 429 (opinion of Alito, J.). For that reason, "society's expectation has been that law enforcement agents and others would not—and indeed, in the main, simply could not—secretly monitor and catalogue every single movement of an individual's car for a very long period." Id., at 430.

Allowing government access to cell-site records contravenes that expectation. Although such records are generated for commercial purposes, that distinction does not negate Carpenter's anticipation of privacy in his physical location. Mapping a cell phone's location over the course of 127 days provides an all-encompassing record of the holder's whereabouts. As with GPS information, the time-stamped data provides an intimate window into a person's life, revealing not only his particular movements, but through them his "familial, political, professional, religious, and sexual associations." Id., at 415 (opinion of Sotomayor, J.). These location records "hold for many Americans the 'privacies of life.' " Riley, 573 U. S., at ___ (slip op., at 28) (quoting Boyd, 116 U. S., at 630). And like GPS monitoring, cell phone tracking is remarkably easy, cheap, and efficient compared to traditional investigative tools. With just the click of a button, the Government can access each carrier's deep repository of historical location information at practically no expense.

In fact, historical cell-site records present even greater privacy concerns than the GPS monitoring of a vehicle we considered in Jones. Unlike the bugged container in Knotts or the car in Jones, a cell phone—almost a "feature of human anatomy," Riley, 573 U. S., at ___ (slip op., at 9)—tracks nearly exactly the movements of its owner. While individuals regularly leave their vehicles, they compulsively carry cell phones with them all the time. A cell phone faithfully follows its owner beyond public thoroughfares and into private residences, doctor's offices, political headquarters, and other potentially revealing locales. See id., at ___ (slip op., at 19) (noting that "nearly three-quarters of smart phone users report being within five feet of their phones most of the time, with 12% admitting that they even use their phones in the shower"); contrast Cardwell v. Lewis, 417 U. S. 583, 590 (1974) (plurality opinion) ("A car has little capacity for escaping public scrutiny."). Accordingly, when the Government tracks the location of a cell phone it achieves near perfect surveillance, as if it had attached an ankle monitor to the phone's user.

Moreover, the retrospective quality of the data here gives police access to a category of information otherwise unknowable. In the past, attempts to reconstruct a person's movements were limited by a dearth of records and the frailties of recollection. With access to CSLI, the Government can now travel back in time to retrace a person's whereabouts, subject only to the retention polices of the wireless carriers, which currently maintain records for up to five years. Critically, because location information is continually logged for all of the 400 million devices in the United States—not just those belonging to persons who might happen to come under investigation—this newfound tracking capacity runs against everyone. Unlike with the GPS device in Jones, police need not even know in advance whether they want to follow a particular individual, or when.

Whoever the suspect turns out to be, he has effectively been tailed every moment of every day for five years, and the police may—in the Government's view—call upon the results of that surveillance without regard to the constraints of the Fourth Amendment. Only the few with- out cell phones could escape this tireless and absolute surveillance.

The Government and Justice Kennedy contend, however, that the collection of CSLI should be permitted because the data is less precise than GPS information. Not to worry, they maintain, because the location records did "not on their own suffice to place [Carpenter] at the crime scene"; they placed him within a wedge-shaped sector ranging from one-eighth to four square miles. Brief for United States 24; see post, at 18–19. Yet the Court has already rejected the proposition that "inference insulates a search." Kyllo, 533 U. S., at 36. From the 127 days of location data it received, the Government could, in combination with other information, deduce a detailed log of Carpenter's movements, including when he was at the site of the robberies. And the Government thought the CSLI accurate enough to highlight it during the closing argument of his trial. App. 131.

At any rate, the rule the Court adopts "must take account of more sophisticated systems that are already in use or in development." Kyllo, 533 U. S., at 36. While the records in this case reflect the state of technology at the start of the decade, the accuracy of CSLI is rapidly approaching GPS-level precision. As the number of cell sites has proliferated, the geographic area covered by each cell sector has shrunk, particularly in urban areas. In addition, with new technology measuring the time and angle of signals hitting their towers, wireless carriers already have the capability to pinpoint a phone's location within 50 meters. Brief for Electronic Frontier Foundation et al. as Amici Curiae 12 (describing triangulation methods that estimate a device's location inside a given cell sector).

Accordingly, when the Government accessed CSLI from the wireless carriers, it invaded Carpenter's reason- able expectation of privacy in the whole of his physical movements.

B

The Government's primary contention to the contrary is that the third-party doctrine governs this case. In its view, cell-site records are fair game because they are "business records" created and maintained by the wireless carriers. The Government (along with Justice Kennedy) recognizes that this case features new technology, but asserts that the legal question nonetheless turns on a garden-variety request for information from a third-party witness. Brief for United States 32–34; post, at 12–14.

The Government's position fails to contend with the seismic shifts in digital technology that made possible the tracking of not only Carpenter's location but also everyone else's, not for a short period but for years and years. Sprint

Corporation and its competitors are not your typical witnesses. Unlike the nosy neighbor who keeps an eye on comings and goings, they are ever alert, and their memory is nearly infallible. There is a world of difference between the limited types of personal information addressed in Smith and Miller and the exhaustive chronicle of location information casually collected by wireless carriers today. The Government thus is not asking for a straightforward application of the third-party doctrine, but instead a significant extension of it to a distinct category of information.

. . .

Our decision today is a narrow one. We do not express a view on matters not before us: real-time CSLI or "tower dumps" (a download of information on all the devices that connected to a particular cell site during a particular interval). We do not disturb the application of Smith and Miller or call into question conventional surveillance techniques and tools, such as security cameras. Nor do we address other business records that might incidentally reveal location information. Further, our opinion does not consider other collection techniques involving foreign affairs or national security. As Justice Frankfurter noted when considering new innovations in airplanes and radios, the Court must tread carefully in such cases, to ensure that we do not "embarrass the future." Northwest Airlines, Inc. v. Minnesota, 322 U. S. 292, 300 (1944).[4]

IV

Having found that the acquisition of Carpenter's CSLI was a search, we also conclude that the Government must generally obtain a warrant supported by probable cause before acquiring such records. Although the "ultimate measure of the constitutionality of a governmental search is 'reasonableness,' " our cases establish that warrantless searches are typically unreasonable where "a search is undertaken by law enforcement officials to discover evidence of criminal wrongdoing." Vernonia School Dist. 47J v. Acton, 515 U. S. 646, 652–653 (1995). Thus, "[i]n the absence of a warrant, a search is reasonable only if it falls within a specific exception to the warrant requirement." Riley, 573 U. S., at ___ (slip op., at 5).

The Government acquired the cell-site records pursuant to a court order issued under the Stored Communications Act, which required the Government to show "reasonable grounds" for believing that the records were "relevant and material to an ongoing investigation." 18 U. S. C. §2703(d). That showing falls well short of the probable cause required for a warrant. The Court usually requires "some quantum of individualized suspicion" before a search or seizure may take place. United States v. Martinez-Fuerte, 428 U. S. 543, 560–561 (1976). Under the standard in the Stored Communications Act, however, law enforcement need only show that the cell-site evidence might be pertinent to an ongoing investigation—a "gigantic" departure from the probable cause rule, as the Government explained below. App. 34. Consequently, an order issued under

Section 2703(d) of the Act is not a permissible mechanism for accessing historical cell-site records. Before compelling a wireless carrier to turn over a subscriber's CSLI, the Government's obligation is a familiar one—get a warrant.

Justice Alito contends that the warrant requirement simply does not apply when the Government acquires records using compulsory process. Unlike an actual search, he says, subpoenas for documents do not involve the direct taking of evidence; they are at most a "constructive search" conducted by the target of the subpoena. Post, at 12. Given this lesser intrusion on personal privacy, Justice Alito argues that the compulsory production of records is not held to the same probable cause standard. In his view, this Court's precedents set forth a categorical rule—separate and distinct from the third-party doctrine—subjecting subpoenas to lenient scrutiny without regard to the suspect's expectation of privacy in the records. Post, at 8–19.

But this Court has never held that the Government may subpoena third parties for records in which the suspect has a reasonable expectation of privacy. Almost all of the examples Justice Alito cites, see post, at 14–15, contemplated requests for evidence implicating diminished pri- vacy interests or for a corporation's own books.[5] The lone exception, of course, is Miller, where the Court's analysis of the third-party subpoena merged with the application of the third-party doctrine. 425 U. S., at 444 (concluding that Miller lacked the necessary privacy interest to contest the issuance of a subpoena to his bank).

Justice Alito overlooks the critical issue. At some point, the dissent should recognize that CSLI is an entirely different species of business record—something that implicates basic Fourth Amendment concerns about arbitrary government power much more directly than corporate tax or payroll ledgers. When confronting new concerns wrought by digital technology, this Court has been careful not to uncritically extend existing precedents. See Riley, 573 U. S., at ___ (slip op., at 10) ("A search of the information on a cell phone bears little resemblance to the type of brief physical search considered [in prior precedents].").

If the choice to proceed by subpoena provided a categorical limitation on Fourth Amendment protection, no type of record would ever be protected by the warrant requirement. Under Justice Alito's view, private letters, digital contents of a cell phone—any personal information reduced to document form, in fact—may be collected by subpoena for no reason other than "official curiosity." United States v. Morton Salt Co., 338 U. S. 632, 652 (1950). Justice Kennedy declines to adopt the radical implications of this theory, leaving open the question whether the warrant requirement applies "when the Government obtains the modern-day equivalents of an individual's own 'papers' or 'effects,' even when those papers or effects are held by a third party. " Post, at 13 (citing United States v. Warshak, 631 F. 3d 266, 283–288 (CA6 2010)). That would be a sensible exception, because it would prevent the subpoena doctrine from overcoming any reasonable expectation of privacy. If the third-party doctrine does not apply to the "modern-day equivalents of an individual's own 'papers' or 'effects,' " then the clear implication is that the documents should receive full Fourth Amendment protection. We simply think that such protection should extend as well to a detailed log of a person's movements over several years.

This is certainly not to say that all orders compelling the production of documents will require a showing of probable cause. The Government will be able to use subpoenas to acquire records in the overwhelming majority of investigations. We hold only that a warrant is required in the rare case where the suspect has a legitimate privacy interest in records held by a third party.

Further, even though the Government will generally need a warrant to access CSLI, case-specific exceptions may support a warrantless search of an individual's cell-site records under certain circumstances. "One well-recognized exception applies when ' "the exigencies of the situation" make the needs of law enforcement so compelling that [a] warrantless search is objectively reasonable under the Fourth Amendment.' " Kentucky v. King, 563 U. S. 452, 460 (2011) (quoting Mincey v. Arizona, 437 U. S. 385, 394 (1978)). Such exigencies include the need to pursue a fleeing suspect, protect individuals who are threatened with imminent harm, or prevent the imminent destruction of evidence. 563 U. S., at 460, and n. 3.

As a result, if law enforcement is confronted with an urgent situation, such fact-specific threats will likely justify the warrantless collection of CSLI. Lower courts, for instance, have approved warrantless searches related to bomb threats, active shootings, and child abductions. Our decision today does not call into doubt warrantless access to CSLI in such circumstances. While police must get a warrant when collecting CSLI to assist in the mine-run criminal investigation, the rule we set forth does not limit their ability to respond to an ongoing emergency.

*   *   *

As Justice Brandeis explained in his famous dissent, the Court is obligated—as "[s]ubtler and more far-reaching means of invading privacy have become available to the Government"—to ensure that the "progress of science" does not erode Fourth Amendment protections. Olmstead v. United States, 277 U. S. 438, 473–474 (1928). Here the progress of science has afforded law enforcement a powerful new tool to carry out its important responsibilities. At the same time, this tool risks Government encroachment of the sort the Framers, "after consulting the lessons of history," drafted the Fourth Amendment to prevent. Di Re, 332 U. S., at 595.

We decline to grant the state unrestricted access to a wireless carrier's database of physical location information. In light of the deeply revealing nature of CSLI, its depth, breadth, and comprehensive reach, and the inescapable and automatic nature of its collection, the fact that such information is gathered by a third party does not make it any less deserving of Fourth Amendment protection. The Government's acquisition of the cell-site records here was a search under that Amendment.

The judgment of the Court of Appeals is reversed, and the case is remanded for further proceedings consistent with this opinion.

It is so ordered.

5.3.1   Criminal Procedure – Search & Seizure of DNA
DNA, DNA collection from arrestees since 1995
Maryland v. King

In *Illinois v. Wealer*, the use of DNA data banks was relatively new, where eleven states had such legislation to provide for DNA data banks. Only two other challenges to the collection of DNA samples from incarcerated persons had arisen at the time of this case.

Illinois v. Wealer
(App. Ct.,Ill., 2d D., 1994)

. . . .

It is beyond dispute that the State has a legitimate interest in deterring and prosecuting recidivist acts committed by sex offenders. Its interest is especially compelling when we consider that sex offenders frequently target children as their victims. Additionally, the State has an interest in establishing the identity of convicted sex offenders where traditional methods of identification might prove otherwise inadequate or inconclusive. Moreover, in addition to solving future crimes, the use of DNA evidence can be used to aid identification of repeat offenders who attempt to otherwise conceal or alter their identity. See Jones, 962 F.2d at 308.

The statutorily mandated DNA testing scheme is closely related to the State's interest in deterring and prosecuting recidivist acts committed by sex offenders because it provides an improved technological method for identifying and eliminating potential suspects.

Next, the privacy interest that a convicted sex offender has in his or her identity is minimal. The analogy to fingerprints is convincing because the blood and saliva sampling mandated under section 5-4-3 infringes on similar privacy interests. See Olivas, 122 Wash. 2d at , 856 P.2d at 1093 (Utter, J., Concurring).

"When a suspect is arrested upon probable cause, his identification becomes a matter of legitimate state interest and he can hardly claim privacy in it. We accept this proposition because the identification of suspects is relevant not only to solving the crime for which the suspect is arrested, but also for maintaining a permanent record to solve other past and future crimes. This becomes readily apparent when we consider the universal approbation of 'booking' procedures that are followed for every suspect arrested for a felony, whether or not the proof of a particular suspect's crime will involve the use of fingerprint identification. * * * While we do not accept even this small level of intrusion for free persons without

Fourth Amendment constraint [citation], the same does not hold true for those lawfully confined to the custody of the state." Jones, 962 F.2d at 306.

This article collects recent notable decisions and scholarship appearing in the aftermath of Maryland v. King.

Unwarranted DNA Sampling: The Legacy of Maryland v. King[7]
By Ken Strutin, Published on May 11, 2014

DNA forensics is about information, privacy and the presumption of innocence. It has become the determinant for identification, solving cold cases and exonerating the innocent. At its core, it is an inestimable library of personal data. Thus, courts and legislatures have been attempting to balance the interests of the individual in protecting their genetic information with the usefulness and necessity of that same data for criminal investigation.

In *Maryland v. King*, 133 S.Ct. 1958 (2013), the U.S. Supreme Court legitimized warrantless DNA sampling from felony arrestees as a booking procedure.1 In fact, they proclaimed genetic identification the new fingerprint.2 Still, the information that can potentially be gleaned from a person's genome is incalculable compared with the finite data revealed by traditional biometrics.3 In the wake of this decision, the states will have the opportunity to reconsider their DNA collection laws,4 whether to amend them or for those without to enact them,5 under the Federal and their respective state constitutions.6 At the same time, the Court's decision has enlivened the debate over the end result of arrestee sampling,7 i.e., the expansion of forensic databases and the applications for the use of this data.8 And it should be noted that any DNA or forensic database is a composite of intertwined informational and legal values that pose competing and conflicting questions about the analytics (accuracy, reliability and validity) of the data and the lawfulness (constitutionality) of its gathering.

Holding: When officers make an arrest supported by probable cause to hold a suspect for a serious offense and bring him to the station to be detained in custody, taking and analyzing a cheek swab of the arrestee's DNA is, like fingerprinting and photographing, a legitimate police booking procedure that is reasonable under the Fourth Amendment.[8]

This article collects recent notable decisions and scholarship appearing in the aftermath of Maryland v. King.9

---

[7] http://www.llrx.com/features/dnasampling.htm .
[8] SCOTUS website http://www.scotusblog.com/case-files/cases/maryland-v-king/ .

CASES

Maryland v. King, 569 U.S. ___ (2013), 133 S.Ct. 1958 (2013)

"In light of the context of a valid arrest supported by probable cause respondent's expectations of privacy were not offended by the minor intrusion of a brief swab of his cheeks. By contrast, that same context of arrest gives rise to significant state interests in identifying respondent not only so that the proper name can be attached to his charges but also so that the criminal justice system can make informed decisions concerning pretrial custody. Upon these considerations the Court concludes that DNA identification of arrestees is a reasonable search that can be considered part of a routine booking procedure. When officers make an arrest supported by probable cause to hold for a serious offense and they bring the suspect to the station to be detained in custody, taking and analyzing a cheek swab of the arrestee's DNA is, like fingerprinting and photographing, a legitimate police booking procedure that is reasonable under the Fourth Amendment."

Haskell v. Harris, No. 10-15152 (9th Cir. March 20, 2014)

"California law requires that all persons arrested for or charged with any felony or attempted felony submit DNA samples for inclusion in law enforcement databases. Cal. Penal Code S 296(a)(2), (4). Plaintiffs brought a class action under 42 U.S.C. S 1983, alleging that the law is unconstitutional on its face and as applied to the certified class, which includes "[a]ll persons who are, or will be, compelled to submit to the search and seizure of their body tissue and DNA under California Penal Code S 296(a)(2)(C) solely by reason of the fact that they have been arrested for, or charged with, a felony offense by California state or local officials." The district court denied a motion for a preliminary injunction, Haskell v. Brown, 677 F. Supp. 2d 1187, 1189-90 (N.D. Cal. 2009), and plaintiffs appealed, 28 U.S.C. S 1292(a)(1).

Plaintiffs' facial and as-applied challenges turn on essentially the same question: Is California's DNA collection scheme constitutional as applied to anyone "arrested for, or charged with, a felony offense by California state or local officials?" After *Maryland v. King*, 133 S.Ct. 1958 (2013), the answer is clearly yes. Plaintiffs' counsel conceded as much at oral argument. Given that concession, plaintiffs cannot show that the district court abused its discretion in denying a preliminary injunction that would apply to the entire class. See *Winter*, 555 U.S. at 20; *Alliance for the Wild Rockies*, 632 F.3d at 1131.

Plaintiffs ask us to enter a preliminary injunction applicable only to a smaller class consisting of individuals arrested for certain felonies that are not, in plaintiffs' view, covered by *Maryland v. King*. But we are a court of review, not first view: We are limited to deciding whether the district court abused its discretion in denying the injunction plaintiffs sought. See *Bull v. City & Cnty. of S.F.*, 595 F.3d 964, 967-68 (9th Cir. 2010) (en banc). If plaintiffs believe they're entitled to a preliminary injunction as to a smaller class, they are free to seek it from the district court and we will review it if and when it is presented to us."

Pretzantzin v. Holder, 725 F.3d 161 (2nd Cir. 2013)

"Still, we find [Maryland v.] King's description of identity-related evidence telling. In finding that "name alone cannot address [the government's] interest in identity," the Court noted that other relevant forms of identification include fingerprints, "name, alias, date and time of previous convictions and the name then used, photograph, Social Security number, or [DNA] profile." Id. at 1972. This broad concept of "identity," when read in conjunction with the Government's proffered interpretation of Lopez-Mendoza's identity statement as precluding the suppression of all identity-related evidence, would render the inventory or booking search exception to the Fourth Amendment's warrant requirement superfluous. After all, if DNA is identity-related evidence, and Lopez-Mendoza precludes the suppression of all identity-related evidence, then why bother to couch Maryland's DNA Collection Act within the booking exception at all? And if identity-related evidence includes fingerprints, and Lopez-Mendoza precludes the suppression of all identity-related evidence, then what are we to make of controlling precedent mandating the suppression of this insuppressible evidence? See, e.g., Hayes v. Florida, 470 U.S. 811, 816-17, 105 S.Ct. 1643, 84 L.Ed.2d 705 (1985) (holding fingerprints properly suppressed when defendant was arrested without probable cause, taken to police station without consent, and detained and fingerprinted for investigatory purposes); Taylor v. Alabama, 457 U.S. 687, 692-93, 102 S.Ct. 2664, 73 L.Ed.2d 314 (1982) (concluding that "[t]he initial fingerprints [] were themselves the fruit of petitioner's illegal arrest...." (citation omitted)); accord Davis v. Mississippi, 394 U.S. 721, 727, 89 S.Ct. 1394, 22 L.Ed.2d 676 (1969). Given such peculiar consequences, it is clear that we cannot read Lopez-Mendoza's identity statement as establishing a rule of evidence."

United States v. Kriesel, 720 F.3d 1137 (9th Cir. 2013)

"Kriesel argued to the district court that the government had no legitimate reason for retaining the blood sample — which of course has within it not only the limited information the government has analyzed for his DNA profile, but his entire unanalyzed genome. The district court ruled the government had a legitimate purpose in retaining the blood samples that generate the CODIS profiles in order to ensure that the matches to forensic evidence, identified through CODIS searches, are accurate. The court found no reason at this time to believe the government would use the blood for other purposes, many of which are already prohibited by statute. The district court therefore granted judgment to the government, and we affirm on a similar basis."

King v. State, 434 Md. 472, 76 A.3d 1035 (2013)

"Because "the exclusionary rule is not a remedy [the courts] apply lightly." Sanchez-Llamas v. Oregon, 548 U.S. 331, 347, 126 S.Ct. 2669, 2680, 165 L.Ed.2d 557 (2006), and the Legislature made no indication that suppression is the proper remedy for a violation of the DNA Collection Act, we decline to find any suppression remedy here. Thus, even if a State violation of the Act of the caliber alleged here had been proven, which we find no evidence of, the trial court denied properly King's motion to suppress the DNA database match and there is no reversible error."

BRIEFS

Brief of Genetics, Genomics and Forensic Science Researchers in Maryland v. King, 54 Jurimetrics J. 43 (2013)

"In Maryland v. King, 133 S.Ct. 1958 (2013), the Supreme Court held that Maryland's statute requiring DNA samples from individuals arrested for crimes of violence or burglary did not violate the Fourth Amendment. One factor in the Court's analysis is the extent to which the forensic DNA profiles invade medical privacy. The majority stated that "[t]he argument that the testing at issue in this case reveals any private medical information at all is open to dispute." With respect to this dispute, eight scientists and two law professors filed a brief in support of neither party seeking to explain what current science tells us about the information conveyed by the thirteen short tandem repeats known as "CODIS markers," the variations in DNA generally used in the United States for forensic identification. This publication consists of the core of the brief along with a foreword about the continuing legal significance of the issue."

Warrantless, Pre-Arrest DNA Testing and a Suspect's Right to Refuse: Amicus Brief filed in State of Maine v. Spencer Glover (Maine Supreme Judicial Court 2014), SSRN (2013)

"When law enforcement seeks to obtain a warrantless, pre-arrest DNA sample from an individual, that individual has the right to say "No." If silence is to become a "badge of guilt," then the right to silence — under the United States and Maine Constitutions — might become a thing of the past. Allowing jurors to infer consciousness of guilt from a pre-arrest DNA sample violates the Fourth Amendment to the United States and Maine Constitutions."

LAW REVIEWS
Dethroning King: Why the Warrantless DNA Testing of Arrestees Should Be Prohibited Under State Constitutions, SSRN (2013)

"In Maryland v. King, the Supreme Court ruled that a state statute mandating the warrantless DNA testing of all people arrested for violent felonies did not violate the Fourth Amendment of the Constitution. The 5-4 majority held that the government had a legitimate interest in the identification of arrestees, which overrode the arrestees' reduced expectations of privacy. Despite the Court's contention, arrestees are presumed innocent and thus have an expectation of privacy much closer to an ordinary citizen than a convicted offender. Although the Court determined that governments have a legitimate government interest in "identifying" the arrestees, the "identification" is really ordinary, investigative police work, which cannot overcome the violation of the arrestees' reasonable expectations of privacy.

The majority also found the DNA testing to be essentially the same as fingerprinting, ignoring that DNA testing is intrusive and not used for identification and can reveal much more information about a person than fingerprinting. Furthermore, the suspicionless DNA testing for the purposes of investigation is not exempt from the Warrant Clause under any other common exception, including the special needs, incident to arrest, or exigent circumstances doctrines. If the Court's identification justification is sufficient, there will be no stopping the warrantless DNA testing of individuals any time they are asked for identification by law enforcement, such as during traffic stops. Allowing carte blanche DNA testing places an individual's most intimate information at risk of being disseminated, whether by accidental or intentional governmental abuse.

This Comment argues that states should hold that the warrantless DNA testing of arrestees is unconstitutional under their state constitutional provisions analogous to the Fourth Amendment. The doctrine of federalism allows a state to grant more protections to its citizens under the state constitution than those provided by the United States Constitution. By simply requiring law enforcement agencies to obtain a warrant supported by probable cause before obtaining the DNA of arrestees, state courts will ensure that the privacy rights of innocent-until-proven-guilty arrestees are maintained."

How the DNA Act Violates the Fourth Amendment Right to Privacy of Mere Arrestees and Pre-Trial Detainees, 59 Loy. L. Rev. 157 (2013)

"In light of the [Maryland v.] King decision, this comment proposes that the current DNA Act violates the fundamental notions of privacy established by the Fourth Amendment, and, thus, it is unconstitutional. Once an individual's DNA is taken and submitted into a federal database, there are no guarantees or unfailing safety measures for retrieval of that DNA if the arrest is subsequently voided, or if the charges are thrown out or dismissed. The statute [42 U.S.C. S 14135a] should be modified to prevent this invasion of privacy and to ensure the protections provided by the Fourth Amendment to persons whose arrests or pre-trial detentions do not result in eventual conviction.

Section II of this comment lays out the background procedural processes and jurisprudence that are essential for an understanding of the laws regarding DNA collection and profiling. This section explains the acts governing DNA sampling and analysis as well as the safeguards instituted to prevent abuse of DNA collection. Section II also details the right to privacy protected by the Fourth Amendment and how the case law concerning its application to DNA testing has evolved over the years. Additionally, this section describes the circuit split regarding the application of the Fourth Amendment to the DNA Act and addresses the two different approaches.

Section III of this comment proposes amending the DNA Act, while also maintaining Congress's intended purpose in passing the Act. Section III suggests that Congress either remove "arrestees and pre-trial detainees" from the statute or make alterations to the DNA Act and its regulations to place the burden of retrieving and expunging the DNA profile on the government. It also suggests that the DNA not be kept indefinitely and that definitive safeguards be implemented. Alternatively, this section proposes that courts should properly apply the requirements and analysis of what constitutes "legitimate governmental interests" and the importance of privacy interests. Additionally, Section III includes defenses to this proposed solution and a critique of the current statute and its limited precedential application after its expanded revision. This section further argues that courts treat the government's interests in DNA collection for "identification" purposes as a pretext, when the underlying intent to gain such information is to aid in solving other crimes. By upholding the DNA Act, courts guarantee that the government's interests in obtaining DNA to aid in solving past crimes will always trump an individual's interest in and expectation of privacy, which contravenes the purpose of the Fourth Amendment. Finally, Section IV summarizes the concerns regarding the current DNA Act and criticizes the precedent that allows for the deterioration of rights protected by the Fourth Amendment."

Indecent Exposure: Genes Are More Than a Brand Name Label in the DNA Database Debate, 42 U. Balt. L. Rev. 561 (2013)

"Before we started expanding the use of DNA databases, we should have considered three things: (1) would expansion increase investigative outcomes; (2) are those outcomes worth the consequences; and (3) is the advancement of DNA technology fixed? While the first may have been a no-brainer, it seems that we have not given any real thought to the other two. It seems likely that with the Supreme Court's decision this year, DNA databases and the populations housed within them will continue to explode in numbers. As citizens, DNA and the concept of turning it over freely has become as routine as giving private information over to the likes of Facebook, LinkedIn, and other social media outlets. We are indifferent to the number of situations that call for the submission of genetic material to medical providers, businesses selling at-home genetic tests, ancestry websites, and other public and private institutions. The reality is that troves of our genetic data are "persistent and widely shared" and incredibly difficult for us later to "access, to verify, or to correct."

It should not surprise us, then, that the criminal justice system wants to collect DNA from an ever-increasing spectrum of people who come into contact with it. The notion of privacy and the presumption of innocence are now blurred figures in this landscape. These concerns do not pertain to simply the collection of DNA profiles and samples, but also to the other information that may be kept. While criminal investigations and medical research previously operated in different genetic spheres, those spheres are starting to converge. When DNA is collected on arrest and uploaded into the database, it is not simply translated into an identity-free criminal bar code. Ultimately, that digitized profile must link to a name, to a location, and possibly to a criminal record. Other records may also be available, especially for released offenders because police must be able to track that person down if there is a hit in the database later. Ultimately, we may find that when police do contact a database offender they may also be able to tell that person his or her predisposition to kidney disease.

In the wake of the [Maryland v.] King case, the fingerprint-DNA analogy has overstayed its welcome. Nonetheless, it seems that it is not slated for retirement any time soon despite enduring concerns about the expansion of DNA collection. If the extension of DNA databases is in fact inevitable, then it should likewise be foreseeable that DNA technology may advance and outpace the restrictions once thought sufficient to keep databases sufficiently void of identifying information. As for now, it seems we would rather be content to operate databases at the margins of technology and tolerate a certain margin of error when things go awry. The criminal justice system hungers for the ability to solve crime and convict the guilty. Databases certainly feed that insatiable beast, but we need to respect that DNA is not the tame dormouse we once thought it to be."

License, Registration, Cheek Swab: DNA Testing and the Divided Court, 127 Harv. L. Rev. 161 (2013)

"Maryland v. King looks on its face like just another Fourth Amendment dispute — with civil libertarians on one side and law enforcement on the other — and garnered no special attention. But King is no ordinary Fourth Amendment case. At first glance, King simply upheld the Fourth Amendment constitutionality of a state statute authorizing the collection of DNA from arrestees. But the opinion represents a watershed moment in the evolution of Fourth Amendment doctrine and an important signal for the future of biotechnologies and policing. This Comment places King into context from three different vantage points, each one step removed. First, this Comment reads between the lines of the majority opinion, in light of the greater constellation of facts and claims placed before the Court, to underscore the significance of what was not said about the constitutionality of arrestee DNA collection. It next considers King as it exemplifies the judicial response to forensic DNA typing more generally, and imagines its precedential value in future biometric cases. Finally, the Comment closes by situating King in the broader landscape of the Court's recent Fourth Amendment jurisprudence and analyzing its insights for the evolution of the field as a whole."

Maryland v. King and the Wonderful, Horrible DNA Revolution in Law Enforcement, 11 Ohio St. J. Crim. L. 295 (2013)

"In Maryland v. King, the Supreme Court held that a Maryland statute authorizing forced DNA sampling from those arrested for certain serious felonies, for inclusion in Maryland's offender DNA database, did not violate the Fourth Amendment. At oral argument, Justice Alito declared that King was "perhaps the most important criminal procedure case that this Court has heard in decades." That statement, while perhaps dramatic, reflects how the DNA revolution has transformed crime solving. We are flooded daily with media reports about unresolved cases cracked by a "cold hit" between DNA from a crime scene and a convicted felon's DNA database profile. Maryland's law, which adds the DNA profiles of arrestees of serious crimes to the convicted felon profiles already in the state offender database, is squarely a part of this crime-solving frenzy. One might be forgiven, then, for predicting that an opinion upholding that law would be an unapologetic paean to the crime-solving virtues of DNA databases. Instead, the majority reconceptualizes the law as deploying DNA typing as a "routine booking procedure," and focuses exclusively on the state's interest in confirming arrestees' identities and determining arrestees' criminal history before making bail decisions.

In Part I of this essay, I [Andrea L. Roth] offer an explanation for the majority's curious logic. Part of the explanation is obvious: five justices were not ready to hold that a suspicionless search conducted primarily for crime-solving is legal so long as it is "reasonable." But the Court might also have been concerned that a crime-solving rationale would justify expanding databases beyond arrestees for serious offenses to arrestees for minor traffic offenses or even the general public, results that the justices-and other privileged Americans who are lucky enough never to have been arrested for a serious offense-might not quietly abide. In Part II, I explain that while the dissent is right in pointing out the Court's revisionist view of the law, the Court still might have written a coherent opinion upholding it. I ultimately suggest in Part III, however, that the norm the Court's opinion seems to set-drawing the line at arrestees-is the worst possible result. As long as arrestees are going to be swept up in the dragnet, the best policy choice - one that would avoid the severe racial inequities in current databases, maximize DNA's crime-solving power, and ensure a robust privacy debate, is a universal citizen database."

Maryland v. King: Policing and Genetic Privacy, 11 Ohio St. J. Crim. L. 281 (2013)

"With its decision in Maryland v. King, the Supreme Court finally stepped into the debate about the use of DNA databases in the American criminal justice system. With King, the Court decided a newly emerging database issue rather than an old one: whether the Fourth Amendment prohibits the collection of DNA samples from arrestees without a warrant or any individualized suspicion. According to the five member King majority, such compulsory collections are reasonable Fourth Amendment searches, given the outcome of a balancing of interests between the individual and government. The problem with King is that it may become influential in ways that weren't fully contemplated by the Supreme Court. While some may lament the micromanagement of policing by the modern Supreme Court's jurisprudence, the reality is that police investigation practices are unevenly regulated. Indeed, what King reveals is the extent to which the Court leaves many matters untouched by Fourth Amendment constraints and subjects them, for better or worse, to the control of the other political branches (as well to likely squabbling in the lower courts). This essay discusses three notable revelations in the Court's decision about the future of policing and genetic privacy. As the essay argues, what the Court introduces it also fails to regulate or even guide in any significant sense."

Maryland v. King: Sacrificing the Fourth Amendment to Build Up the DNA Database, 73 Md. L. Rev. 667 (2014)

"Although DNA technology is undoubtedly a powerful crime fighting tool, the [Maryland v.] King Court's assessment of the DNA collection of arrestees under the reasonableness balancing test is a misguided judicial response to the immediate benefits of new technology, and it leaves room for government abuse. Unlike searches of physical places and things, a search of someone's DNA is unique with respect to the physical intrusion necessary to effectuate the search and the amount of data rendered by the search. While DNA searches require limited physical invasion of the human body, they yield a considerable amount of aggregated data. Thus, these types of searches are complex and require special consideration. The King Court, however, wrongly applied the reasonableness balancing test. Instead, the Court should have relied on a line of cases that involves searching data on seized computers, which are more comparable to cases on collecting and searching DNA data. If the Court had done so, the Court would have found that similar to the requirement to obtain a search warrant to search data on seized computers, the government should be required to obtain a search warrant before entering an arrestee's DNA profile into a DNA database to search for a "hit.""

Maryland v. King: The Case for Uniform, Nationwide DNA Collection and DNA Database Laws in the United States, 23 Information & Communications Technology Law 77 (2014)

"The recent United States Supreme Court pronouncement in Maryland v. King that the police may readily take a DNA cheek swab of a suspect after an arrest for a serious offense poses challenging Fourth Amendment questions. Moreover, private DNA databases built by healthcare centers raise concerns such as the security of the data from government intrusions and whether information from a DNA database might be sold. In this article, I [Vikram Iyengar] advocate for a uniform national infrastructure of DNA collection and retention laws, and legislative and judicial safeguards on third-party use and disclosure of citizens' DNA information."

On the 'Considered Analysis' of Collecting DNA Before Conviction, 60 UCLA L. Rev. Disc. 104 (2013)

"For nearly a decade, DNA-on-arrest laws eluded scrutiny in the courts. For another five years, they withstood a gathering storm of constitutional challenges. In Maryland v. King, however, Maryland's highest court reasoned that usually fingerprints provide everything police need to establish the true identity of an individual before trial and that the state's interest in finding the perpetrators of crimes by trawling databases of DNA profiles is too "generalized" to support "a warrantless, suspicionless search." The U.S. Supreme Court reacted forcefully. Chief Justice Roberts stayed the Maryland judgment, writing that "given the considered analysis of courts on the other side of the split, there is a fair prospect that this Court will reverse the decision below." The full Court then granted a writ of certiorari. This essay briefly examines the opinions listed by the Chief Justice and finds their analysis incomplete. I [David H. Kaye] outline the Fourth Amendment questions that a fully considered analysis must answer, identify questionable dicta on the definition of "searches" and "seizures" in the opinions, describe a fundamental disagreement over the analytical framework for evaluating the reasonable warrantless searches or seizures, and criticize a creative compromise in one of the opinions that would allow sample collection without DNA testing before conviction. I conclude that the Supreme Court not only must assess the actual interests implicated by pre-conviction collection and profiling of DNA but also should articulate the appropriate framework for evaluating the reasonableness of warrantless searches in general."

Policing by Numbers: Big Data and the Fourth Amendment, 89 Wash. L. Rev. 35 (2014)

"The age of "big data" has come to policing. In Chicago, police officers are paying particular attention to members of a "heat list": those identified by a risk analysis as most likely to be involved in future violence. In Charlotte, North Carolina, the police have compiled foreclosure data to generate a map of high-risk areas that are likely to be hit by crime. In New York City, the N.Y.P.D. has partnered with Microsoft to employ a "Domain Awareness System" that collects and links information from sources like CCTVs, license plate readers, radiation sensors, and informational databases. In Santa Cruz, California, the police have reported a dramatic reduction in burglaries after relying upon computer algorithms that predict where new burglaries are likely to occur. Unlike the data crunching performed by Target, Walmart, or Amazon, the introduction of big data to police work raises new and significant challenges to the regulatory framework that governs conventional policing. This article identifies three uses of big data and the questions that these tools raise about conventional Fourth Amendment analysis. Two of these examples, predictive policing and mass surveillance systems, have already been adopted by a small number of police departments around the country. A third example

— the potential use of DNA databank samples — presents an untapped source of big data analysis. While seemingly quite distinct, these three examples of big data policing suggest the need to draw new Fourth Amendment lines now that the government has the capability and desire to collect and manipulate large amounts of digitized information."

Response: Maryland v. King: Per Se Unreasonableness, the Golden Rule, and the Future of DNA Databases, 127 Harv. L. Rev. F. 39 (2013)

"In License, Registration, Cheek Swab: DNA Testing and the Divided Court, Professor Erin Murphy deftly summarizes and situates the Supreme Court's opinion in Maryland v. King. As she observes, the case can be read narrowly or broadly. Murphy reads the case broadly, suggesting that King is "a watershed moment" that portends "a new Fourth Amendment in town" and that its "reimagination of the idea of 'identity'" "arguably invite[s] a new era of genetic identification." Here, I [David H. Kaye] offer a less dramatic view of the doctrinal significance of King and the limits of the majority's identification theory. I also offer a precept for officials seeking to expand or improve DNA databases in this new era."

Suspicionless DNA Collection from Arrestees Violates the Fourth Amendment, But Easier Expunction of DNA Records Can Help Mitigate the Harm, SSRN (2013)

"Suspicionless DNA collection from pre-conviction arrestees should be treated as a violation of the Fourth Amendment when it is conducted without a valid search warrant. The predominant policy justifications for that DNA collection (1) as a crime-fighting tool and/or (2) a modern identification tool, like high-tech versions of fingerprints, are not compelling enough to justify treating the process as comporting with the Fourth Amendment. Arrestees do not have the same low expectation of privacy as prisoners or convicts, and treating them as if they do violates their legal presumption of innocence. The public interest in fighting crime and identifying arrestees also fits within the ordinary role of law enforcement, meaning that those activities do not qualify for the "special needs" exception to the individualized suspicion required for most Fourth Amendment searches and seizures.

However, since the Supreme Court upheld suspicionless arrestee DNA collection, analysis, and aggregation in a nationwide DNA database (in Maryland v. King, 133 S.Ct. 1958 (2013)), participating states should adopt measures requiring automatic expunction of the DNA records of any arrestees who are not convicted within a reasonable amount of time from when they were arrested for the crime that led to the collection of their DNA."

Twenty-First Century Surveillance: DNA "Data-Mining" and the Erosion of the Fourth Amendment, 51 Hous. L. Rev. 229 (2013)

"This Comment argues that the Court should not have reversed the Maryland Court of Appeals' decision because expansion of state DNA statutes threatens both the personal liberties of unconvicted citizens, as well as the integrity of already burdened crime labs. In response to the Court's decision, this Comment proposes that Congress should constrain existing federal DNA legislation, thus requiring all fifty states that contribute to the federal database to comply with the stricter federal standards. Specifically, Congress should amend the federal legislation by: (1) requiring the automatic deletion of the DNA sample upon dismissal of charges; (2) postponing the creation of the DNA profile from the DNA sample until the arrestee is convicted; and (3) mandating that DNA samples be immediately deleted following the creation of the DNA profile."

Why DNA Databasing Is Good for Maryland: A DNA Analyst's Perspective, 42 U. Balt. L. Rev. 591 (2013)

"From a purely scientific point of view, more data is better. Drawing conclusions from small sets of data increases the likelihood that something has been missed, overlooked, or declined to be considered. Excluding data is limiting. When a crime is committed, there is a perpetrator. From the perspective of providing service to the citizens in the region and being as scientifically precise as possible, excluding data sets means all possible outcomes are perhaps not being explored. In the context of a scientific endeavor, gathering as much information as possible and practicable is prudent and beneficial to the results of the analysis. Having an expanded DNA database, filled with profiles of eligible and lawfully collected samples, benefits a laboratory's ability to arrive at conclusions, rather than leaving a sample as "unknown." As stated previously, the national database contains over 400,000 "unknowns" in the forensic index. Our goal as forensic DNA scientists, police agencies, and policy makers should be to decrease, or ideally, eliminate those unknowns, prevent future criminal activity, and provide answers to the citizens we serve. One powerful way to do this is by continuing to expand the DNA database to include the DNA profiles of arrestees.

Continuing to add DNA profiles to forensic DNA databases across the nation will lead to lower levels of crime through prevention, lower costs for enforcement, and safer neighborhoods. Using illogical rationale to prevent collections and limit the size and scope of these databases increases the likelihood of higher crime rates and lower case closure rates. In terms of societal benefit, having the tools necessary to prevent crime and identify those who commit crime through objective evidence is a goal all should agree is worth accomplishing."

Why So Contrived? The Fourth Amendment and DNA Databases After Maryland v. King, SSRN (2014)

"In Maryland v. King, 133 S.Ct. 1958 (2013), the Supreme Court narrowly upheld the constitutionality of routine collection and storage of DNA samples and profiles from arrestees. Oddly, the majority confined its analysis to using DNA for certain pretrial decisions rather than directly endorsing DNA's more obvious value as a tool for generating investigative leads in unsolved crimes. This article suggests that this contrived analysis may have resulted from both existing Fourth Amendment case law and the desire to avoid intimating that a more egalitarian and extensive DNA database system also would be constitutional. It criticizes the opinions in King for failing to clarify the conditions that prompt balancing tests as opposed to per rules for ascertaining the required reasonableness of searches and seizures. It urges the adoption of a more coherent doctrinal framework for scrutinizing not just DNA profiling, but all forms of biometric data collection and analysis. Finally, it considers what King implies for more aggressive DNA database laws."

+++++

Abandoned DNA

Excerpt from Kevin Hartnett, Globe Correspondent, *The DNA in your garbage* (May 2013)[9]

. . .

TO THE EXTENT that the legal system is grappling with abandoned DNA, it's chiefly in the criminal realm. Police are making more active use of DNA all the time, collecting and storing the information it contains, and a vigorous debate is underway about the privacy rights we have over our DNA in the context of an investigation. Later this spring the Supreme Court will decide, in the case Maryland v. King, whether the police can force a suspect to give a DNA sample when he or she has merely been arrested—but not yet convicted—for a crime.

"Abandoned DNA" comes into play when the police don't have a DNA sample, and can't force a suspect to give one up. In Washington in 2003, police posed as a fictitious law firm and sent a letter with a return envelope to a murder suspect named John Nicholas Athan, inviting him to participate in a fake class-action lawsuit. He replied, and police lifted DNA from Athan's saliva on the seal of the envelope and used it to convict him of the killing. The Washington State Supreme Court reviewed the technique and ruled it permissible, explaining that as soon as a letter goes in the mail, "The envelope, and any saliva contained on it, becomes the property of the recipient."

What might at first seem like clever police work strikes Joh as a very slippery slope. In treating DNA the same way we treat the envelope it came on, she suggests, we miss some important differences. First, DNA is uniquely hard to hang onto: It's in stray hairs and on chewing gum, and we constantly give it away without choosing to. "What can a person do to so stop shedding DNA?" she asks. Second, there is a meaningful difference between physical objects that contain DNA and the information encoded on them. The former is just spit on the sidewalk; the latter reveals facts about us that we may not even want to know ourselves, and we'd like to think that the law can also make that distinction.

That might sound very subjective—that the difference between a molecule of gum and a molecule of DNA is how we feel about it—but privacy law does sometimes hinge on just that. In a landmark 1967 decision, the Supreme Court expanded Fourth Amendment rights, which prohibit illegal searches and seizures, to include what Justice John Harlan called the "reasonable expectation of privacy"—which, to genetic-privacy advocates, clearly applies to DNA.

---

[9] https://www.bostonglobe.com/ideas/2013/05/11/the-dna-your-garbage-for-grabs/sU12MtVLkoypL1qu2iF6IL/story.html .

"Your DNA is like your house, it's as private as you can get," said Sheldon Krimsky, professor of urban and environmental policy at Tufts University and author of the book "Genetic Justice." "It has information about you, your family, your siblings. I think individuals, if given an understanding of what's in their DNA, would have an expressed expectation of privacy."

One proposal for how far privacy law should protect our DNA came recently from David Gusella, a third-year law student at Boston College. In an article in the Boston College Law Review in March, he pointed out that when police pick up abandoned DNA, there should be a clear limit to the information they can draw from it. They should be allowed to sequence it for traits related to appearance (because, he argued, we can't reasonably expect our appearance to remain private when we step out in public) but not anything beyond that. Other scholars argue, however, that it's more effective to set limits on when the police can even collect DNA—because once they have it, it's unrealistic to imagine they will use some parts and not others.

While people are talking about law enforcement uses of abandoned DNA, there has been almost no debate about another potential risk: private individuals taking each other's genetic material. Joh is one of the few scholars working on the issue. She argued in the Boston University Law Review in 2011 that sequencing someone else's genome without consent should be classified as felony theft—a charge whose seriousness would help establish social and legal norms recognizing DNA as an exceptional kind of property.

Genetic material does enjoy some protections, in theory: Eleven states have genetic information laws that are written broadly enough to conceivably punish someone for sequencing another person's genetic information without consent. (In 2011, Massachusetts legislators considered a sweeping Genetic Bill of Rights that would have protected abandoned DNA, but the legislation never became law.) But the penalties are minimal, and no cases have been brought under the laws.

Still, even if DNA theft by private citizens might sound like science fiction, it has happened. In 2002, film producer Stephen Bing was implicated in a paternity suit after private investigators hired by billionaire Kirk Kerkorian used DNA from Bing's discarded dental floss to prove that he (and not Kerkorian) was the father of a young child. Similarly, in 2002 British police thwarted a scheme to use an attractive woman to take a strand of hair from Prince Harry—with the intention of using it to prove that he was not in fact Prince Charles's son. In 2006, the United Kingdom became the first country to pass a law that made it illegal for private citizens to sequence another person's DNA without permission.

. . .OTHER POTENTIAL ABUSES of abandoned DNA are currently possible but still untried. George Annas, a bioethicist Boston University, wrote in the New England Journal of Medicine about how abandoned DNA could be exploited by political campaigns to reveal embarrassing facts about their rivals. (Imagine the headlines that would have resulted if, in 1984, Democratic operatives had been able to show that Ronald Reagan carried the ApoE gene, which conveys a high risk for Alzheimer's.)

Joh thinks that a first step in encouraging courts and legislatures to grant greater protection against unauthorized DNA analysis is to stop calling the genetic material "abandoned" in the first place. "People think, well, if it's abandoned, why should I worry about it?" Joh proposes the more provocative label of "DNA theft."

This semantic struggle points to an underlying challenge: We're still just beginning to understand what DNA means to us. Is it just a molecule, or is it us? Until we have a better sense of what our DNA really tells us, what it can and can't reveal about a person, it's going to be hard to pin down exactly how it should be treated legally.

Given this still emerging picture, experts agree that privacy rights around abandoned DNA are unlikely to change anytime soon. Krimsky, for one, thinks it will probably take a scandal. "There hasn't been a good enough case where there's enough damage done," he said. "I guarantee if there was a political candidate who had his DNA taken by a citizen and his political life is ruined, you'd see some action taken."

Will DNA collection be simply a "plain view" search? Since it can be collected on discarded cups will all DNA collection become "not a search"?

5.3.2 Criminal Procedure – Fifth Amendment Right Against Self-Incrimination

Cybersecurity

The Fifth Amendment provides for several individual rights and protections including protection from being forced to be a witness against oneself in a criminal proceeding.

The origin of self-incrimination in recent western history can be seen in coerced testimony in England in the Seventeenth Century, when interrogators forced confessions using torture to determine an individual's religious affiliation. Their silence was an admission of guilt, and this is the aspect of incrimination that was particularly distasteful. Much of the inspiration for the Bill of Rights came from oppressive legal practices in England, and this particular protection is embodied in the Fifth Amendment of the U.S. Constitution.

The Fifth Amendment provides that "[n]o person … shall be compelled in any criminal case to be a witness against himself."[10]

The colloquial phrase, "plead the Fifth" is based on this constitutional protection. In a criminal proceeding, the right against self-incrimination permits the defendant the right not to take the witness stand to testify against their will. However, if the defendant takes the stand to testify, then the privilege is deemed waived; that is, there can be no partial testimony and still maintain protection under the Fifth Amendment.

The act of silence is not permitted to be considered by a jury as an admission of guilt or otherwise in their decisionmaking process. Clarified by the U.S. Supreme Court in 2001, the

---

[10] 5th Amend., U.S. Const.

court opined in *Ohio v. Reiner*,[11] where the U.S. Supreme Court held that "a witness may have a reasonable fear of prosecution and yet be innocent of any wrongdoing. The [Fifth Amendment right against self-incrimination] serves to protect the innocent who otherwise might be ensnared by ambiguous circumstances."

What if a defendant "pleads the Fifth" when asked for his or her password?

Based on an understanding of the U.S. Supreme Court search for analogies in emerging technologies cases, the obvious analogy to a password is a physical key, which unlocks boxes, doors, and anything else that has a physical presence. Or could it be more like a combination lock where the code is held in memory? Those are exactly the two analogies that were argued by the prosecutor and the defendant, respectively.

A key differs from a combination lock, because a combination is held in an individual's mind as the "expression of the contents of an individual's mind" so held the U.S. Supreme Court of a combination lock.

The following excerpt is from an order in just such a case where the U.S. District Court heard a case where the defendant invoked the Fifth Amendment protection against self-incrimination and filed a motion to suppress the order for her to reveal her password to her laptop. Her laptop contained documents likely to be evidence of financial and real estate criminal fraud.

Excerpt of the Judge's Order in Case 1:10-cr-00509-REB Document 247 Filed 01/23/12 USDC Colorado:

United States v. Fricosu
No. 10-cr-00509-REB-02

. . . .

II. CONCLUSIONS OF LAW

The Fifth Amendment provides that "[n]o person . . . shall be compelled in any criminal case to be a witness against himself." U.S. CONST. Amend. V. Nevertheless, "the Fifth Amendment does not independently proscribe the compelled production of every sort of incriminating evidence." Fisher v. United States, 425 U.S. 391, 408, 96 S.Ct. 1569, 1579, 48 L.Ed.2d 39 (1976). Instead, "the privilege protects a person only against being incriminated by his own compelled testimonial communications." Id., 96 S.Ct. at 1580.

Although the privilege applies typically to verbal or written communications, an act that implicitly communicates a statement of fact may be within the purview of the privilege as well. United States v. Hubbell, 530 U.S. 27, 36, 120 S.Ct. 2037, 2043, 147 L.Ed.2d 24 (2000); Doe v. United States, 487 U.S. 201, 209, 108 S.Ct. 2341,

The contents of the computer are not, and are not claimed to be, privileged. See Doe I, 104 S.Ct. at 1241-42 (documents that are prepared or compiled voluntarily lack the element of compulsion and are not protected by the Fifth Amendment); In re Grand Jury Subpoena to Boucher, 2009 WL 424718 at *2

---

[11] 532 U.S. 17 (2012).

(D. Vt. Feb. 19, 2009) (same, with respect particularly to contents of a laptop computer).

The defendant had acknowledged that he sometimes downloaded child pornography unknowingly from online newsgroups, but stated that he deleted all such files when he realized their contents. 2347, 101 L.Ed.2d 184 (1988) (Doe II). More specifically in the context of this case, "[a]lthough the contents of a document may not be privileged, the act of producing the document may be." United States v. Doe, 465 U.S. 605, 612, 104 S.Ct. 1242, 1242, 79 L.Ed.2d 552 (1984) (Doe I). Production itself acknowledges that the document exists, that it is in the possession or control of the producer, and that it is authentic. Hubbell, 120 S.Ct. at 2043. The small universe of decisions dealing with the Fifth Amendment issues implicated by compelling a witness or defendant to provide a password to an encrypted computer or otherwise permit access to its unencrypted contents are instructive here.

In In re Grand Jury Subpoena to Boucher, 2007 WL 4246473 (D. Vt. Nov. 29, 2007) (Boucher I), a laptop computer was found in the defendant's car during a search incident to his crossing the border from Canada into the United States. During the initial search, an officer opened the computer and without entering a password was able to view its files, revealing thousands of images of what appeared to be, based on the names of the files, adult and some child pornography. An agent of the Bureau of Immigration and Customs Enforcement ("ICE") was called in, who asked the defendant to show him where these images were located on the computer.

The defendant navigated to a drive "Z," which contained several images of child pornography. After the defendant was arrested and the laptop seized, the computer was found to be password protected. When agents were unable to decrypt the computer, the grand jury issued a subpoena demanding the defendant produce any documents reflecting any passwords associated with the computer. Boucher I, 2007 WL 4246473 at *1-2. Noting that under prevailing Supreme Court precedent, a defendant cannot be compelled to reveal the contents of his mind, the magistrate judge found that the act of producing the password was testimonial and, therefore, privileged. Id. at *4-*6. Accord United States v. Kirschner, 2010 WL 1257355 at *3-4 (E.D. Mich. March 30, 2010).

On appeal of that decision, the grand jury revised its request to require the defendant to produce, not the password itself, but rather an unencrypted version of the Z drive. In re Grand Jury Subpoena to Boucher, 2009 WL 424718 at *2 (D. Vt. Feb.19, 2009) (Boucher II). Because of the revision to the request, the district court denied the motion to quash. The court noted that "[w]here the existence and location of the documents are known to the government, no constitutional rights are touched, because these matters are a foregone conclusion," that is, they "add[] little or nothing to the sum total of the Government's information." Id. at *3 & *4 (quoting Fisher, 96 S.Ct. at 1581) (internal quotation marks omitted). Likewise, the defendant's production was not necessary to authenticate the drive because he had already admitted possession of the computer, and the government had agreed not to use his act of production as evidence of authentication. Id. at *4. Accord United States v. Gavegnano, 2009 WL 106370 at *1 (4th Cir. Jan. 16, 2009) (where government independently proved that defendant was sole user and possessor of computer, defendant's revelation of password not subject to suppression).

There is little question here but that the government knows of the existence and location of the computer's files. The fact that it does not know the specific content of any specific documents is not a barrier to production. See Boucher II, 2009 WL 424718 at *3 (citing In re Grand Jury Subpoena Duces Tecum Dated Oct. 29, 1992) (United States v. Doe), 1 F.3d 87, 93 (2nd Cir. 1993), cert. denied, 114 S.Ct. 920 (1994)).

Additionally, I find and conclude that the government has met its burden to show by a preponderance of the evidence that the Toshiba Satellite M305 laptop computer belongs to Ms. Fricosu, or, in the alternative, that she was its sole or primary user, who, in any event, can access the encrypted contents of that laptop computer. The uncontroverted evidence demonstrates that Ms. Fricosu acknowledged to Whatcott during their recorded phone conversation that she owned or had such a laptop computer, the contents of which were only accessible by entry of a password. Of the three laptop computers found and seized during the execution of the search warrant of Ms. Fricosu's residence, only one was encrypted, the Toshiba Satellite M305. That laptop computer was found in Ms. Fricosu's bedroom, and was identified as "RS.WORKGROUP.Ramona." None of defendant's countervailing arguments – the suggestions that the computer might have been moved during the search, that someone else may have randomly designated the computer account as "Ramona," or that the fact that the hard drive was imaged before it was read somehow undermines its validity or Special Agent Johnson testified in detail as to the verification procedures he used to ensure that the imaged copy was what it purported to be. Proof at the level of abstraction that Ms. Fricosu suggested was necessary at the hearing is not necessary and probably ultimately not available in any event – is sufficient to alter my conclusion that it is more likely than not that the computer belonged to and was used by Ms. Fricosu.

Accordingly, I find and conclude that the Fifth Amendment is not implicated by requiring production of the unencrypted contents of the Toshiba Satellite M305 laptop computer. It is clear that the All Writs Act enables the court to issues orders to effectuate an existing search warrant. See United States v. New York Telephone Co., 434 U.S. 159, 172, 98 S.Ct. 364, 372, 54 L.Ed.2d 376 (1977) ("This Court has repeatedly recognized the power of a federal court to issue such commands under the All Writs Act as may be necessary or appropriate to effectuate and prevent the frustration of orders it has previously issued in its exercise of jurisdiction otherwise obtained."); see also In re Application of United States for an Order Authorizing Disclosure of Location Information of a Specified Wireless Telephone, – F.Supp.2d – , 2011 WL 3424470 at *44 (D. Md. Aug. 3, 2011) (citing cases in which All Writs Act used to effectuate existing search or arrest warrant). Moreover, the government has offered Ms. Fricosu immunity, precluding it from using her act of producing the unencrypted contents of the laptop computer against her. (See Gov't Motion App., Exh. 1.) Accordingly, the writ should issue.

THEREFORE, IT IS ORDERED as follows:
1. That the government's Application Under the All Writs Act Requiring Defendant Fricosu To Assist in the Execution of Previously Issued Search Warrants [#111] filed May 6, 2011, is GRANTED;
2. That Ms. Fricosu's Motion for Discovery – Seized Hard Drive [#101], filed April 27, 2011, is GRANTED;
3. That on or before February 6, 2012, the government SHALL PROVIDE counsel for defendant, Ramona Camelia Fricosu, with a copy of the hard drive of the Toshiba Satellite M305 laptop computer, serial number 98158161W;
4. That on or before February 21, 2012, defendant, Ramona Camelia Fricosu, SHALL PROVIDE counsel for the government in this case with an unencrypted copy of the hard drive of the Toshiba Satellite M305 laptop computer, serial number 98158161W; and
5. That the government SHALL BE precluded from using Ms. Fricosu's act of production of the unencrypted contents of the computer's hard drive against her in any prosecution.

Dated January 23, 2012, at Denver, Colorado.
BY THE COURT:
Robert E. Blackburn
United States District Judge

So the court opined that the defendant could not be compelled to reveal her password, but she could be ordered to produce an unencrypted harddrive, which the court ordered.

5.3.3 Export Controls on Emerging Technologies

Introduction
There are three federal departments delegated the implementation of the regulatory framework for export and import administration. The Department of Commerce, the Department of State and the Department of Treasury. Within those departments, the Export Administration Regulations (EAR) are administered by the Bureau of Industry and Security in the U.S. Department of Commerce. The International Traffic in Arms Regulations (ITAR) are administered by the Directorate of Defense Trade Controls, U.S. Department of State. The Office of Foreign Assets regulations are implemented by the Office of Foreign Assets Control in the U.S. Department of Treasury.
There are two different lists of items for export, the Commerce Control List (CCL) which is part of the U.S. Department of Commerce implementation and contains dual use items that are

also commercial. These items are typically designed for commercial purposes but also have military applications (computers, pathogens, civilian aircraft, etc.), as well as test equipment, materials and the software and technology. The second list for ITAR implementation identifies each item with an export controls classification number (ECCN). It covers military items found on the United States Munitions List (USML), such as munitions and defense articles, most space related technologies because of the application of these materials to missile technology, and technical data related to defense articles and services, such as providing assistance for the design and use of defense items.

The countries to which exports are prohibited are typically designated by the U.S. Congress and the list is codified at 22 CFR 126.1 and is updated, often. This is a changing area driven by international policy and diplomacy and should be carefully checked for the most recent updates because it changes often. The OFAC also administers economic sanctions which focus on the end-user or country and may limit transfer of technologies and assistance to OFAC's list of sanctioned countries. OFAC also has a "Specially Designated Nationals and Blocked Persons List". It also prohibits payments or providing "value" to nationals of sanctioned countries and certain entities, but if OFAC could allow the export with the granting of a license.

Defining an export

An export is a shipment or transmission of items out of the United States.
An item, which is collective term, per EAR is a commodity (something you can hold, has substance, etc.), software or technology.
Then there are also reexports which are also controlled. A reexport is a shipment or transmission of items subject to the EAR from one foreign country to another. This rule causes a lot of foreign companies to "design out" controlled U.S. commodities from their products. Technology and information – non-tangible can also be exported.

The regulations include any item in U.S. trade (goods, technology, information) U.S. items wherever located, even internationally, providing a defense service or ITAR technical data to a foreign national in the U.S. or abroad. The regulations exclude items in the public domain as well as artistic or non-technical publications (maps, children's books, sheet music, calendars, film).

Penalties for EAR violations include civil fines up to $250,000 per violation or double the value of the transaction. A denial of export privileges can also be used for any length of time. Penalities for ITAR include criminal offenses. Each criminal violation may result in a fine of not more than $1,000,000 or imprisonment of not more than 20 years, or both. Civil penalties are also available for a fine of not more than $500,000.

Deemed Exports and Defense Services

"Deemed exports" can mean access to controlled technology and source code by a foreign national in the U.S. and does not require the perpetrator to be outside of the country. It only requires a general intent to transfer the information.

The EAR defines a deemed export as the release of technology or source code subject to the EAR to a foreign national in the U.S. This can be a foreign or visiting faculty, research assistants or students. This can apply to something as simple as a tour of a laboratory, exchanging phone calls or emails or having visual inspections. Transferring ITAR technical data to another or performing a defense service, even training, on behalf of a foreign person in the U.S. or abroad can result in a "deemed export" determination. The transfer of information does not apply to U.S. Citizens, permanent residents and those with U.S. asylum protection.

If there is a need for transfer, a license could be obtained for the transfer of an item or information on the CCL or the USML technology lists to a non-permanent resident or foreign national. If the item is on the Commerce Control List (CCL), then a license may be required from Commerce or State.

Anyone violating this requirement may be placed on a "denied persons list" and be prohibited from engaging in any expoert.

Fundamental Research Exclusion

National Security Decision Directive (NSDD) 189, National Policy on the Transfer of Scientific, Technical and Engineering Information issued 9/21/85 established national policy for controlling the flow of this information produced in federally funded fundamental research at colleges, universities and laboratories.(Reaffirmed in letter from Condoleezza Rice, Asst. to the President for Security Affairs on 11/1/01.)

Fundamental Research Definition

The definition of fundamental research is:

Basic and applied research in science and engineering, the results of which ordinarily are published and shared broadly within the scientific community, as distinguished from proprietary research and from industrial development, design, production, and product utilization, the results of which ordinarily are restricted for proprietary or national security reasons. (NSDD 189).

The Fundamental Research Exclusion (FRE) can be lost if the university based research accepts restrictions on the publication of the results of project with those restrictions. Or if the research is part of an industry contract or testing agreement. The export programs EAR/ITAR have a "carve-out" for delay of publication for a pending patent application if the Principal Investigator has If the PI has made such an agreement.

The Fundamental Research Exception can also be lost if the agreement requires sponsor approval prior to publication, as distinct from a simple "review" before publication. It is acceptable to comment but not to approve.

Travel outside the U.S.

The Department of Commerce and the Department of State have regulations that affect: travel outside of the United States, which applies to physically taking items with you on a trip such as a laptop, encryption products on your laptop, a cell phone, data/technology, blueprints, drawings, schematics or other "tools of the trade" Giving access to a foreign person outside the United States to controlled information is a risk.

The Office of Foreign Assets Control (OFAC) has regulations that affect: money transactions and the exchange of goods and services in certain countries – providing "value". Particularly travel to these sanctioned countries: Balkans, Belarus, Burma, Cote d'Ivoire, Cuba, Democratic Republic of the Congo, Iran, Iraq, Former Liberian Regime of Charles Taylor, North Korea, Sudan, Syria, and Zimbabwe can be a problem. Before doing business with particular persons, the people who are prohibited for such contacts are listed on the Commerce, State, and OFAC have "lists".

The cost of noncompliance

For EAR, criminal penatlies can be $50,000 to $1 million or 5 times value of export, whichever is greater, per violation, 10 years imprisonment. Civil: revocation of exporting privilege can result in fines of $10,000 to $120,000 per violation. For example, Bass-Pro was fined $510,000 for shipping guns without a license. Dr. Thomas Butler, Texas Tech University, was sentenced to two years in prison for making fraudulent claims and unauthorized exports (plague bacteria) to a listed country, Tanzania. ITT was fined $100,000,000 for exporting night vision materials without license

For ITAR, criminal penalties up to $1 million per violation and 10 years imprisonment are possible. Civilly, seizure and forfeiture of article, revocation of exporting privilege, up to $500,000 fine per violation is possible. Professor Roth, University of Tennessee, was convicted in 2008 and sentenced to four years in prison for carrying his laptop to China with sensitive information on the harddrive. Raytheon fined $25,000, Hughes Electronics and Boeing Satellite Systems were fined $32 million; Boeing was fined $4.2 million and Lockheed Martin was fined $13 million.

For OFAC, criminal fines can be $50,000 to $10,000 per violation and 10 to 30 years imprisonment. Civilly, fines can be $11,000 to $1million per violation. For example, Augsburg College, Minnesota, was fined $9,000 for traveling to Cuba four times for a total of $36,000. In 2009, Thermon Manufacturing, in Texas was fined $14,613 for three shipments to Sudan. Disclosure after discovering the violation can help reduce the penalty.

Two convictions

Dr. Thomas Butler, Texas Tech University was convicted of forty-seven counts of a sixty-nine count indictment and was sentenced to two years in prison in 2004. He was placed on the denied persons list, and a felony conviction prevents him from obtaining the necessary clearances to work with Yersinia pestis, which was his research area.

Professor John Roth, University of Tennessee, was sentenced to 48 months for violating the Arms Export Control Act by illegally exporting technical information relating to USAF research contracts. He was developing plasma technology for use on an advanced form of an unmanned air vehicle (UAV). Prof. Roth gave ITAR technical data to a Chinese and an Iranian student in his laboratory. While in China, he downloaded his project from a Chinese colleague's computer. Testimony showed that Prof. Roth had been warned by his compliance officer of this risks.

_____

6.1.1   Economic Espionage –cybersecurity, biotechnology
The first case prosecuted under the Economic Espionage Act of 1996[12]

United States v. Chung
659 F.3d 815 (9th Cir. 2011)

Excerpt on the *United States v. Chung* case, from Case Reports, 125 *Harvard Law Review* 2177-2184 (2012):

CRIMINAL LAW — ECONOMIC ESPIONAGE — NINTH CIRCUIT UPHOLDS FIRST TRIAL CONVICTION UNDER § 1831 OF THE ECONOMIC ESPIONAGE ACT OF 1996. — United States v. Chung, 659 F.3d 815 (9th Cir. 2011), cert. denied, No. 11-1141, 2012 WL 929750 (U.S. Apr. 16, 2012). Congress enacted the Economic Espionage Act of 19961 (EEA or Act), the first federal statute criminalizing the misappropriation of trade secrets, to equip federal prosecutors with a potent weapon against foreign and domestic theft of commercial information. Despite a startling escalation in the rate and scale of economic espionage,2 surprisingly few cases have been prosecuted under the Act.3 Recently, in United States v. Chung, 4 the Ninth Circuit upheld the first trial conviction under § 1831 of the EEA.5 Although Chung is a notable step in the battle against economic espionage, its precedential value is nominal: the court left every element of the § 1831 analysis equivocal, shed scant light on the purpose of the EEA, and offered little guidance regarding the relevance of civil trade secret jurisprudence for EEA interpretation. The doctrinal uncertainty left in Chung's wake, combined with powerful federal disincentives to prosecute EEA cases in the face of ambiguity, threatens to thwart the EEA's deterrent purpose. Future courts, then, should take an active role in clarifying the Act. In interpreting the EEA and in deciding which civil trade secret standards to import to the EEA context, courts should uphold the Act's national security objectives by adopting an expansive reading of its terms.

---

[12] 18 U.S.C. §§ 1831–1839 (1996).

The FBI's news release upon the indictment of individuals for stealing biotechnology trade secrets in corn seeds. This is the first case to uncover a biotechnology economic espionage case that has been brought to an indictment and trial. Here is the FBI's news release:

Six Chinese Nationals Indicted for Conspiring to Steal Trade Secrets from U.S. Seed Companies [13]

U.S. Attorney's Office December 19, 2013	• **Southern District of Iowa**(515) 473-9300

DES MOINES, IA—United States Attorney Nicholas A. Klinefeldt announced the indictment on December 17, 2013, against six Chinese nationals for conspiracy to steal trade secrets from U.S. seed companies. The indictment alleges that from on or about April 2011 to on or about December 2012, Mo Hailong, Li Shaoming, Wang Lei, Wang Hongwei, Ye Jian, and Lin Yong conspired to steal the trade secrets of several U.S.-based seed manufacturing companies and transport those trade secrets to China for the benefit of their China-based seed company. Mo Hailong was previously charged by criminal complaint on Tuesday, December 10, 2013.

Mo Hailong is employed as the director of International Business of the Beijing Dabeinong Technology Group Company, which is part of DBN Group. DBN Group is believed to be a Chinese conglomerate with a corn seed subsidiary company, Kings Nower Seed.

Li Shaoming is chief executive pfficer of Beijing Kings Nower Seed S & T Co., Ltd. Beijing Kings Nower Seed S&T Co. (BKN) is the wholly owned seed subsidiary of DBN. Beijing Kings Nower Seed is headquartered in Beijing, China.

Wang Lei is a citizen and resident of China and the vice chairman of Beijing Kings Nower Seed S&T Co. Ltd.

Wang Hongwei is believed to be a resident of Quebec, Canada. Wang Hongwei is believed to be a citizen of both Canada and China.

Ye Jian is a citizen and resident of China and a research manager for Beijing Kings Nower Seed S&T Co. Ltd.

Lin Yong is a citizen and resident of China and an employee for Beijing Kings Nower Seed S&T Co. Ltd.

The defendants are alleged to have conspired to steal inbred corn seed from Dupont Pioneer, Monsanto, and LG Seeds. This "inbred" or "parent" line of seed constitutes valuable intellectual property of a seed producer. After stealing the inbred corn seed, the conspirators attempted to covertly transfer the inbred corn seed to China. The estimated

---

[13] https://www.fbi.gov/omaha/press-releases/2013/six-chinese-nationals-indicted-for-conspiring-to-steal-trade-secrets-from-u.s.-seed-companies .

loss on an inbred line of seed is approximately five to eight years of research and a minimum of 30 to 40 million dollars.

The public is reminded that an indictment is merely a charge, and that the defendants are presumed innocent until and unless proven guilty.

United States v. Lee

Ex-Valspar Worker in Wheeling Admits Stealing Trade Secrets[14]

March 3, 2011

A former Valspar Corp. employee admitted to stealing trade secrets from the paint maker with plans to take them to a new employer in China.

David Yen Lee, 54, of Jersey City, New Jersey, pleaded guilty today to theft of a trade secret with intent to economically benefit someone other than its owner before U.S. District Judge Robert .

"Guilty, sir," he told the judge.

According to court papers, Lee, who holds a doctorate in chemistry, worked as a technical director at the Wheeling facility of Minneapolis-based Valspar from 2006 to 2009, when he left to take a job in Shanghai with Osaka, Japan- based Nippon Paint Co. Nippon Paint wasn't a defendant in the case.

When he was arrested in March 2009, Lee had a pocket-size computer "thumb drive" containing Valspar data in his possession, federal agents said. The information he took is worth $7 million to $20 million, Assistant U.S. Attorney Jessica Romero told Gettleman today.

Lee, whose crime is punishable by as long as 10 years in prison and a $250,000 fine, is scheduled to be sentenced on Nov. 23. The U.S. will recommend a sentence of about 5 1/2 years, Romero said. Lee, who is free on bail, and his lawyer, Daniel Rubenstein, declined to comment after the hearing.

The case is U.S. v. Lee, 09cr290, U.S. District Court, Northern District of Illinois (Chicago).

---

[14] http://www.dailyherald.com/article/20100902/business/309029930/ .

Chapter 7

Tort Law and Emerging Technologies

6.1.2 Tort Law—Basics

In general, tort law is the area of civil law that directs the tortfeasor to compensate the injured party when they have caused the injury, either intentionally or unintentionally.

What is a tort?

A tort is a civil wrong that is either intentional or unintentional, but may come from the same act as a criminal case (Remember the O.J. Simpson criminal case and then the civil case?). There are two categories of torts. The intentional torts are committed with intent. There are five general ones: assault, battery, false imprisonment, intentional infliction of emotional distress, and trespass. The unintentional torts include negligence and nuisance. Each of these torts has a set of "elements" which all must be met in order to be proven in court. Tort law is state law, not federal law, but each state has the same basic elements for proving a tort. Mainly they differ in the way they determine liability. In civil cases the parties are called the plaintiff, which is the party suing or claiming to be injured and the defendant is the one who acted and against whom the case is brought. The burden to prove these elements is on the accuser, or the plaintiff. (Note that it is the complainant in criminal law, rather than the plaintiff, that begins a legal action, and it is the state in criminal law not the individual victim who actually brings the case.)

Not to keep you in the dark any longer, here are the elements of the five general intentional torts:

Assault has three elements. Intent will always be one of the elements in the intentional torts, and for assault the second is apprehension of harm and the third is causation.

Battery has three elements. First, an intent to commit a harmful touching; second, the action results in an actual offensive contact; and three, there is causation between the act and the touching.

False imprisonment has four elements. First, intent to confine the plaintiff; second, an actual confinement preventing the plaintiff from leaving; third, a causal link; and fourth, an awareness of the plaintiff of the confinement. The law of torts across the nation has been summarized and distilled into a general set of principles to help understand torts, called a "restatement". The Restatement (2nd) of Torts, §31, defines false imprisonment:

An actor is subject to liability to another for false imprisonment if:

(a) he acts intending to confine the other or a third person within boundaries fixed by the actor, and

(b) his act directly or indirectly results in such a confinement of the other, and

(c) the other is conscious of the confinement or is harmed by it.

Trespass to land also includes the element of intent, but it is a general intent of actually being on the land, perhaps without knowing one is trespassing. The Restatement (2nd) of Torts, section 329, states: A trespasser is a person who enters or remains upon land in the possession of another without a privilege to do so created by the possessor's consent or otherwise. There are several other kinds of trespass, too.

Intentional infliction of emotional distress has four elements: 1. intent to cause or reckless disregard or the probability of causing emotional distress; 2. outrageous conduct by the defendant; 3. actual damages or suffering; and 4. causation of the emotional distress by the plaintiff's outrageous conduct.

The Unintentional torts

The unintentional torts lack the common element of intent, but the general concept is that although intent may not be present, the extent of the recklessness, carelessness or neglect may give rise to a wrong that should be compensated because of these actions. Negligence and product liability are unintentional torts.

For negligence, first, there must be a duty to the plaintiff; second that duty must have been breached by the defendant; third, there must be a link between the injuries and the acts of the defendant, called "proximate cause" and the risk has to be a foreseeable one; fourth, the plaintiff must have suffered damages as a result of all of the above.

There are some defenses like assumption of risk, attractive nuisance and consent which arise in Halloween Tort Law and can help a defendant.

Product liability is the result of a product that has either a design defect, a manufacturing defect or a marketing defect that renders it strictly liable for the harm it causes. The strict liability standard means that it does not matter how careful the manufacturer was in the process, the mere production of it makes the manufacturer strictly liable for the harm.

Defenses to product liability could be statutorily created or if the product is used in a way that was clearly not intended.

[Excerpt from Sutton, Law and Biotechnology (2007)]

Intentional torts with potential applicability to biotechnology issues include trespass, trespass to land, conversion, private nuisance and public nuisance. Torts have sought as remedies for damages in both human tissues as well as damages from genetically engineered crops. The first case, a landmark case in establishing that human tissues are not property, sets analyzes the theories of trespass and conversion for profiting on unique tissue taken from a patient, without his consent or remuneration for their commercialization. The second case raises the issues of conversion, private nuisance and public nuisance in the unique damages that can be done by genetically engineered crops in contaminating other crops which become economic losses.

The intentional torts have not proven to be successful legal tools for recovery from damages from the products and practices of biotechnology. The following article suggests that among the intentional torts, trespass to land and conversion may be the most promising.

Excerpt from Julie A. Davies and Lawrence C. Levine, "SYMPOSIUM: Biotechnology and the Law: Biotechnology's Challenge to the Law of Torts," 32 McGeorge L. Rev. 221 (Fall 2000)

There may be liability for intentional torts in the biotechnology context. The two intentional torts most likely to arise are trespass to land and conversion. A. Trespass to Land Use of genetically engineered crops creates a significant risk of trespass to land. Trespass to land arises where a defendant intentionally enters the land of another or intentionally causes something to enter the land of another. Although intent is required, it is the intent to enter the land, not the intent to trespass, that is key. Thus, if a defendant enters the plaintiff's land reasonably believing that she has permission to do so, or even under a reasonable belief that the property is hers, she will be liable for trespass to land.

In the biotechnology context, if the defendant knows that it is substantially certain that seeds from her pesticide-resistant plants will find their way on to the plaintiff's property, she can be liable for trespass to land. Further, she is liable for all harm that ensues as a result of the trespass. Genetically engineered crops pose a real risk of trespass to land liability if they cross-pollinate with neighboring plants or otherwise contaminate the land of adjoining land owners.

B. Conversion.

The intentional tort that thus far has received the most attention in the biotechnology context is the tort of conversion. Conversion arises when a defendant intentionally exercises "dominion and control over a chattel which so seriously interferes with the right of another to control it that the actor may justly be required to pay the other the full value of the chattel." Although an intentional tort, as with trespass to land, it is simply the intent to do the act - here the exercise of dominion and control - that gives rise to liability.

The propriety of a conversion action in the biotechnology context was first considered in the now-famous case of Moore v. Regents of the University of California. Moore had been undergoing medical care for hairy-cell leukemia, a rare and potentially fatal form of cancer. As part of the medical treatment for the disease, Moore's spleen was removed, a standard treatment for the disease. The defendants used Moore's spleen to develop a cell-line that was patented and highly valuable. Moore had no knowledge of the defendants' commercial use of his cells. In fact, Moore was induced to make about a dozen trips to the defendants under the guise of continuing medical treatment when, in fact, the trips were solely to assist the defendants with their ongoing commercial use of Moore's cells. Moore sued, alleging several torts including conversion. A divided California Supreme Court reversed an appellate court that had permitted Moore to pursue a conversion claim.

The Moore decision was a tremendous victory for the biotechnology industry. The decision foreclosed a conversion action against those who exercised dominion and control over the patient's tissue samples without the patient's consent. The majority determined that Moore's cells were not property and, thus, could not be converted.

The court admitted that its conclusion was reached in an effort to protect medical research, which, the majority believed, could have been harmed by permitting conversion liability. The impact of Moore remains substantial and its application to biotechnological harms is yet to be seen. For example, one author argues that the tort of conversion should apply in the context of the misappropriation of human eggs and embryos, notwithstanding the restrictive holding of Moore. Such an action, however, may well be foreclosed if a court elects to adopt the California Supreme Court's reasoning in Moore.

6.1.3 Tort Law
In Re Starlink Corn Products Liability Litigation

In Re Starlink Corn Products Liability Litigation
212 F. Supp. 2d 828 (N.D. Ill., E. Div., 2002)

Memorandum Opinion and Order by Judge James B. Moran This controversy arises from the discovery of genetically modified corn in various food products. Plaintiffs disseminated a product that contaminated the entire United States' corn supply, increasing their costs and depressing corn prices. Plaintiffs have filed a 57-count master second amended consolidated class action complaint, alleging common law claims for negligence, strict liability, private nuisance, public nuisance and conversion on behalf of a nationwide class of corn farmers. . . . Defendants filed a motion to dismiss, arguing that the Federal Insecticide, Fungicide and Rodenticide Act (FIFRA), 7 U.S.C. §§ 136 et seq., preempts plaintiffs' state law claims, that the economic loss doctrine bars any recovery, and that the complaint fails to state a claim under any of plaintiffs' purported legal theories. For the following reasons, defendants' motion to dismiss is granted in part and denied in part.

BACKGROUND

Aventis genetically engineered a corn seed to produce a protein known as Cry9C that is toxic to certain insects. The seeds are marketed under the brand name StarLink. Garst is a licensee who produced and distributed Starlink seeds. Aventis applied to register Starlink with the EPA, which is responsible for regulating insecticides under FIFRA, 7 U.S.C. §§ 136 et seq. The EPA noted that Cry9C had several attributes similar to known human allergens, and issued only a limited registration, permitting Starlink use for such purposes as animal feed, ethanol production and seed increase, but prohibiting its use for human consumption. Consequently, segregating it from non-StarLink corn, which was fit for human consumption, became of utmost importance.

A little background about normal practices for cultivating, harvesting and distributing corn demonstrates the extensive steps necessary to prevent StarLink corn from entering the food supply.Corn replicates by the transfer of pollen from one corn plant to another, including cross-pollination from one breed to another. Once airborne, corn pollen can drift over considerable distances, meaning that different corn varieties within a farm, and from neighboring farms, regularly cross-breed.

With few exceptions, there are not procedures in place to segregate types of corn. Different corn breeds within an individual farm are commingled at the harvesting stage. Corn from hundreds of thousands of farms is then further commingled as it is gathered, stored and shipped through a system of local, regional and terminal grain elevators. Elevators, storage and transportation facilities are generally not equipped to test and segregate corn varieties. The commingled corn is then marketed and traded as a fungible commodity.

In light of these general practices in the corn industry, the EPA required special procedures with respect to StarLink. These included mandatory segregation methods to prevent StarLink from commingling with other corn in cultivation, harvesting, handling, storage and transport, and a 660-foot "buffer zone" around StarLink corn crops to prevent cross-pollination with non-StarLink corn plants. The limited registration also made Aventis responsible for ensuring these restrictions were implemented, obligating it (a) to inform farmers of the EPA's requirements for the planting, cultivation and use of StarLink; (b) to instruct farmers growing StarLink how to store and dispose of the StarLink seeds, seed bags, and plant detritus; and (c) to ensure that all farmers purchasing StarLink seeds signed a contract binding them to these terms before permitting them to grow StarLink corn.

StarLink was distributed throughout the United States from approximately May 1998 through October 2000. The limited registration initially limited StarLink cultivation to 120,000 acres. In January 1999, Aventis petitioned the EPA to raise this limit to 2.5 million acres. The EPA agreed, subject to an amended registration that required Aventis to (a) inform purchasers (i.e. "Growers") at the time of StarLink seed corn sales, of the need to direct StarLink harvest to domestic feed and industrial non-food uses only;(b) require all Growers to sign a "Grower

Agreement" outlining field management requirements and stating the limits on StarLink corn use;(c) deliver a Grower Guide, restating the provisions stated in the Grower Agreement, with all seed;(d) provide all Growers with access to a confidential list of feed outlets and elevators that direct grain to domestic feed and industrial uses;(e) write to Growers prior to planting, reminding them of the domestic and industrial use requirements for StarLink corn;(f) write to Growers prior to harvest, reminding them of the domestic and industrial use requirements for StarLink corn;(g) conduct a statistically sound follow-up survey of Growers following harvest, to monitor compliance with the Grower Agreement.

Over this 29-month period, StarLink cultivation expanded from 10,000 acres to 350,000 acres.

In October 2000, after numerous reports that human food products had tested positive for Cry9C, a wave of manufacturers issued recalls for their corn products. On October 12, 2000, Aventis, at EPA's urging, applied to cancel the limited registration, effective February 20, 2001. Fear of StarLink contamination nonetheless continues to affect corn markets. Many U.S. food producers have stopped using U.S. corn, replacing it with imported corn or corn substitutes. South Korea, Japan and other foreign countries have terminated or substantially limited imports of U.S. corn. Grain elevators and transport providers are now mandating expensive testing on all corn shipments.

Plaintiffs allege that the widespread StarLink contamination of the U.S. corn supply is a result of defendants' failure to comply with the EPA's requirements. Aventis did not include the EPA-mandated label on some StarLink packages, did not notify, instruct and remind StarLink farmers of the restrictions on StarLink use, proper segregation methods and buffer zone requirements, and did not require StarLink farmers to sign the obligatory contracts. Prior to the 2000 growing season Aventis allegedly instructed its seed representatives that it was unnecessary for them to advise StarLink farmers to segregate their StarLink crop or create buffer zones because Aventis believed the EPA would amend the registration to permit StarLink use for human consumption. In July 2001, however, an EPA Scientific Advisory Panel reaffirmed its previous position on StarLink's allergenic qualities. Further, the FDA has declared StarLink to be an adulterant under the Food, Drug and Cosmetic Act.. . .

II.   Economic Loss Doctrine. This rule limits the types of damages plaintiffs may recover in tort. Physical injuries to persons or property are compensable; solely economic injuries are not. The difficult question is defining what constitutes an "economic" injury. . . .

Non-StarLink corn crops are damaged when they are pollinated by StarLink corn. The pollen causes these corn plants to develop the Cry9C protein and renders what would otherwise be a valuable food crop unfit for human consumption. Non-StarLink corn is also damaged when it is commingled with StarLink corn. Once mixed, there is no way to re-segregate the corn into its edible and inedible parts. The entire batch is considered tainted and can only be used for the domestic and industrial purposes for which StarLink is approved. None of that supply can ever be used for human food.There are at least four different points along the supply chain at which StarLink could have entered the food corn supply, all of which are consistent with the complaint: (1) plaintiffs unknowingly purchased seed containing the Cry9C protein, i.e. their suppliers' inventory had been contaminated; (2) plaintiffs' crops were contaminated by pollen from StarLink corn on a neighboring farm; (3) plaintiffs' harvest was contaminated by commingling with StarLink corn in a transport or storage facility; and (4) food manufacturers commingled the corn within their raw material storage or processing activities.

The first situation would fall within the economic loss doctrine. Plaintiffs could have negotiated contractual protection from their suppliers and simply did not get what they had bargained for. In the fourth, plaintiffs would have suffered no harm to their property because the corn was commingled after they had relinquished their ownership interest in it. Scenarios 2 and 3, however, present viable claims for harm to their crops. [Resolving the complaint's ambiguous phraseology in plaintiffs' favor, we find that they have sufficiently alleged that their crops were contaminated at some point within that chain.]

The StarLink situation does not fit neatly into traditional economic loss doctrine analysis. Plaintiffs here had no commercial dealings with defendants or defendants' customers. This is more than a lack of direct privity, and not a situation where a party could have negotiated warranty or indemnity protection and chose not to. Plaintiffs had no opportunity to negotiate contractual protection with anyone. Still, as the access cases aptly demonstrate, the economic loss doctrine has grown beyond its original freedom-of-contract based policy justifications. Farmers' expectations of what they will receive for their crops are just that, expectations. Absent a physical injury, plaintiffs cannot recover for drops in market prices. Nor can they recover for any additional costs, such as testing procedures, imposed by the marketplace. But if there was some physical harm to plaintiffs' corn crop, the lack of a transaction with defendants affects what will be considered "other property." [This includes corn commingled at grain elevators because plaintiffs retain ownership rights to corn stored there. Each contributing farmer owns a pro rata share of the entire, now tainted, supply.] Assuming plaintiffs did not buy corn seeds with the Cry9C protein, it cannot be said that a defective part of their crop injured the whole, that a defective product was integrated into a system or that the harm to their crop was a foreseeable consequence of the seeds' failure to perform. These facts are distinguishable from Hapka, 458 N.W.2d at 688 (holding farmer who purchased diseased seeds could not recover for harm to rest of crop). Plaintiffs' seeds, as purchased, were adequate. The StarLink contaminant was wholly external.

Nor does the StarLink controversy present the unlimited or speculative damage concerns common in access cases. There are a finite number of potential plaintiffs -- only non-StarLink corn farmers -- who can claim injury. This may be a sizeable group, and the damages may be tremendous, but the fact that defendants are alleged to have directly harmed a large number of plaintiffs is not a defense. StarLink's effects on commercial corn farmers are distinct and qualitatively different from society at large. And damages are easily measured through price changes because corn is a regularly traded commodity with a readily measurable market. Further, as discussed above, the contamination of plaintiffs' corn supply is a physical injury.To the extent plaintiffs allege that their crops were themselves contaminated, either by cross-pollination in the fields or by commingling later in the distribution chain, they have adequately stated a claim for harm to property. Once plaintiffs have established this harm they may be entitled to compensation for certain economic losses. . . .

IV. ConversionConversion is defined as "an intentional exercise of dominion or control over a chattel which so seriously interferes with the right of another to control it that the actor may justly be required to pay the other the full value of the chattel." Restatement (Second) of Torts § 222A. Plaintiffs argue that defendants' role in contaminating the corn supply amounts to a conversion of their property.

We disagree. The defining element of conversion, the one that distinguishes it from a trespass to chattels, is the extent of interference with the owner's property rights. If the damage is minor, in duration or severity, plaintiff may only recover for the diminished value. But if the damage is sufficiently severe, plaintiff may recover full value. Conversion is akin to a forced judicial sale. The defendant pays full value for the chattel, and receives title to it. Restatement § 222A comment c. Here, plaintiffs have not alleged that defendants destroyed their crops or deprived them of possession. Plaintiffs retained possession and still had total control over the corn. Most, if not all of it, was ultimately sold to third parties. The only damages were a lower price, for which plaintiffs could be compensated without forcing a sale.

It is possible to convert a chattel by altering it, without completely destroying it. In particular, commingling fungible goods so that their identity is lost can constitute a conversion. Restatement § 226 comment e. To do so, however, the perpetrator must alter the chattel in a way that is "so material as to change the identity of the chattel or its essential character." Restatement § 226 comment d. At worst, StarLink contamination changed plaintiffs' yield from being corn fit for human consumption to corn fit only for domestic or industrial use. Plaintiffs do not claim they were growing the corn to eat themselves, but for sale on the commodity markets. The crops were still viable for the purpose for which plaintiffs would normally use them, for sale on the open market. That the market had become less hospitable does not change the product's essential character. As above, the severity of the alteration is indicated by the decrease in market price. This could arguably constitute a trespass to chattels, but does not rise to the level of conversion.Lastly, negligence cannot support a conversion claim. It requires intent. Restatement § 224. The complaint alleges that defendants did not take adequate precautions to ensure that StarLink corn was adequately segregated. Nowhere do plaintiffs claim that defendants intentionally commingled StarLink and non-StarLink corn, or deliberately contaminated the food supply. Even if defendants negligently failed to prevent cross-pollination and commingling, they would not be liable for conversion.

V. Nuisance

A. Private [Nuisance]

The complaint alleges that defendants created a private nuisance by distributing corn seeds with the Cry9C protein, knowing that they would cross-pollinate with neighboring corn crops. [The private nuisance claims appear to be premised exclusively on cross-pollination in the fields, not commingling later in the distribution chain.]

A private nuisance is a nontrespassory invasion of another's interest in the private use and enjoyment of land." Restatement (Second) of Torts § 821D. We agree that drifting pollen can constitute an invasion, and that contaminating neighbors' crops interferes with their enjoyment of the land. The issue is whether defendants are responsible for contamination caused by their product beyond the point of sale.

Commingling could not constitute a private nuisance because it does not involve an invasion of any private interests in land. By contrast, the public nuisance claims, discussed below, may be premised on commingling because "unlike a private nuisance, a public nuisance does not necessarily involve interference with use or enjoyment of land." Restatement § 821B comment h.

Defendants argue that they cannot be liable for any nuisance caused by StarLink because they were no longer in control of the seeds once they were sold to farmers. But one can be liable for nuisance "not only when he carries on the activity but also when he participates to a substantial extent in carrying it on." Restatement § 834. Plaintiffs maintain that defendants' design of the StarLink technology, distribution of the seeds and, most importantly, their failure to fulfill their EPA-mandated duties, constitutes substantial participation.The paradigm private nuisance case involves a suit between two neighboring landowners, one of whom alleges that the other's activities are somehow interfering with the first's enjoyment of the land. Suing the manufacturer of the product that the neighbor was using appears to be an extension of nuisance law into an area normally regulated by product liability. But there is precedent for such an application under certain circumstances, and it does fit within the definition of a nuisance. . . .Suppose, however, that [the manufacturer] had not taken steps to alert customers of the risks of the product, or intentionally marketed the product to customers who it knew or should have known would dispose of [it] in a manner that would harm the environment. Nothing in the opinion in City of Bloomington would preclude the imposition of liability on the manufacturer under those facts. . .

.   This brings us to the case at bar, which is much closer to mainstream nuisance doctrine than either the asbestos or gun cases. In the asbestos cases, the plaintiffs had themselves purchased the product, consented to having it installed on their property and then sued the manufacturer when it turned out to be harmful. There was no invasion of a neighboring property and plaintiffs had exclusive access to the nuisance-causing agent. Here, plaintiffs did not purchase StarLink seeds, and have alleged that pollen from neighboring farms did enter their premises.

Aside from the presence of an invasion, the fact that the alleged nuisance occurred on another's property means that, unlike asbestos purchasers, plaintiffs had no ability to access or control the nuisance themselves. In the gun cases, manufacturers successfully argued that they should not be held responsible for third parties' intentional misuse of their products. Here, however, plaintiffs have not alleged that StarLink farmers defied the manufacturers' instructions, but rather that the instructions themselves violated the EPA's mandates. Moreover, the gun cases alleged a public nuisance and did not implicate plaintiffs' ability to enjoy land or anyone's unreasonable use of land. Private nuisance jurisprudence has always focused on the use and enjoyment of land.

Plaintiffs here have alleged that they are unable to enjoy the profits of their land (selling food corn), because of an unreasonable activity on neighboring land (growing StarLink corn).Another critical factor here is the impact of the limited registration, which negates many of the concerns courts have expressed about holding manufacturers liable for post-sale nuisances. For example, they emphasized that the manufacturers did not have any control over how the purchasers had used their products, or any access to abate the nuisance. Aventis, on the other hand, had an affirmative duty to enforce StarLink farmers' compliance with the Grower Agreements.

This arguably gave Aventis some measure of control over StarLink's use, as well as a means to abate any nuisance caused by its misuse. This mirrors Page County Appliance Center, supra, where the court found the manufacturer's ongoing service contract with the purchaser gave defendant enough access and control to create a question of fact as to its contribution to the nuisance. Aventis' duties under the limited registration were, by comparison, even more extensive. Similarly, defendants' failure to give StarLink farmers the warnings mandated by the limited registration, and (ultimately incorrect) representations that StarLink need not be segregated because the EPA was going to approve it for human consumption, are also arguably the type of culpable conduct relied upon. . .

In summary, of the states involved here Iowa, Wisconsin and Illinois have all held a manufacturer liable for a nuisance related to its product beyond the point of sale. . . .The lack of state precedent matching these precise facts does not preclude us from applying widely accepted Restatement law to new factual situations. Residue from a product drifting across property lines presents a typical nuisance claim. All parties who substantially contribute to the nuisance are liable. The unique obligations imposed by the limited registration arguably put Aventis in a position to control the nuisance. On a motion to dismiss we may not speculate whether the as yet undeveloped facts will constitute substantial contribution. To the extent the allegations comport with our preemption analysis above, they do state a valid claim for private nuisance.

B. Public [Nuisance]

Plaintiffs also assert that StarLink's contamination of the general food corn supply constitutes a public nuisance. Beyond defendants' argument that they lacked control over the alleged nuisance, discussed above, they assert that plaintiffs cannot establish special harm. At the outset, we note the limited depth of review courts typically undertake on a motion to dismiss a public nuisance claim.

The pleading requirements are not strenuous because the 'concept of common law public nuisance elude[s] precise definition.' ... The unreasonableness of the defendant's actions and the substantialness of the right invasion, which lead to the determination of nuisance, are questions of fact for the jury.'To state a claim, plaintiffs must allege "an unreasonable interference with a right common to the general public." Restatement § 821B(1).

The Restatement sweeps broadly in defining a "public right," including "the public health, the public safety, the public peace, the public comfort or the public convenience." Restatement § 821B(2)(a). Contamination of the food supply implicates health, safety, comfort and convenience, and certainly satisfies this permissive standard.To state a private action for public nuisance, plaintiffs must also demonstrate that they have been harmed differently than the general public. Restatement § 821C.

The harm must be of a different type, not merely a difference in severity or imposing a disproportionate share of the burden on plaintiffs. Among the Restatement's specific examples are physical harm to chattels, § 821C comment d, and pecuniary loss to businesses, § 821C comment h. Both are present here.

The closest analogy and most pertinent discussion is in Burgess v. M/V Tamano, 370 F. Supp. 247, 250 (D. Me. 1973). There, commercial fisherman alleged that an oil spill harmed local waters and marine life. The court found that although fishing the waters was a right of the general public, it affected commercial fishermen differently because they depended on it for their livelihood. This was consistent with the general principle that pecuniary loss to the plaintiff will be regarded as different in kind 'where the plaintiff has an established business making commercial use of the public right with which the defendant interferes ....'" Id., quoting Prosser, Law of Torts, § 88 at 590 (4th ed. 1971).

Here, plaintiffs are commercial corn farmers. While the general public has a right to safe food, plaintiffs depend on the integrity of the corn supply for their livelihood.Defendants maintain that because plaintiffs purport to represent a group so numerous as a nationwide class of corn farmers, their damages cannot be considered special or unique. But the special damages requirement does not limit the absolute number of parties affected so much as it restricts the types of harm that are compensable. Class actions and special damages are not mutually exclusive. Commercial corn farmers, as a group, are affected differently than the general public.

CONCLUSION

For the foregoing reasons, defendants' motion to dismiss is granted with respect to the claims for conversion . . . . The motion is denied with respect to the claims for negligence per se, public nuisance, private nuisance . . . . The negligence and strict liability claims are dismissed to the extent they rely on a failure to warn, but may proceed under the theories outlined above.

6.2.1 Tort Law
Moore v. Board of Regents of the Univ of Calif

Moore v. Regents of University of California

793 P.2d 479 (1990)

OPINION by: Judge J. Panelli

I. Introduction

We granted review in this case to determine whether plaintiff has stated a cause of action against his physician and other defendants for using his cells in potentially lucrative medical research without his permission. Plaintiff alleges that his physician failed to disclose preexisting research and economic interests in the cells before obtaining consent to the medical procedures by which they were extracted. The superior court sustained all defendants' demurrers to the third amended complaint, and the Court of Appeal reversed. We hold that the complaint states a cause of action for breach of the physician's disclosure obligations, but not for conversion.

II. Facts

Our only task in reviewing a ruling on a demurrer is to determine whether the complaint states a cause of action. Accordingly, we assume that the complaint's properly pleaded material allegations are true and give the complaint a reasonable interpretation by reading it as a whole and all its parts in their context. . . . The plaintiff is John Moore (Moore), who underwent treatment for hairy-cell leukemia at the Medical Center of the University of California at Los Angeles (UCLA Medical Center). The five defendants are: (1) Dr. David W. Golde (Golde), a physician who attended Moore at UCLA Medical Center; (2) the Regents of the University of California (Regents), who own and operate the university; (3) Shirley G. Quan, a researcher employed by the Regents; (4) Genetics Institute, Inc. (Genetics Institute); and (5) Sandoz Pharmaceuticals Corporation and related entities (collectively Sandoz).

Moore first visited UCLA Medical Center on October 5, 1976, shortly after he learned that he had hairy-cell leukemia. After hospitalizing Moore and "withdr[awing] extensive amounts of blood, bone marrow aspirate, and other bodily substances," Golde n1 confirmed that diagnosis. At this time all defendants, including Golde, were aware that "certain blood products and blood components were of great value in a number of commercial and scientific efforts" and that access to a patient whose blood contained these substances would provide "competitive, commercial, and scientific advantages." . . .

On October 8, 1976, Golde recommended that Moore's spleen be removed. Golde informed Moore "that he had reason to fear for his life, and that the proposed splenectomy operation . . . was necessary to slow down the progress of his disease." Based upon Golde's representations, Moore signed a written consent form authorizing the splenectomy.

Before the operation, Golde and Quan "formed the intent and made arrangements to obtain portions of [Moore's] spleen following its removal" and to take them to a separate research unit. Golde gave written instructions to this effect on October 18 and 19, 1976. These research activities "were not intended to have . . . any relation to [Moore's] medical . . . care." However, neither Golde nor Quan informed Moore of their plans to conduct this research or requested his permission. Surgeons at UCLA Medical Center, whom the complaint does not name as defendants, removed Moore's spleen on October 20, 1976.

Moore returned to the UCLA Medical Center several times between November 1976 and September 1983. He did so at Golde's direction and based upon representations "that such visits were necessary and required for his health and well-being, and based upon the trust inherent in and by virtue of the physician-patient relationship . . . ." On each of these visits Golde withdrew additional samples of "blood, blood serum, skin, bone marrow aspirate, and sperm." On each occasion Moore traveled to the UCLA Medical Center from his home in Seattle because he had been told that the procedures were to be performed only there and only under Golde's direction.

"In fact, [however,] throughout the period of time that [Moore] was under [Golde's] care and treatment, . . . the defendants were actively involved in a number of activities which they concealed from [Moore] . . . ." Specifically, defendants were conducting research on Moore's cells and planned to "benefit financially and competitively . . . [by exploiting the cells] and [their] exclusive access to [the cells] by virtue of [Golde's] ongoing physician-patient relationship . . . ."

Sometime before August 1979, Golde established a cell line from Moore's T-lymphocytes. FN2 On January 30, 1981, the Regents applied for a patent on the cell line, listing Golde and Quan as inventors. "[B]y virtue of an established policy . . ., [the] Regents, Golde, and Quan would share in any royalties or profits . . . arising out of [the] patent." The patent issued on March 20, 1984, naming Golde and Quan as the inventors of the cell line and the Regents as the assignee of the patent. (U.S. Patent No. 4,438,032 (Mar. 20, 1984).)

SELECTED NOTES

FN2 A T-lymphocyte is a type of white blood cell. T-lymphocytes produce lymphokines, or proteins that regulate the immune system. Some lymphokines have potential therapeutic value. If the genetic material responsible for producing a particular lymphokine can be identified, it can sometimes be used to manufacture large quantities of the lymphokine through the techniques of recombinant DNA. (See generally U.S. Congress, Office of Technology Assessment, New Developments in Biotechnology: Ownership of Human Tissues and Cells (1987) at pp. 31-46 (hereafter OTA Report); see also fn. 29, post.) While the genetic code for lymphokines does not vary from individual to individual, it can nevertheless be quite difficult to locate the gene responsible for a particular lymphokine. Because T-lymphocytes produce many different lymphokines, the relevant gene is often like a needle in a haystack. (OTA Rep., supra, at p. 42.) Moore's T-lymphocytes were interesting to the defendants because they overproduced certain lymphokines, thus making the corresponding genetic material easier to identify. (In published research papers, defendants and other researchers have shown that the overproduction was caused by a virus, and that normal T-lymphocytes infected by the virus will also overproduce. See fn. 30, post.)

Cells taken directly from the body (primary cells) are not very useful for these purposes. Primary cells typically reproduce a few times and then die. One can, however, sometimes continue to use cells for an extended period of time by developing them into a "cell line," a culture capable of reproducing indefinitely. This is not, however, always an easy task. "Longterm growth of human cells and tissues is difficult, often an art," and the probability of succeeding with any given cell sample is low, except for a few types of cells not involved in this case. (OTA Rep., supra, at p. 5.)

. . . The Regent's patent also covers various methods for using the cell line to produce lymphokines. Moore admits in his complaint that "the true clinical potential of each of the lymphokines . . . [is] difficult to predict, [but] . . . competing commercial firms in these relevant fields have published reports in biotechnology industry periodicals predicting a potential market of approximately $ 3.01 Billion Dollars by the year 1990 for a whole range of [such lymphokines] . . . ."

With the Regents' assistance, Golde negotiated agreements for commercial development of the cell line and products to be derived from it. Under an agreement with Genetics Institute, Golde "became a paid consultant" and "acquired the rights to 75,000 shares of common stock." Genetics Institute also agreed to pay Golde and the Regents "at least $ 330,000 over three years, including a pro-rata share of [Golde's] salary and fringe benefits, in exchange for . . . exclusive access to the materials and research performed" on the cell line and products derived from it. On June 4, 1982, Sandoz "was added to the agreement," and compensation payable to Golde and the Regents was increased by $ 110,000. "[T]hroughout this period, . . . Quan spent as much as 70 [percent] of her time working for [the] Regents on research" related to the cell line. . .

B. Conversion

Moore also attempts to characterize the invasion of his rights as a conversion -- a tort that protects against interference with possessory and ownership interests in personal property. He theorizes that he continued to own his cells following their removal from his body, at least for the purpose of directing their use, and that he never consented to their use in potentially lucrative medical research. Thus, to complete Moore's argument, defendants' unauthorized use of his cells constitutes a conversion. As a result of the alleged conversion, Moore claims a proprietary interest in each of the products that any of the defendants might ever create from his cells or the patented cell line. No court, however, has ever in a reported decision imposed conversion liability for the use of human cells in medical research. n15 While that fact does not end our inquiry, it raises a flag of caution. (See fn. 16.) In effect, what Moore is asking us to do is to impose a tort duty on scientists to investigate the consensual pedigree of each human cell sample used in research.

To impose such a duty, which would affect medical research of importance to all of society, implicates policy concerns far removed from the traditional, two-party ownership disputes in which the law of conversion arose. Invoking a tort theory originally used to determine whether the loser or the finder of a horse had the better title, Moore claims ownership of the results of socially important medical research, including the genetic code for chemicals that regulate the functions of every human being's immune system.

We have recognized that, when the proposed application of a very general theory of liability in a new context raises important policy concerns, it is especially important to face those concerns and address them openly. [declining to expand negligence law to encompass theory of "clergyman malpractice"];[declining to apply tort remedies for breach of the covenant of good faith in the employment context]; [declining to apply strict products liability to pharmaceutical manufacturers].) Moreover, we should be hesitant to "impose [new tort duties] when to do so would involve complex policy decisions", especially when such decisions are more appropriately the subject of legislative deliberation and resolution. This certainly is not to say that the applicability of common law torts is limited to the historical or factual contexts of existing cases. But on occasions when we have opened or sanctioned new areas of tort liability, we "have noted that the 'wrongs and injuries involved were both comprehensible and assessable within the existing judicial framework.'"

Accordingly, we first consider whether the tort of conversion clearly gives Moore a cause of action under existing law. We do not believe it does. Because of the novelty of Moore's claim to own the biological materials at issue, to apply the theory of conversion in this context would frankly have to be recognized as an extension of the theory. Therefore, we consider next whether it is advisable to extend the tort to this context. 1. Moore's Claim Under Existing Law "To establish a conversion, plaintiff must establish an actual interference with his ownership or right of possession. . . . Where plaintiff neither has title to the property alleged to have been converted, nor possession thereof, he cannot maintain an action for conversion." Since Moore clearly did not expect to retain possession of his cells following their removal, to sue for their conversion he must have retained an ownership interest in them. But there are several reasons to doubt that he did retain any such interest. First, no reported judicial decision supports Moore's claim, either directly or by close analogy. Second, California statutory law drastically limits any continuing interest of a patient in excised cells. Third, the subject matters of the Regents' patent -- the patented cell line and the products derived from it -- cannot be Moore's property.

Neither the Court of Appeal's opinion, the parties' briefs, nor our research discloses a case holding that a person retains a sufficient interest in excised cells to support a cause of action for conversion. We do not find this surprising, since the laws governing such things as human tissues, transplantable organs, blood, fetuses, pituitary glands, corneal tissue, and dead bodies deal with human biological materials as objects sui generis, regulating their disposition to achieve policy goals rather than abandoning them to the general law of personal property. It is these specialized statutes, not the law of conversion, to which courts ordinarily should and do look for guidance on the disposition of human biological materials.

Not only are the wrongful-publicity cases irrelevant to the issue of conversion, but the analogy to them seriously misconceives the nature of the genetic materials and research involved in this case. Moore, adopting the analogy originally advanced by the Court of Appeal, argues that "[i]f the courts have found a sufficient proprietary interest in one's persona, how could one not have a right in one's own genetic material, something far more profoundly the essence of one's human uniqueness than a name or a face?" However, as the defendants' patent makes clear -- and the complaint, too, if read with an understanding of the scientific terms which it has borrowed from the patent -- the goal and result of defendants' efforts has been to manufacture lymphokines.

Lymphokines, unlike a name or a face, have the same molecular structure in every human being and the same, important functions in every human being's immune system. Moreover, the particular genetic material which is responsible for the natural production of lymphokines, and which defendants use to manufacture lymphokines in the laboratory, is also the same in every person; it is no more unique to Moore than the number of vertebrae in the spine or the chemical formula of hemoglobin.

The next consideration that makes Moore's claim of ownership problematic is California statutory law, which drastically limits a patient's control over excised cells. Pursuant to Health and Safety Code section 7054.4, "[n]otwithstanding any other provision of law, recognizable anatomical parts, human tissues, anatomical human remains, or infectious waste following conclusion of scientific use shall be disposed of by interment, incineration, or any other method determined by the state department [of health services] to protect the public health and safety." Clearly the Legislature did not specifically intend this statute to resolve the question of whether a patient is entitled to compensation for the nonconsensual use of excised cells. A primary object of the statute is to ensure the safe handling of potentially hazardous biological waste materials. Yet one cannot escape the conclusion that the statute's practical effect is to limit, drastically, a patient's control over excised cells. By restricting how excised cells may be used and requiring their eventual destruction, the statute eliminates so many of the rights ordinarily attached to property that one cannot simply assume that what is left amounts to "property" or "ownership" for purposes of conversion law.

2. Should Conversion Liability Be Extended?

As we have discussed, Moore's novel claim to own the biological materials at issue in this case is problematic, at best. Accordingly, his attempt to apply the theory of conversion within this context must frankly be recognized as a request to extend that theory. While we do not purport to hold that excised cells can never be property for any purpose whatsoever, the novelty of Moore's claim demands express consideration of the policies to be served by extending liability rather than blind deference to a complaint alleging as a legal conclusion the existence of a cause of action. There are three reasons why it is inappropriate to impose liability for conversion based upon the allegations of Moore's complaint.

First, a fair balancing of the relevant policy considerations counsels against extending the tort. Second, problems in this area are better suited to legislative resolution. Third, the tort of conversion is not necessary to protect patients' rights. For these reasons, we conclude that the use of excised human cells in medical research does not amount to a conversion.

Of the relevant policy considerations, two are of overriding importance. The first is protection of a competent patient's right to make autonomous medical decisions. That right, as already discussed, is grounded in well-recognized and long-standing principles of fiduciary duty and informed consent. This policy weighs in favor of providing a remedy to patients when physicians act with undisclosed motives that may affect their professional judgment. The second important policy consideration is that we not threaten with disabling civil liability innocent parties who are engaged in socially useful activities, such as researchers who have no reason to believe that their use of a particular cell sample is, or may be, against a donor's wishes.

To reach an appropriate balance of these policy considerations is extremely important. In its report to Congress, the Office of Technology Assessment emphasized that "[u]ncertainty about how courts will resolve disputes between specimen sources and specimen users could be detrimental to both academic researchers and the infant biotechnology industry, particularly when the rights are asserted long after the specimen was obtained. The assertion of rights by sources would affect not only the researcher who obtained the original specimen, but perhaps other researchers as well. "Biological materials are routinely distributed to other researchers for experimental purposes, and scientists who obtain cell lines or other specimen-derived products, such as gene clones, from the original researcher could also be sued under certain legal theories [such as conversion].

Furthermore, the uncertainty could affect product developments as well as research. Since inventions containing human tissues and cells may be patented and licensed for commercial use, companies are unlikely to invest heavily in developing, manufacturing, or marketing a product when uncertainty about clear title exists." (OTA Rep., supra, at p. 27.) Indeed, so significant is the potential obstacle to research stemming from uncertainty about legal title to biological materials that the Office of Technology Assessment reached this striking conclusion: "[R]egardless of the merit of claims by the different interested parties, resolving the current uncertainty may be more important to the future of biotechnology than resolving it in any particular way." (OTA Rep., supra, at p. 27.)

We need not, however, make an arbitrary choice between liability and nonliability. Instead, an examination of the relevant policy considerations suggests an appropriate balance: Liability based upon existing disclosure obligations, rather than an unprecedented extension of the conversion theory, protects patients' rights of privacy and autonomy without unnecessarily hindering research. To be sure, the threat of liability for conversion might help to enforce patients' rights indirectly. This is because physicians might be able to avoid liability by obtaining patients' consent, in the broadest possible terms, to any conceivable subsequent research use of excised cells.

Unfortunately, to extend the conversion theory would utterly sacrifice the other goal of protecting innocent parties. Since conversion is a strict liability tort, it would impose liability on all those into whose hands the cells come, whether or not the particular defendant participated in, or knew of, the inadequate disclosures that violated the patient's right to make an informed decision. In contrast to the conversion theory, the fiduciary-duty and informed-consent theories protect the patient directly, without punishing innocent parties or creating **disincentives to the conduct of socially beneficial research.**

———————————————

Chapter 8

Intellectual Property Law and Emerging Technologies

6.2.2   Intellectual Property Law --Basics

Intellectual Property Basics
The constitutional authority for patents is found in the U.S. Constitution. Article One, section 8, clause 8, which states:

> The Congress shall have power ... To promote the progress of science and useful arts, by securing for limited times to authors and inventors the exclusive right to their respective writings and discoveries;

What is a Patent?
There are three types of patents: (1) Utility patents may be granted to anyone who invents or discovers any new and useful process, machine, article of manufacture, or composition of matter, or any new and useful improvement thereof; (2) Design patents may be granted to anyone who invents a new, original, and ornamental design for an article of manufacture; and (3) Plant patents may be granted to anyone who invents or discovers and asexually reproduces any distinct and new variety of plant.

What Is a Trademark or Servicemark?
A trademark is a brand name. A trademark or service mark includes any word, name, symbol, device, or any combination, used or intended to be used to identify and distinguish the goods/services of one seller or provider from those of others, and to indicate the source of the goods/services. (U.S. PTO website).

What is a Copyright?
Copyright is a form of protection provided to the authors of "original works of authorship" including literary, dramatic, musical, artistic, and certain other intellectual works, both published and unpublished.

The requirements for a patent include: (1) utility ; (2) novelty, nonobviousness ; and (3) written requirement.

Identifying the appropriate prior art is part of the process. The rule describes this: . . . even if an invention is new, a patent may not be obtained "if the differences between the subject matter sought to be patented and the prior art are such that the subject matter as a whole would have been obvious at the time the invention was made to a person having ordinary skill in the art to which said subject matter pertains."

It must be "an advance in the art" and "not a trivial advance" or an "extension over something else."

Further, the invention must be duplicated from the patent without "undue experimentation' by some who is a person of ordinary skill in the ar. In "the field of biotechnology, a person of ordinary skill in the art may well be a person with a Ph.D., because the average biotech scientist has a Ph.D. "

The invention must have novelty , which means it must be new or a novel innovation, something not anticipated.

The Written Description Requirement, the published guidance for examiners in evaluating biotechnology patents requires the following procedure: (1) compare what the applicant possesses and what the applicant claims; (2) determine whether there is sufficient written description to inform a skilled artisan that the applicant is in possession of the claimed invention as a whole; (3) for species claims, determine whether the application: (i) includes a reduction to practice; (ii) is complete based on the drawings; or (iii) identifies sufficient distinguishing characteristics to show the applicant was in possession of the claimed invention; and (4) for genus claims, determine whether the application: (i) describes a representative number of species by reduction to practice, drawings, or disclosure of identifying characteristics; or (ii) disclosed functional characteristics correlated with structure or a combination of identifying characteristics that indicate the inventor was in possession of the claimed invention.

Biotechnology Patent Issues

The USPTO applied the Brenner standards to biotechnology patent applications and required human clinical data to demonstrate biotechnology invention utility.
In 1995, the USPTO issued guidance for biotechnology patent utility.

With regard to the nonobviousness criteria, this became an important issue in the fast moving field of biotechnology, and raised the question about what is "state of the art" ? Because the state of the art changed so rapidly, the U.S. PTO wrote that ". . . it is important for the examiner to keep in mind that the question to be answered is whether the claimed invention would have been obvious in view of the state of the art at the time the invention was made, not at the time it is being examined."

In Graham v. John Deere Co., the Supreme Court set forth three factual inquiries to be used in considering whether an invention is obvious or nonobvious: (i) determining the scope and content of the prior art; (ii) ascertaining the differences between the prior art and the claims at issue; and (iii) resolving the level of ordinary skill in the pertinent art.

Also, secondary considerations such as unexpected results, commercial success, long-felt need, and the failure of others are to be considered in evaluating the obviousness or nonobviousness of an invention.

In the nonobviousness analysis, consider: (a) the claimed invention must be considered as a whole; (b) the references must be considered as a whole and must suggest the desirability and thus the obviousness of making the combination; (c) the references must be viewed without the benefit of impermissible hindsight afforded by the claimed invention; and (d) reasonable expectation of success is the standard by which obviousness is determined.

The enabling requirement, for biotechnology was reinforced by The Federal Circuit, U.S. Court of Appeals, by invalidating broad biotechnology claims requiring "undue experimentation." Enabling Requirement Criteria can be analyzed using the Wands factors which are: (1) the quantity of experimentation required; (2) the amount of guidance provided; (3) the presence or absence of working examples; (4) the nature of the invention; (5) the state of the prior art; (6) the relative skill of those in the art; (7) the predictability of the art; and (8) the breadth of the claims.

Nanotechnology and Patent Law

The U.S. PTO found that patents that might otherwise be called "nanotechnology" were called by many descriptions and were found in many different classes of patents in many categories. In order to help with the prior art for both applicants and examiners, a new class was created for nanotechnology: Class 977 Nanotechnology. In this class, a "cross-reference art collection" exists for nanotechnology and provides for disclosures related to: (i) Nanostructure and chemical compositions of nanostructure; (ii) Device that include at least one nanostructure; (iii) Mathematical algorithms, e.g., computer software, etc., specifically adapted for modeling configurations or properties of nanostructure; (iv). Methods or apparatus for making, detecting, analyzing, or treating nanostructure; and (v). Specified particular uses of nanostructure.

As used above, the term "nanostructure" is defined to mean an atomic, molecular, or macromolecular structure that: (a) Has at least one physical dimension of approximately 1-100 nanometers; and (b) Possesses a special property, provides a special function, or produces a special effect that is uniquely attributable to the structure s nanoscale physical size.
Two notes describe the content of the Class 977 collection:

(2) Note. Class 977 generally does not cover chemical or biological structures, per se, specifically provided for elsewhere. That is, a compound, element, or composition of matter of nanoscale dimension is not considered to be sufficient by itself for placement in Class 977. Compounds, elements, composites, and compositions of matter of nanoscale dimension are placed in the U.S. Patent Classification system (USPC) where such compounds, elements, composites, and compositions of matter are classifiable unless they have particularly shaped configurations (e.g., fullerenes or fullerene-like structures, etc.) formed during manufacture which impart special properties or functions to the nanostructural assemblage related to the altering of basic chemical or physical properties attributed to the nanoscale.

(3) Note. Special properties and functionalities should be interpreted broadly, and are defined as those properties and functionalities that are significant, distinctive, non-nominal, noteworthy, or unique as a result of the nanoscale dimension. In general, differences in

properties and functionalities that constitute mere differences of scale are insufficient to warrant inclusion of the subject matter in Class 977.

Robots and Patent Law

A new class was created for robots, Class 901. Robots, as well as a collection of art of robot-related patents. The robot art collection is described as follows:

> This collection provides for a reprogrammable, multifunction manipulator designed to move devices through variable programmed motions for the performance of changeable tasks on a repetitive basis without human intervention and all subcombinations thereof specialized for use with such manipulator.

Synthetic Biology—the Rebels

The community of scientists in synthetic biology has coalesced around the iGEM competition for high school and undergraduate students to build a biological machine in competition. In order to move rapidly and improve on the discoveries that are made in the course of the competition, there has been a tacit rejection of the traditional patent system in exchange for the open source concept which was prevalent in the early days of computer programming. Open source advocates believe patents stifle innovation and prevent other inventors from using prior art without infringing thereby destroying the ability to move the science and technology forward. They also feel that patents that are granted too broadly leave little room for innovation, which has been seen in biotechnology, particularly genetics.

6.2.3   Intellectual Property Law--Recording Industry Association of America

Copyright, among the three basic types of intellectual property law, has probably had the biggest impact from emerging technologies, in particular, digital works that are preserved, published and passed along through electronic communication.

6.2.3   Intellectual Property—Copyright
Copyright, Using litigation to make examples in society of IP theft, Recording Industry case
Copyright flows from the same constitutional basis as patents and with the same general approach—statutorily created exclusive rights to foster progress. The U.S. Constitution, Article One, section 8, clause 8 states:

> The Congress shall have power ... To promote the progress of science and useful arts, by securing for limited times to authors and inventors the exclusive right to their respective writings and discoveries;. . .

Elements of copyright

To have copyrightable subject matter there is only a threshold for protection required and to exhibit only a modicum of originality and be fixed in a "tangible medium of expression." A notice of copyright is required on all works published prior to 1989; but registration of copyright is not required to be valid. However, if the party making the infringement claim files suit, then the work must have been created by the party bringing suit, or the employer in a "work for hire" work and it must be formally registered.

The duration of copyright has changed with legislation over the years. Currently, the duration of copyright is for the life of the author, plus 70 years, or 95 years from first publication in the case of anonymous works (or 120 years from year of creation, whichever comes first.)

Philosophical perspectives on copyright

In 1769, Millar v. Taylor, Lord Justice Mansfield opined: "From what source, then is the common law drawn, which is admitted to be so clear in respect of the copy before publication? From this argument – because it is just, that an author should reap the pecuniary profits of his own ingenuity and labor."

Philosophical basis of copyright

Copyright is based on two philosophical underpinnings: natural law and utilitarian approaches. The natural law approach recognizes personhood and the right in that person's own creations and ownership of that work. The utilitarian approach is primarily for the public good, and secondarily for the benefit of the author. The utilitarian approach is the basis in the U.S. ". . . to promote the Progress of Science and useful Arts."

The Digital Age

By the early 1990s, Congress passed several amendments to the Copyright Act to address fears of reproducing content through digital means. The Audio Home Recording Act of 1992 regulates the design of digital audio tape technology and imposes a tax on the sale of devices and blank tapes to compensate copyright holders for home copying. The Digital Performance Right in Sound Recordings Act of 1995 affords creators and owners of sound recordings a basis for earning income on digital streams and webcasts. The No Electronic Theft (NET) Act of 1996 expands criminal enforcement for digital piracy. The Digital Millennium Copyright Act (DMCA) of 1998 affords to copyright owners rights against those who circumvent copy protection technologies and leaves online service providers protected from liability for infringing acts of their subscribers subject to various limitations.

The Betamax case, 1984

This case demonstrates a fair use based on the question of whether a recording device for television programming was "fair use", an exception to copyright law and a defense to infringement.

A major electronics manufacturer developed a video tape recording device that viewers could use to watch their selected television shows when they wanted to at a later time. This "time-shifting" which was a recording of a complete TV program in real-time for viewing later, was feared to cause great economic loss in the television programming content industry.

Several major film studios filed a copyright infringement suit against the electronics manufacturer claiming the device could be used for copyright infringement.

In 1984's Sony v. Universal Studios (aka the Betamax case), the Supreme Court held that time-shifting with a VCR did meet the "fair use" standard. The courts noted that the private, non-commercial home taping of free television programs for later viewing was not infringing and was not economically damaging.

Napster case

The Napster case, Capitol Records v. Bertelsmann, attracted much public attention because it affected the public's entertainment interests. The court opined: "Applying this standard to the case at bar, it is apparent that plaintiffs' "indexing" theory falls well short of meeting the requirements for establishing direct copyright infringement. Rather than requiring proof of the actual dissemination of a copyrighted work or an offer to distribute that work for the purpose of its further distribution or public performance, plaintiffs' theory is premised on the assumption that any offer to distribute a copyrighted work violates section 106(3).

This is not sufficient to satisfy plaintiffs' burden of proving that Napster or its users directly infringed their copyrighted musical compositions and sound recordings, as they must do if they are to hold defendants secondarily liable for that infringement. Accordingly, the court holds that defendants are entitled to summary judgment on this issue."

Napster case appeal

The Ninth Circuit ultimately concluded that Napster's direct knowledge of copyright infringement by users of its software and its ability to control that activity through the index of file names maintained on its central servers created a responsibility to remove links to infringing content and engage in policing its network.

Napster was forced into bankruptcy. While this case was pending, a new generation of P2P service providers developed and the Grokster case began.

Grokster case

The Grokster case, Metro-Goldwyn Mayer Studios v. Grokster, 543 U.S. 913 (2005), seemed like it might be a victory for content providers, when Grokster lost against the studios. In Grokster, the company had encouraged and invited infringement making statements that were clear to that effect. The court opined: "We hold that one who distributes a device with the object of promoting its use to infringe copyright, as shown by clear expression or other affirmative steps taken to foster infringement, is liable for the resulting acts of infringement of third parties." This seeming victory for content providers really provided a recipe for how to avoid this outcome in the next version of a file sharing website.

In RIAA v. Verizon Internet Services, 351 F.3d 1229 (D.C. Cir. 2003), subpoena power had been limited to find file sharers, to only the IP address of the computer, but without the physical address and knowing the jurisdiction it was extremely difficult and time consuming to sue individual file sharers, but after Grokster and Napster cases, the content industries started suing individual file-sharers and sought to identify individuals.

Capitol Records, Inc. v. Thomas, 579 F.Supp.2d 1210 (D. Minn. 2008) was the first file-sharing case to go to trial against an individual. The trial judge reversed a $220,000 verdict against the file sharer and ordered a new trial based on the question whether making a file folder available was distribution ,and whether the activity amounted to "and to authorize". If "authorize" constituted making a file available, then individuals were meeting the standard for infringement. Over 30,000 individual law suits were filed bu the Recording Industry of Association of America (RIAA).

The Electronic Frontier Foundation, a non-profit advocacy group for open internet and free access, wrote:

> Five years into the RIAA's campaign, it has become all too clear (if there
> were ever any doubt) that suing music fans is not a viable business model for
> the recording industry. (Sept. 2008).

In 2008, RIAA abandoned its individual law suit effort after a backlash of bad publicity. Thereafter, the RIAA shifted its pressure to Online Service Providers to notify customers, set up monitoring and warn file sharers of protected content, and block them from uploading.

"Fair use" and the internet

The availability of images that are copyrighted through the internet presents infringement opportunities, but where does "fair use" end and "infringement" begin? *In Perfect 10, Inc. v. Amazon.com*, 487 F.3d 701 (9th Cir. 2007), the court asked whether a search engine can provide thumbnail images of infringing content that has been posted on the internet? In this case, Perfect 10 is a business that provides its subscribers with images of women. Copyright infringers who had obtained the images posted them on the internet where they were now infringing. The search engine collected thumbnails of these images in its searches, and Perfect 10 claimed this was infringement.

The court used the four factor fair use test: (1) Purpose and character of the use; (2) the nature of the copyrighted work; (3) the amount and substantiality of the portion used; and (4) the effect of use on the market.

In the Perfect 10 case, the 9th Circuit opined: "Having undertaken a case-specific analysis of all four factors (downloading images to a cell phone from google search engine), we now weigh all those factors together 'in light of the purposes of copyright'."

We note that Perfect 10 has the burden of proving that it would defeat Google's affirmative fair use defense. In this case, Google has put Perfect 10s thumbnail images (along with millions of other images) to a use fundamentally different than the use intended by Perfect 10.

In doing so, Google has provided a significant benefit to the public. Weighing this significant transformative use against the unproven use of Google's thumbnails for cell phone downloads, and considering the other fair use factors, all in light of the purpose of copyright, we conclude that Google's use of Perfect 10's thumbnails is a fair use...

Remix culture

"Remix culture" is a term frequently used by Stanford law professor and Creative Commons founder Lawrence Lessig to describe a growing society of amateur creators who blend media and materials to develop new works, and the social context that fosters the growth of that community. This suggests a growing societal acceptance of this kind of use of copyrighted material and perhaps a shift in what will be called "fair use."

Society's Consideration of Digital Rights and Aggressive Enforcement

Being too aggressive created a backlash in the RIAA litigation against 30,000 individuals, including stroke victims and children.

Aaron Schwartz case

When Aaron Swartz committed suicide when he was faced with seven felony charges and decades in prison, another backlash followed. Aaron Swartz set up a server inside a closet on the MIT campus and downloaded the content of JSTOR presumptively with a plan to post it and make it available for free. He advocated open source and detested the hoarding of content by services that charged for their content.

The Attorney General, Massachusetts, aggressively pursued a criminal prosecution, and was criticized for it, after Aaron Schwartz committed suicide prior to a hearing. He was being charged with seven felonies, with six counts in the federal criminal complaint. The counts alleged were: (1) wire fraud; (2) computer fraud; (3) unlawfully obtaining information from a protected computer; (4) Recklessly damaging a protected computer; (5) aiding and abetting; (6) and criminal forfeiture.

Aggressive enforcement tactics like this one, may be technically correct, but the backlash from the public from extraordinarily high fines and jail sentences will likely result in an eventual shift in the law in file sharing and content providers will need to update their technological model if they want to continue to have customers.

Chapter 9

Banking and Finance Law and Emerging Technologies
Prof. Catherine Christopher

6.3.1. Emerging technologies in banking and finance law

A financial institution is any firm that engages in financial activities; this is a deliberately broad, umbrella term that encompasses banks, insurance companies, securities firms, holding companies, and firms that offer many other complementary services. A bank is a specific kind of financial institution—generally speaking, banks take deposits and make loans, whereas insurance companies and securities firms engage in other financial services. Financial institutions send information, promises (contracts), and funds around the world via a network that is dizzying in its size, scope, and speed.

Financial institutions serve an important role as economic intermediaries. Banks, for instance, allow you to put your money in one centralized location and direct the bank—the intermediary—to send that money to people you owe. That's what happens when you write a check or pay with a debit or credit card. Globally, intermediaries have proliferated to allow each economic actor to interact with more customers, counterparties, etc.

This makes things easier for buyers and sellers, because the network of intermediaries do a lot of the heavy lifting to make actual transactions happen. Third-party intermediaries solve a lot of problems: they serve as clearinghouses, keepers of ledgers, etc. (Governments want to make sure these important intermediaries are safe and honest, which is why financial institutions are heavily regulated.)

But each financial intermediary charges a small fee for its services. A 2% fee may not seem like much, but in the aggregate, a lot of the world's GDP is bound up in transaction fees. For example, it is estimated that in 2013, credit- and debit-card payments alone generated $250 billion in fees. These fees are borne by the merchants, but to be sure, they are built into the prices of the goods and services consumers are purchasing.

Despite the speed with which each intermediary processes transactions, increases in global connectivity are beginning to make brick-and-mortar firms look slow. Most deposits into checking accounts don't clear until overnight or, in some cases, for several days. Sending actual money—not just setting up a payment—on a weekend or a national holiday is effectively impossible.

Another criticism of the traditional banking system is that it is not fully inclusive, that is, that not all people have access to the banking system. A shocking number of people around the world, and even within the United States, do not have meaningful access to bank accounts. These individuals must rely on informal, and largely unregulated, financial service providers like prepaid cards, check cashers, auto title loan companies, and others.

The World Bank estimates that in 2014, 33.1% of people over the age of 15 in Argentina had bank accounts. In India, that percentage is 35.2%, and in China, 63.8%. Compare these figures with the percentages of people who have bank accounts in Great Britain (97.2%), Germany (98.1%), and Japan (96.4%). By the World Bank's estimate, only 88.0% of Americans have bank accounts. The following excerpt discusses the number of "unbanked" people in America, and the consequences of being unbanked.

Excerpt: Catherine Martin Christopher, Mobile Banking: the Answer for the Unbanked in America?, 65 CATHOLIC U. L. REV. (forthcoming 2016).

About ten percent of the adult population in the United States is unbanked, meaning they do not currently have a bank account. Two-thirds of these people have never had a bank account. (The fact that a third of unbanked people used to have bank accounts means that getting a bank account is not the same thing as keeping one.)

In addition to those who are unbanked, another seventeen percent of American adults are underbanked, meaning they do have a bank account but also utilize alternative financial service providers like check cashers, payday lenders, pawn shops, auto title lenders, or prepaid cards. The unbanked use alternative financial service providers or simply operate in cash. The FDIC estimates that 29% of unbanked households are cash-only.

In America, there are undeniable—and troubling—correlations between banking status and race, age, employment, and other characteristics. [As of late 2014, t]wenty percent of Black households and 18% of Hispanic households are unbanked, compared with just 3.6% of white households. Being unbanked skews young: households where the householder is under age 24 are unbanked at a rate of 15.7%, and households headed by someone between 25 and 34 are unbanked at a rate of 12.5%. Households experiencing unemployment are unbanked at a rate of 23.0%, and households where the householder does not have a high school degree are unbanked at 25.1%. Immigration status, too, is correlated with being unbanked: foreign-born non-citizens living in the US are unbanked at a rate of 22.7%.

Even more significant than race, age, or employment status, however, is income level. Households earning less than $15,000 per year are unbanked at a rate of 27.2%, and those earning between $15,000 and $30,000 per year are unbanked at a rate of 11.4%. Overall, unbanked Americans are disproportionately nonwhite, young, and poor.

A. Why people are unbanked

When the unbanked are asked why they do not have a bank account, the most common answer is that they do not have enough money to warrant an account. Relatedly, many unbanked people also cite high or unpredictable account fees as the reason for not having a bank account. These individuals, mostly poor, typically transact relatively small amounts of money, and they find (or fear) that minimum balance requirements, overdraft fees, and other bank account features are more expensive than the value of the account. In short, most unbanked Americans feel a bank account costs more than it's worth.

Some unbanked people had bank accounts previously, indicating that account retention, as well as account acquisition, is a problem. The Federal Reserve found in 2013 that 34 percent of currently unbanked people "had a bank account at some point in the past." The most common reasons for discontinuing bank account use were the same as those of people who have never had bank accounts: that the customers didn't have enough money to warrant the account, the account fees were too high or unpredictable, or that the customers didn't like dealing with or didn't trust banks.

These previously banked individuals may have discontinued their accounts for reasons of their own, or they may have had their accounts terminated for misuse of the account. Misuse can have long-term ramifications: Most banks rely on ChexSystems, a consumer-reporting "software that records consumers with poor banking practices" or who have engaged in "account mishandling[.]"ChexSystem retains information for five years, and banks use this information in their screening process, allowing them to refuse accounts for individuals who have been flagged. While this system presumably keeps "high risk or fraudulent customers" out of the banking system, it also punishes some who have made innocent mistakes.

Another common reason for being unbanked is distrust or dislike of banks. In its biennial survey of unbanked and underbanked Americans, the FDIC found 34.2% of unbanked respondents cited this as one of the reasons for being unbanked, and 15% cited it as the main reason. Many people who used to have bank accounts report that they "'[got] in trouble,' that is, over-drafting an account and failing—or in some cases refusing—to pay the requisite penalties." These experiences left some people "with strong, negative feelings towards financial institutions[.]"

The other side of the don't-like-banks coin is that some people feel they get better service at alternative financial service locations. The unbanked have little choice in using alternative financial services for their transactional needs, but underbanked people, who by definition do have bank accounts, use alternative financial services voluntarily. This is largely due to increased convenience: alternative financial service providers are often open longer hours than bank branches, and deliver cash or credit on the spot. Alternative financial service providers also typically charge up-front fees, whereas unbanked people often perceive bank accounts as having "penalties and hidden costs."

Banks, for their part, have little financial incentive to offer traditional banking products specifically to the unbanked: because these individuals make such small transactions and carry small balances, banks do not expect significant profit from these customers.

B. What it means to be unbanked

Bank accounts serve several important, if basic, purposes: they offer an opportunity to deposit and save, access to a secure and inexpensive payment system, physical security, access to credit, and the convenience of locating all these services under one roof at lower costs. In short, they provide financial and physical security. Alternative financial service providers, on the other hand, offer these services at significant expense or do not offer them at all.

1. Savings & deposits

Bank accounts facilitate savings because they are a place to deposit and store funds that are not being spent. Savings, in turn, allow individuals to "buy homes, pay for education, or start small businesses; all of which are proven measures to develop assets and accumulate wealth."

Some deposited funds, typically those in savings accounts, accrue interest. All funds on deposit with regulated state and federal banks are insured by the FDIC, within statutory limitations. Check-cashers, in contrast, do not offer a place to keep funds on deposit, and offer no interest or insurance. Prepaid cards offer a place to keep funds on deposit, but typically do not offer interest. Funds stored on prepaid cards are also not typically insured; Bluebird, for instance, offers "pass-through" FDIC insurance, meaning that Bluebird's parent company, American Express, places Bluebird-deposited funds at FDIC-insured banks. If those banks fail, the FDIC will insure them, but if American Express fails, the funds may not be insured.

2. Payment systems

Bank accounts, especially transaction accounts, typically allow the customer to direct a transaction from her own account to the account of another, either by check, debit, or electronic transfer. Most of these services are free—banks typically do not charge a fee for writing a check, and debit fees are typically paid by the merchant rather than the bank customer. Alternative financial service providers, on the other hand, do charge significant fees to deliver payments to utility companies, for example, or to issue money orders.

Bank transfers can also be arranged and conducted promptly. Checks can be written on the spot and handed over, debit transactions take place almost as quickly as a PIN can be entered, and electronic transfers can be arranged at any time of day or night on a bank's website or mobile app. Customers of alternative financial service providers are not so lucky; they must go to the physical location and stand in line before they can conduct their business. Cashing paper checks, whether at a bank or at an alternative financial service provider, is economically inefficient when compared to electronic transactions; debit and electronic payments can be processed far more cheaply. By one estimate, every paper check that is replaced by an electronic transfer saves $1. By shifting more payments from paper checks to electronic transfers, the cost savings and increased efficiency are significant.

3. Security

When funds are on deposit at a bank, they are far safer than when stored at home or in a pocket. Not only are most deposited funds insured by the FDIC, but the physical cash is safer from theft, fire, or natural disaster, because the bank building has better security. Patrons of check-cashing stores, on the other hand, are at significant risk of robbery or mugging: it's highly likely that people walking out of a check-casher have a large amount of cash on their persons, and criminals know that. That these people cash paychecks at regular, predictable intervals only increases their risk of theft.

4. Access to credit

For those with bank accounts, banks and other regulated financial institutions are often the first stop for reliable, affordable credit. Home mortgage and auto loans are available at reasonable interest rates, and credit cards provide shorter-term credit for other purchases.

The unbanked and underbanked, however, often rely on fringe banking institutions such as payday lenders, auto title loan companies, and pawn shops for credit: "These lenders are often usurious, sometimes predatory, and almost always much worse for low-income individuals than the services offered by traditional banks to their customers. For instance, the average annual income for an unbanked family is $25,500, and about 10% of that income, or $2412, goes to the fees and interest paid to access credit or other financial services—services that those with bank accounts often get for free."

As with deposits and payment systems, those most in need of credit and least able to pay for it are charged more dearly.

Because fringe banks do not report their loans to credit bureaus, utilizing these services also hinders individuals' ability to establish their own creditworthiness. Instead, payday and car title loan customers are often sucked into a vicious cycle of rolling over their loans time and again, accruing crippling additional fees.

5. Convenience and lower cost

Banks and regulated financial institutions offer numerous services and products under their roofs and through affiliated institutions; they also offer multiple access points, with ATMs and expanding internet and mobile banking services to complement personal interaction at physical and branch locations.

They also offer basic financial services for low or no cost. For example, banks do not charge fees to deposit funds. When a paycheck is deposited, the bank customer is entitled to the face amount of the check.

The unbanked and underbanked, on the other hand, spend considerable amounts of time and effort conducting simple transactions, driving to and from alternative financial service providers, waiting in line, and delivering payments to vendors and creditors. Check-cashers charge significant fees to cash a check, and do not offer a place to keep those funds on deposit. (One study found that people earning $12,000 per year pay an annual average of $250 simply to cash their paychecks at check-cashers.) These fees are charged despite the fact that the vast majority of these checks are paychecks and government benefit payments, which carry extremely low risk of being returned for having insufficient funds. As one observer wrote, "There is absolutely no good reason why a person earning $20,000 per year should spend $240 a year to access their own hard-earned money. This, however, is what millions of Americans are doing."

Individuals who use check-cashers are in effect paying a fee to access their own money, a fee which banks would not impose. Because the poor are more likely to use check-cashers, while the middle- and upper-class are more likely to use banks, these fees are being paid by those least able to afford them.
[End of excerpt]

In the United States and around the world, both banked and unbanked people are seeking safe, cheap ways of storing and sending money. Emerging technologies, especially those using internet and mobile platforms, hold great promise for a variety of economic actors. Digital currencies such as Bitcoin and Litecoin operate peer-to-peer; that is, they work across networks of individuals and do away with financial intermediaries completely. Without intermediaries, transactions happen in a matter of minutes rather than hours or days, and fees are generally much lower per transaction than intermediated transactions. (On the other hand, traditional payment systems are capable of bearing heavier traffic loads: the Bitcoin protocol can process about seven transactions per second, compared with Visa's ability to process 10,000 in the same amount of time.)

Because they are virtual, digital currencies also have a few characteristics that traditional payment systems don't. For example, digital currency can be transferred to any digital wallet anywhere in the world, crossing international borders just as easily as crossing the street. Digital currencies also make it feasible to send far smaller payments, which benefits individuals making remittances to family members in other countries.

Because they are decentralized rather than intermediated, digital currencies are largely unregulated—this feature is a benefit for some users, who dislike government oversight in such matters, but for other users, lack of government involvement makes digital currencies unreliable. Moreover, digital currencies require a level of computer literacy most people do not have. This means that either digital currency use is restricted to those tech-savvy enough to participate, or it requires new digital currency intermediaries to interface with the currencies on the users' behalves.

Mobile phone technology may also be an emerging technology that changes the way individuals interact with banking and finance systems. In developing nations such as Kenya and South Africa, mobile phone technology has leapfrogged over traditional, land-based methods of communication. Programs such as WIZZIT and M-Pesa facilitate fast and cheap transfers of funds via the users' mobile phones. Mobile phone technology has also been used to facilitate microlending, loans of small amounts of money for short periods of time. (Microlending has been tremendously useful in developing nations.) Mobile phone technology may also be able to increase access to the banking system in the United States.

6.3.2   Banking/Finance Law – Bitcoin

In this segment, we explore the groundbreaking digital currency Bitcoin, including how it works, why people use it, and how it may be used in the future.

Excerpt: Catherine Martin Christopher, Why on Earth Do People Use Bitcoin?, 2 Bus. & Bankr. L.J. 1 (2014).

Since I began reading, writing, and speaking about Bitcoin, I often find myself describing it to people who've never heard of it.

"It's a digital currency," I explain. "It exists solely on the internet. It's not backed by any government, or a company, or by the price of gold. It's a computer code that's run on thousands of computers, all networked together over the internet.

"The code solves a series of math problems," I continue. (I have my spiel pretty well down by now.) "All the computers networked together work to solve these really complicated math problems, and the solution to each problem is a long string of letters and numbers that is a bitcoin. Once a bitcoin is generated, it's randomly awarded to one of the computers in the network, and the code starts in on solving the next math problem."

I then explain mining versus buying: "If you want to, you can download the Bitcoin software onto your computer and contribute your computing power to solving the math problems. You might do this in the hopes of being rewarded with a bitcoin once it's generated. That's called mining for bitcoins. But it would probably take you a couple of years to mine a bitcoin from your home computer, so if you don't want to wait that long, you can just buy some from a website, a digital currency exchange. You give them dollars and they give you bitcoins." If I'm really testing the boundaries of Bitcoin-newbies' patience, I'll also throw in, "You may have heard of a big FBI bust of a website called Silk Road, in early October, 2013. Silk Road was a website that matched up buyers and sellers, kind of like eBay, except that there were illegal drugs and weapons for sale, so long as the parties transacted in Bitcoin. Silk Road used Bitcoin because your Bitcoin account doesn't have your name attached to it."
Plenty of people look pretty shell-shocked by this point in my talk, so this is where I usually pause for questions.

"People spend real money on this?" is a frequent question I hear. Yes, they do – in late October, 2013, a single bitcoin cost about $200 (which was actually more than a bitcoin was worth before Silk Road was shut down). In November, 2013, after some positive media coverage in China and a U.S Senate hearing that signaled the currency's legitimacy, the price of one bitcoin shot up over $900, and as of this writing, it remains high.
[End of excerpt]

People use Bitcoin for a variety of reasons. It's somewhat functional as a currency: you can exchange bitcoins for (some) goods and services. Not every vendor accepts bitcoins, of course, but those who do are enthusiastic about it. You may end up paying less for the products you buy because the transaction fees are lower for Bitcoin than for dollars. On the other hand, the exchange rate for bitcoins is quite volatile, so you risk paying something other than the true price because of the exchange rate.

On another level, because bitcoins are things that can be bought low and sold high, many investors and speculators buy them in the hopes of turning a profit. Bitcoin is popular among criminals, too, because value can be transferred without a name, address, or social security number. (More on criminal applications in the next section.)
Bitcoin may be useful in parts of the world where national currency is ineffective. Bitcoin has been proposed as a way to protect individual savings from the effects of hyperinflation, or as a way to keep goods and services flowing when war or political disruption makes banks hard to reach.

Initially, however, Bitcoin was popular as a libertarian ideal: currency without government involvement. The next excerpt explores this idea.

Excerpt: Catherine Martin Christopher, Bitcoin's Complex Relationship with Trust (forthcoming).

Bitcoin is not the world's first digital currency, but it is the first to solve what's known as the double-spending problem. Digital currency systems must find a way to prevent units of the currency from being electronically duplicated. Most digital files, such as an email attachment, can be downloaded multiple times, which is not a good feature for a currency because it expands the money supply indefinitely and sellers cannot be sure they are getting an original unit of currency instead of a duplicate.

The double-spending problem is not unique to Bitcoin—fiat currencies have this problem, too. When an individual interacts with a vendor and offers to buy a good or service with a debit or credit card, the vendor cannot really be sure the buyer has money to pay for the item. The double-spending problem in fiat currencies is solved by banks. Banks serve as trusted intermediaries, maintaining account ledgers and verifying to the economic system as a whole in which account money is residing.

Bitcoin solves the double-spending problem with an innovative feature called the blockchain. The blockchain is a public ledger, showing the current wallet location of each bitcoin as well as the history of where every bitcoin has ever been. The blockchain serves two important functions for the money supply. First, it prevents bitcoins from being counterfeited, because each bitcoin is unique and a new one cannot be introduced unless the Bitcoin protocol can verify its origins. Second, it prohibits double-spending because a transfer of bitcoins cannot be made unless the blockchain shows the would-be spender actually owns the coins she purports to transfer. Once a user has transferred coins away from herself, the ledger shows that those coins have moved, and she is unable to spend them again unless they are first returned to her wallet.

While the concept of the ledger is not new (banks have had ledgers for centuries), the innovative feature of the Bitcoin ledger is that it is decentralized. Banks maintain their own ledgers, which are verified periodically (and imperfectly) by government regulators—individual currency users just have to trust that the bank and the regulator are getting it right. The Bitcoin protocol, on the other hand, is operating simultaneously on thousands or millions of computers all straining for consensus. Once consensus is reached that a given transaction is valid, a process that takes a few minutes, that transaction is added to the blockchain. The blockchain itself is publicly available, a transparency banks do not provide.

Because of the blockchain and its decentralized but verifiable ledger, Bitcoin is generally understood to be a "trustless" system. The public ledger feature of the blockchain relies on complex but verifiable cryptography calculations, rather than by human decision-making. It seems no accident that Bitcoin was introduced to the world mere weeks after the spectacular global financial crisis of 2008. During that crisis, it became apparent that trusted intermediaries had in fact gotten themselves far in over their heads—using other people's money—and that regulators either didn't understand what was happening or simply allowed irresponsible over-leveraging. In the aftermath of that crisis, when the world was trying to understand why anyone had thought murky credit default swaps were a good idea, a mathematically-driven, transparent currency system that prohibited coins from being in two places at once seemed like a pretty good idea.

[End of excerpt]

Because Bitcoin exceeds the computer literacy of most people, however, third-party vendors are necessary for most people to participate in the Bitcoin economy. Startups offer Bitcoin storage and security systems, transaction services, and currency exchanges. Ironically, for a "trustless" currency, users must place their trust in these third-party vendors to design effective products resistant to hacking.

Bitcoin advocates and entrepreneurs are excited about what other uses can be found for the blockchain. The frontier of such new For instance, it may possible to encode real property records in the blockchain. Existing property records are thick books maintained in county recordkeeping offices that index deeds alphabetically by name of grantor and grantee, all so we can verify that the person transferring a piece of property is in fact the owner. The blockchain does the same thing. If property records can be put in the blockchain, ownership can be verified automatically by computers, instead of by title searchers who manually page through the record books or online repositories of scanned deed documents.

Furthermore, it may be possible to encode contracts into the blockchain. For instance, if I want to purchase a piece of real property, I may not have enough money to pay for the property all at once. Instead, I may agree to an installment contract from the seller, in which I agree to make a series of payments over a period of time, after which title to the property will pass to me. This simple agreement can be reduced to computer code; a contract is, after all, a series of if-then statements, equivalent to "If I pay $1,000 per month for 30 years, then the property will become mine." Such an agreement can be enshrined in the blockchain, and after payments are made and verified, title to the property passes to me. This is a simplified example of a smart contract, one that is automated and self-executing.

Taking things yet one step further, it may be possible to combine a smart contract with smart property. Imagine, for example, that I'm buying a car instead of a house, and assume I will need to make monthly payments for a few of years to pay off the vehicle. If this is a smart contract, the obligation is recorded on the blockchain, and if I default, ownership of the vehicle will revert to the dealer. Assume further that this car is one that doesn't have a mechanical key, but instead has a fob that automatically unlocks the car if it's in close proximity to the vehicle. If that fob is internet-enabled and connected to the blockchain, and if I fail to make a payment on the car, the fob can be automatically disabled upon my breach of the contract. I'll walk up to the car, but the fob won't unlock it.

Perhaps this all sounds like something out of Aldous Huxley's novel Brave New World. Projects like this are currently in development, however, and they pose interesting questions about the rules of contract law, methods of dispute resolution, and the role of lawyers into the future. For example, what happens when the parties want to modify a contract encoded in the blockchain? Can a debt be forgiven once it's recorded in the blockchain? Will (should) contracting parties still use lawyers to help anticipate potential problems of contract performance?

6.3.3 Banking/Finance Law -- Criminal law implications in banking and finance

Many people associate Bitcoin with criminal activity. Indeed, Bitcoin is popular with criminals because transacting parties can keep their identities hidden, and because payments of any size can be made quickly across national borders.

Perhaps Bitcoin's greatest criminal association is with Silk Road, a website set up by twenty-something Ross Ulbricht. After its establishment in January 2011, Silk Road quickly grew into an eBay-like marketplace, where sellers offered illegal drugs, guns, pornography, and other illicit items in exchange for Bitcoin. By the end of 2012, the website was facilitating $1.2 million in sales each month, from which Ulbricht was earning $92,000 in commissions. After a lengthy and careful sting operation by several cooperating federal agencies, Ulbricht was arrested on October 1, 2013, and was promptly convicted of distributing narcotics over the internet and various related crimes. He was sentenced to life in prison.

Aside from the occasional dramatic tale like Ulbricht's, banking and finance crimes tend to be "white-collar" crimes: securities fraud, market manipulation, or violation of myriad financial laws and regulation. There is a healthy debate about what Bitcoin is and how it should be regulated. The Financial Crimes Enforcement Network (FinCEN, part of the Treasury Department) treats Bitcoin as a currency, regulating (and prosecuting) digital currency exchanges the same way it regulates and prosecutes check cashers and banks. Of note, FinCEN doesn't regulate Bitcoin, just as it doesn't regulate dollars—it regulates transactions denominated in those currencies.

The Internal Revenue Service, on the other hand, considers Bitcoin to be property, and has announced that taxpayers should track their basis in their bitcoins and pay taxes on any gains realized upon the sale of those bitcoins. The IRS rationalizes that Bitcoin's less-than-universal acceptance is strong evidence that it is not, in fact, a currency. Along these same lines, cogent arguments can be made that bitcoins are commodities, which would subject them to regulation by the Commodities Futures Trading Commission, or securities, which would subject them to regulation by the Securities Exchange Commission.

In banking, however—that is, in the portion of the financial industry that takes deposits, makes loans, and offers checking accounts—the overarching criminal law enforcement concerns deal with money laundering and terrorist financing. The following excerpt explains the structure and purpose of current U.S. money-laundering laws, and how they are imperfect tools to curtail criminal activity.

Excerpt: Catherine Martin Christopher, Whack-A-Mole: Why Prosecuting Digital Currency Exchanges Won't Stop Online Money Laundering, 18 LEWIS & CLARK L. REV. 1 (2014). (Copyright, Catherine Martin Christopher)

A. Statutes

Money laundering is criminalized by the intersection of a pair of relatively young statutory schemes: the Money Laundering Control Act of 1986 and the Bank Secrecy Act of 1970. These statutes and their implementing regulations act in concert to deter and criminalize money laundering, which is essentially the process by which individuals disguise the source of illegally obtained funds. Criminals must obscure the origin of criminally derived income so they may spend it without drawing the attention of law enforcement.

Money laundering is a crime because lawmakers sought to make underlying criminal activity more difficult to engage in. Initially, anti-money laundering statutes were enacted in order to hamper the illegal drug trade, though anti-money laundering laws are also used to fight "corruption, organized crime and transnational criminal activity." Theoretically, individuals will be less likely to engage in criminal enterprises if they cannot safely (that is, without law enforcement detection) spend the proceeds of their crimes.

The Money Laundering Control Act of 1986 criminalizes financial transactions (or attempted financial transactions) that "conceal or disguise the nature, the location, the source, the ownership, or the control of the proceeds of specified unlawful activit[ies]." Such "specified unlawful activities" are enumerated in a mind-numbingly long list ranging from dealing controlled substances, murder, and human trafficking, to copyright infringement and violence against maritime fixed platforms. Thus, in order to be guilty of money laundering under the Money Laundering Control Act, an individual must first have committed one of these specified unlawful activities. . . .

In more recent years, especially after the terrorist attacks of September 11, 2001, anti-money laundering laws are also relied upon to prevent terrorism. Terrorism is, in several senses, a very different crime from illegal drug distribution, the initial target of anti-money laundering laws. Individuals who deal in drugs are paid after the illegal conduct has occurred—with those crimes, law enforcement can use anti-money laundering laws to trace the movement of funds back to the individuals who have already committed some other crime. With terrorist financing, however, the movement of funds occurs before the intended crime has been committed. Funds are transacted to prepare for a terroristic act that has not yet occurred—to purchase supplies, for instance, or to train would-be terrorists. In these instances, anti-money laundering laws are used to aid in detective work that will allow law enforcement to disrupt a crime that has not yet occurred. In the case of terrorism, therefore, money is laundered to obscure not its source, but its destination.

Another important distinction between terrorism and other crimes such as drug trafficking is the legality of the origins of the funds in question. Drug traffickers obtain large sums of money (usually in cash) through their illegal endeavors, and the money laundering process is designed to disguise the source of those ill-gotten funds. With terrorism, however, the money may have been obtained from perfectly lawful sources; for example, individuals with lawful, respectable jobs may decide to donate a portion of their salary to terrorist causes. In such instances, it is the intended use of the funds—and the desire to conceal the intended use—that makes the transactions criminal.

Whether related to terrorism, drugs, or other forms of crime, though, money laundering is criminalized only because it is the outgrowth of some underlying crime. Spending income is perfectly legal so long as the funds were legally obtained; only where the funds were earned by (or destined for, in the case of terrorism) illegal means does the "shell" crime of money laundering occur.

B. Regulations

Anti-money laundering laws are in turn enforced through a complex scheme of regulations that require financial institutions to confirm customer identities, maintain certain records, and report certain transactions to government agencies. The Bank Secrecy Act delegates to the Secretary of the Treasury broad authority to require financial institutions to maintain records and make reports that have "a high degree of usefulness in criminal, tax, or regulatory investigations or proceedings" or "a high degree of usefulness in the conduct of intelligence or counterintelligence activities . . . to protect against international terrorism."

Broadly, there are three types of regulations that impact American anti-money laundering efforts: know your customer, recordkeeping, and reporting requirements. Know your customer, or KYC, regulations require that banks implement "risk-based procedures for verifying the identity of each customer to the extent reasonable and practicable." Although the regulations allow for some flexibility based on the institution's size, customer base, types of accounts offered, etc., banks' policies must include collection of a customer's name, date of birth, address, and an identification number (such as a taxpayer ID). Typically, this means checking the drivers' licenses of customers who present themselves at a physical office.

Confirming customer identities becomes murkier, though, when the customer conducts business at an ATM or drive-through teller service, or—most ominously—conducts business online. Even if the bank has complied with the KYC requirements when opening an account, in these non-face-to-face situations, it is more difficult to confirm that the person authorizing the transaction is the actual account holder; the authentication (such as a PIN or online password) may be forged or stolen.

Also of note, other countries have different (read: more lax) KYC requirements. It is possible for an individual in the United States to open a bank account in another country that does not require meaningful customer due diligence, then obtain a bank card that works at American ATMs. Money can be funneled into the foreign bank account with little or no identifying customer information, then accessed as cash in the United States.
The regulations require that financial institutions maintain records of certain transactions as well. Nonbanks are required to maintain records of all transactions over $3,000, while the record retention threshold for banks is $10,000. Such records must be retained for five years.
Moreover, certain transactions trigger a financial institution's obligation to report the transaction to the government. For instance, all financial institutions (other than casinos) are required to report any "deposit, withdrawal, exchange of currency or other payment or transfer" exceeding $10,000. These reports must be filed within 15 days of the transaction, and any financial institution making such a transaction must verify and record the transacting customer's name and address, as well as record the beneficiary's identity, account number, and social security or taxpayer identification number.

More vaguely, financial institutions must report "suspicious" transactions. Regulations describe a "suspicious" transaction as one that involves at least $5,000 where the bank "knows, suspects, or has reason to suspect" that the funds are being laundered, the transaction is designed to evade regulation, or "[t]he transaction has no business or apparent lawful purpose or is not the sort in which the particular customer would normally be expected to engage." For money services businesses, the dollar threshold drops to $2,000. Suspicious transactions must be reported using a Suspicious Activity Report (SAR) filed with the Treasury Department's Financial Crimes Enforcement Network within 30 days of the transaction.

Taken altogether, the regulations are confusing and burdensome. Willful failure to comply with regulations promulgated under the Bank Secrecy Act exposes the financial institution and its employees—not the customer actually making or receiving an illegal transaction—to criminal penalties of up to one year in prison and a $1,000 fine, while willful or grossly negligent failure to comply may lead to civil liability to the United States of up to $10,000. Failure to report coin or currency transactions, failure to report the import or export of monetary instruments over $10,000, or structuring transactions to avoid reporting requirements can result in the financial institution forfeiting "all property, real or personal, involved in the offense and any property traceable thereto."

Potential violations exist everywhere. For example, money transmitting businesses are required to register with the Financial Crimes Enforcement Network, and failure to do so is a punishable offense. Beyond that, operating a money transmitting business without obtaining a license required by the home state also constitutes a federal crime punishable by five years imprisonment or a fine.

These regulations place a heavy burden on financial institutions to perform criminal detection and law enforcement work. In fact, some have suggested that this shifting of police work was intentional, because financial institutions are in a better position and are better capable of detecting criminal activity.

Legislators have thus created another shell in the Russian nesting doll of anti-money laundering laws: it is illegal for financial institutions to fail to report suspicious activity, because that suspicious activity is indicative of money laundering, while money laundering in turn is only illegal because it indicates the commission of an underlying crime. The crime of failing to make SARs is thus significantly attenuated from the root problem: the drug trade, terrorism, or other criminal activity.

Moreover, by requiring KYC and SAR compliance and criminalizing the failure to comply with those regulations, legislators have now shifted the criminal activity (and law enforcement attention) away from the drug dealers, terrorists, and other criminals onto the financial institutions that take those individuals' deposits and effect their financial transactions. To be sure, financial institutions benefit from the transaction fees imposed on money laundering activities, but the institutions themselves may not be wittingly contributing to the underlying criminal activity.

Even more frustrating is the very real possibility that the burdensome reporting requirements are ineffective. The regulations promulgated pursuant to the Patriot Act would likely not have prevented, or even raised suspicion about, the financial transactions that funded the September 11 terrorist attacks. Loopholes in the reporting requirements are constantly being found and exploited by money launderers so the launderers can continue to use the financial system to obscure the source (or purpose) of their funds, while regulators are constantly playing catchup. For instance, money launderers conducted business by wire transfers for some time before regulators realized it and, in 1995, included wire transactions in the reporting requirements. Large transactions have long been broken down into multiple smaller increments in order to fall beneath the reporting requirements—a process known by the hilarious name of "smurfing" —until legislators specifically criminalized this evasive behavior.

Moreover, a SAR is filed long after the horse is out of the barn. Although useful in creating a paper trail, there may be considerable delay (up to 30 days) between the suspicious transaction itself and the filing of the report. Even among those transactions that do raise suspicion, most are not halted—indeed, a suspicious transaction cannot be halted if it is reported days and weeks after it has been completed. If the reporting requirements do not raise sufficient red flags to garner law enforcement attention and allow prevention of terroristic crimes, the utility of SARs is reduced to investigation after the commission of a crime.
[End of Excerpt]

Can a person engage in money laundering with Bitcoin? To answer this question, we must ask whether Bitcoin is money. One court wrote the following:

Excerpt: United States v. Faiella, 39 F. Supp.3d 544 (S.D.N.Y. 2014)
Memorandum Order
JED S. RAKOFF, U.S.D.J.

Defendants in this case are charged in connection with their operation of an underground market in the virtual currency "Bitcoin" via the website "Silk Road." Defendant Faiella is charged with one count of operating an unlicensed money transmitting business in violation of 18 U.S.C. § 1960 ,1 Indictment ("Ind.") ¶ 1 (Count One), and one count of conspiracy to commit money laundering in violation of 18 U.S.C. § 1956(h) , Ind. ¶¶ 3-5 (Count Three). Following indictment, Faiella moved to dismiss Count One of the Indictment on three grounds: first, that Bitcoin does not qualify as "money" under Section 1960; second, that operating a Bitcoin exchange does not constitute "transmitting" money under Section 1960; and third that Faiella is not a "money transmitter" under Section 1960. Following full briefing, the Court heard oral argument on August 7, 2014. Upon consideration, the Court now denies defendant Faiella's motion, for the following reasons:

First, "money" in ordinary parlance means "something generally accepted as a medium of exchange, a measure of value, or a means of payment." Merriam-Webster Online, http://www. merriam-webster.com/dictionary/money (last visited Aug. 18, 2014). As examples of this, Merriam-Webster Online includes "officially coined or stamped metal currency," "paper money," and "money of account" — the latter defined as "a denominator of value or basis of exchange which is used in keeping accounts and for which there may or may not be an equivalent coin or denomination of paper money[.]" Id. Further, the text of Section 1960 refers not simply to "money," but to "funds." In particular, Section 1960 defines "money transmitting" as "transferring funds on behalf of the public by any and all means." 18 U.S.C. § 1960(b)(2) (emphasis added). Merriam-Webster Online defines "funds" as "available money" or "an amount of something that is available for use: a supply of something." Merriam-Webster Online, http://www.merriam-webster.com/dictionary/fund (last visited Aug. 18, 2014). Bitcoin clearly qualifies as "money" or "funds" under these plain meaning definitions. Bitcoin can be easily purchased in exchange for ordinary currency, acts as a denominator of value, and is used to conduct financial transactions. See, e.g., SEC v. Shavers, 2013 U.S. Dist. LEXIS 110018, 2013 WL 4028182, at *2 (E.D. Tex. Aug. 6, 2013) ("It is clear that Bitcoin can be used as money. It can be used to purchase goods or services . . . . [I]t can also be exchanged for conventional currencies . . . .").

If there were any ambiguity in this regard — and the Court finds none — the legislative history supports application of Section 1960 in this instance. Section 1960 was passed as an anti-money laundering statute, designed "to prevent the movement of funds in connection with drug dealing." United States v. Bah, 574 F.3d 106, 112 (2d Cir. 2009) (citing H.R. Rep. No. 107-250(I), at 54 (2001)). Congress was concerned that drug dealers would turn increasingly to "nonbank financial institutions" to "convert street currency into monetary instruments" in order to transmit the proceeds of their drug sales. S. Rep. 101-460, 1990 WL 201710 (1990). Section 1960 was drafted to address this "gaping hole in the money laundering deterrence effort." Id. Indeed, it is likely that Congress designed the statute to keep pace with such evolving threats, which is precisely why it drafted the statute to apply to any business involved in transferring "funds . . . by any and all means." 18 U.S.C. § 1960(b)(2).

Second, Faiella's activities on Silk Road constitute "transmitting" money under Section 1960. Defendant argues that while Section 1960 requires that the defendant sell money transmitting services to others for a profit, see 31 C.F.R. § 1010.100(ff)(5)(i) (2013) (defining "money transmission services" to require transmission of funds to "another location or person"), Faiella merely sold Bitcoin as a product in and of itself. But, as set forth in the Criminal Complaint that initiated this case, the Government alleges that Faiella received cash deposits from his customers and then, after exchanging them for Bitcoins, transferred those funds to the customers' accounts on Silk Road. Ind. ¶ 5; Complaint ¶¶ 14, 17-18. These were, in essence, transfers to a third-party agent, Silk Road, for Silk Road users did not have full control over the Bitcoins transferred into their accounts. Rather, Silk Road administrators could block or seize user funds. See, e.g., Complaint ¶¶ 29, 41. Thus, the Court finds that in sending his customers' funds to Silk Road, Faiella "transferred" them to others for a profit.

Third, Faiella clearly qualifies as a "money transmitter" for purposes of Section 1960. The Financial Crimes Enforcement Network ("FinCEN") has issued guidance specifically clarifying that virtual currency exchangers constitute "money transmitters" under its regulations. See FinCEN Guidance at 1 ("[A]n administrator or exchanger [of virtual currency] is an MSB [money services business] under FinCEN's regulations, specifically, a money transmitter, unless a limitation to or exemption from the definition applies to the person." (emphasis in original)). FinCEN has further clarified that the exception on which defendant relies for its argument that Faiella is not a "money transmitter," 31 C.F.R. § 1010.100(ff)(5)(ii)(F), is inapplicable. See FinCEN Guidance at 4 ("It might be argued that the exchanger is entitled to the exemption from the definition of 'money transmitter' for persons involved in the sale of goods or the provision of services. . . . However, this exemption does not apply when the only services being provided are money transmission services.").

Finally, defendant claims that applying Section 1960 to a Bitcoin exchange business would run afoul of the rule of lenity, constituting such a novel and unanticipated construction of the statute as to operate like an ex post facto law in violation of the Due Process Clause. The Supreme Court has repeatedly stated that the rule of lenity is "reserved . . . for those situations in which a reasonable doubt persists about a statute's intended scope even after resort to 'the language and structure, legislative history, and motivating policies' of the statute'" Moskal v. United States, 498 U.S. 103 , 108 , 111 S. Ct. 461 , 112 L. Ed. 2d 449 (1990) (quoting Bifulco v. United States, 447 U.S. 381 , 387 , 100 S. Ct. 2247 , 65 L. Ed. 2d 205 (1980) (emphasis in original)). Here, as noted, there is no such irreconcilable ambiguity requiring resort to the rule of lenity. Further, defendant's argument that this case constitutes ex post facto judicial lawmaking that violates the Due Process Clause is undermined by Faiella's own statements to the operator of Silk Road that Bitcoin exchanges have "to be licensed, and that law enforcement agencies might "seize [his] funds." Ind. ¶ 51.

For the reasons above, defendant's motion to dismiss is denied. . . .
SO ORDERED.

[End of excerpt]

In this emerging era of high-tech financial crimes, law enforcement face new challenges in detecting and preventing crimes. Law enforcement agencies often work together to investigate and prosecute crimes.

References

Richard Scott Carnell, et al., THE LAW OF BANKING AND FINANCIAL INSTITUTIONS (Wolters Kluwer, 4th ed. 2009)

Nathaniel Popper, DIGITAL GOLD (HarperCollins, 2015)

Paul Vigna & Michael J. Casey, THE AGE OF CRYPTOCURRENCY (St. Martin's Press, 2015)

Jerry Brito, et al., Bitcoin Financial Regulation: Securities, Derivatives, Prediction Markets, and Gambling, 14 Colum. Sci. & Tech. L. Rev. 144 (2014)

Gianni De Nicolo et al., Bank Consolidation, Internationalization, and Conglomeration: Trends and Implications for Financial Risk (IMF Working Paper, July 2003)

Satoshi Nakamoto, Bitcoin: A Peer-to-Peer Electronic Cash System (White paper, 2008)

Nick Szabo, A Formal Language for Analyzing Contracts (White paper, 2002)

Nick Szabo, The Idea of Smart Contracts (White paper, 1997)

The World Bank, Global Financial Development Report: Financial Inclusion (2014)

Chapter 10

Scientific Evidence and Emerging Technologies

7.1.1   Scientific Evidence – Foundation cases, Part 1

Although the Salem Witch Trials occurred before the U.S. Constitution, we cannot totally ignore the impact it had on evidence, scientific evidence and the enduring colloquial phrase that it brought, the "witch hunt." The following is an excerpt from Sutton, *Law and Science* (Carolina Academic Press, 2001).

Witch Trials and Evidence

Johan Kepler, one of the scientists of this period, expressed frustration with the legal system of the time, as being without "harmonies." During his life, he found it necessary to expend much of his time and energy on the judiciary system. Kepler's early work, however, quite apart from science, included his efforts to sell his horoscope readings, but he had such difficulty collecting his fees that he resorted to the court, pro se. He went from court to court in an effort to collect his fees, but only managed to get an unwanted reputation and was laughed at and humiliated in his barrister efforts.13 Some years later, as the imperial mathematician, Kepler then had an outstanding scientific reputation, and was regarded with esteem. Kepler's mother was raised by an aunt who later was burned alive as a witch, and his mother almost suffered this same fate, were it not for Kepler's appearance in court as her advocate.14 After his mother repeatedly had been threatened and tortured as a suspected witch, Kepler intervened. The court records noted that she was acquitted of witchcraft because of the "unfortunate" intervention of Kepler, the imperial mathematician as attorney for the defense. Kepler wrote after this, "let us despise the barbaric neighings which echo through these noble lands, and awaken our understanding and longing for the harmonies."15 Kepler found himself in conflict between the church and his work as well. He was forced to delay the publication of his advancement of Copernicus's works because of pressures from the church.

In spite of this surge in scientific thought, the Roman Catholic Church still refused to give a place to the new thinking about the universe, and in 1616, banned all books which maintained that the earth moves. It was in 1616 that forged minutes of a meeting with Galileo, then 70 years old, and the Cardinal Bellarmine, held claim to have enjoined Galileo Galilei from further teaching or practicing of Copernicanism in any way.16 Acting as the law of the land, the church ended Galileo's open practice of what was then modern science.17 One of the Church's own books, The Malleus Maleficarum, the Witch Hammer, on the procedures for conducting a trial of witches and other heretics in the civil courts and ecclesiastical courts was widely available. It had been written at the behest of the Catholic Church as a procedural manual for the prosecution of witches, and was said to have had a prominent place on the bench of every judge and every magistrate in Europe and later in America.18 This procedural manual was sanctioned by the church in the famous Bull of Pope Innocent VIII wherein every power of the church is summoned for the prosecution of witches. This author's careful review of the ancient text revealed no reference to, or influence of, any scientific thinking of the period.

The early scientific methodology was a refreshing approach to designing an inquiry which would yield answers in an unbiased way in a world which did not seem to have either predictability or order. Some leading scientists sought to extend these new approaches to the state and to society in the hope of bringing order to the seeming chaos.19

The European Witch Hunts
Another window to the influence of science on law in this period—early seventeenth century—is seen in the requirement of what might be called expert testimony in witch trials in France. The search for body marks required the services of either the barbers or the physicians and surgeons. A well-documented set of evidence used in a witch trial, that of a priest, Louis Gaufridi, records the process. The appointment, by the court, of two physicians and two surgeons was made to look for the crucial devil's mark somewhere on his body.20 The medical evidence produced by the physicians and surgeons included the finding of such marks and the piercing of them to observe whether the patient felt pain; if not, witchcraft was assumed to have been proven. The report on the case included the observations of the physicians and surgeons as to the character of the marks, the reaction of the suspect to needle piercing, and the opinion of the doctors as to whether or not the marks originated from normal occurrences. Interestingly, their opinion did not include a conclusion as to whether the suspect was in fact a witch or not.21 Since finding a devil's mark was one of the most convincing forms of evidence required to convict a witch, the activity of "pricking" grew into a profession, and beginning in the 1630s, a guild was formed to promote this trade.22

In spite of the trial of Galileo in 1633 and his subsequent recanting of his beliefs in astronomy,23 Galileo in 1642, discovered how the pendulum acts to provide a timekeeping mechanism. Amidst this revolution in science, witchcraft trials and executions were occurring in both Europe and America, and 1648 marks the first year of an execution for witchcraft in the United States.

In America, the first university, Harvard University was founded in 1636. (Its existence was ensured with the inclusion of the college in the 1692 Colony charter.) The college was founded by the Puritans for the promotion of religion in the colonies, and John Winthrop, a leading Newtonian served on the Harvard faculty.36

Although science was but a hobby, and law a profession in the period, the growing recognition of the influence of science on the law is summed up by Edmund Burke: "What can be more instructive than to search out the first, obscure and scanty fountains of that jurisprudence which now waters and enriches whole nations...— the laws, — sometimes lost and trodden down in the confusion of wars and tumults, and sometimes overruled by the hand of power; then victorious over tyranny; growing stronger, clearer, and more decisive by the violence they had suffered; softened and mellowed by peace and religion; improved and exalted by commerce, by social intercourse, and that great opener of the mind, ingenious science?"37

Massachusetts and the Salem Witchcraft Trials — Influence of Science?

A dark part of American history and one which best illustrates the absence of conclusive science is the Massachusetts witchcraft trials in the 1650s. What is less generally known, is the absence in this trial of professionally trained lawyers. In the appointment of the Commission which was to hear the trials in Salem, not a single Commissioner38 was a member of the bar.

The absence of a professionally trained bar cannot account for the failed defenses of the accused, however, because among the first victims of witchcraft accusations and convictions in New England was a sister to Governor Bellingham, who himself was a lawyer. His sister, Anne Hibbins was executed for witchcraft in 1656 — while he was governor. This occurrence is not unlike similar panics in twentieth century America, where science was disregarded when public fervor demanded political action. The result was an immense influence of policy and law with a basis in inconclusive science.39

Despite important advances in science, it has been observed that no one thought of criticizing theology based upon the newest scientific discoveries. "No one used Newton's law of gravitation to challenge Cotton Mather's remarks about the aerial activities of 'legions of devils'".40 Epileptic-like seizures caused by a fungus called ergot, which grows on damp wheat had been observed in the colonies but had not been attributed to witchcraft in the past.41 That the occurrence of these epileptic-like seizures did not cause the public to question whether these fits were caused by something other than witchcraft supports the notion that no one thought to question theology based on observations in science. It was not until 1976, that a scientific article was published which supported the theory that the fungus ergot was probably responsible for the epileptic-like fits observed in the girls who were thought to be bewitched. When scientific news was finally published, it was newsworthy enough to be reported by the New York Times.42

Perhaps it was the political will and the deep belief in the existence of witchcraft by Sir William Phillip, who had been appointed the first governor under the charter that resulted in the almost-emergency appointment of the witchcraft Commission with its exclusive subject matter of witchcraft and related felonies.43 The date of this commission's founding was June 2, 1692 and it convened in Salem on that same day.

Evidence at the Trials — Theological not Scientific

The French practice of searching for a "devil's mark" also was followed in Salem, likely following the same judicial procedure as directed in The Malleum Maleficarum.44 The proceeding of the Salem trials centered around the evidence of markings on the body of the accused, requiring a court-appointed "expert witness" of the day to examine and report to the court their findings. After all who were willing to testify on any related matter were exhausted, the next process was the hunt for "witch marks" by the jury, in the absence of the "expert witness". But much less was acceptable to convict a witch, as for example the testimony of Tituba, the woman attributed with beginning the witchcraft frenzy, among the young women of Salem Village. Her testimony, consisting of a total of thirty-nine questions, included no questions about body marks, but involved her visions of the "devil", "rats" of various sorts, and a rendition of her travel on sticks — "we ride upon sticks."45

---

13. Ferris, Timothy, Coming of Age in the Milky Way, William Morrow and Company: New York (1988), p. 74.

14. Ferris, p. 74.

15. Ferris, p. 82, quoting Koestler, Arthur, The Sleepwalkers, New York: Grosset & Dunlap (1959) on the life and work of Copernicus, Kepler, and Galileo.

16. Ferris, p. 100.

17. Papal Bull, 1996, Vatican, Rome, Italy. It was not until 1996 that the Church admitted that Galileo had been correct.

18. Summers, Montage, "Introduction" prepared for the 1948 reprint of Heinrich Kramer and James Sprenger, The Malleus Maleficarum, New York: Dover Publications (1971), p. viii.

7. Thomas Jefferson, Notes on the State of Virginia 159-60 (W. Penden, ed., 1955).

8. Goldberg, Stephen, "The Constitutional Status of American Science," 1979 U. Ill. L. For. 1, 5 (1979).

9. Moore v. Gaston County Board of Education, 357 F. Supp. 1037, 1041 (1973).

10. Ferris, Timothy. Coming of Age in the Milky Way, New York: William Morrow and Company, Inc. (1988), p. 82.

11. Goldberg, Steven, Culture Clash, Law and Science in America 17 (1994).

12. Law and the Social Role of Science, ed. Harry W. Jones, (Rockefeller University Press: 1967), "Literature of the Law — Science Confrontation," p. 138.

25. Id. at 39-41.

26. Olson, p. 27.

27. Charles A. Miller, Jefferson and Nature — An Interpretation 11 (1988).

28. Webster's New Encyclopedic Dictionary, Black Dog and Leventhal Publishers, Inc.: New York (1993), p. 1756. Newton's First Law, A force exerted on a body directly will remain at rest or travel in a straight line at constant speed unless it is acted upon by an external force; Newton's Second Law, The resultant force exerted on a body is directly proportional to the acceleration produced by the force. F = ma; Newton's Third Law, To every action there is an equal and opposite reaction; and Newton's Law of Gravitation, Every particle in the universe attracts every other particle with a force that is directly proportional to the product of their masses and inversely proportional to the square of the distance between them. F=g(m1m2).

29. Ferris, Timothy, Coming of Age in the Milky Way, William Morrow and Company: New York (1988), p. 119.

30. Ferris, p. 419.

31. See, Henry Steele Commager, Empire of Reason: How Europe Conceived and America Realized the Enlightenment (1977).

19. Olson, Richard. The Emergence of the Social Sciences, 1642- 1792, New York: Twayne Publishers (1993), p. 10.

20. Summers, Montague, The History of Witchcraft, The Guernsey Press: London, England (1925)(reprinted 1994), p. 72. The devil's mark is made by the Devil, or by the Devil's vicegerent at the Sabbats upon the admission of a new witch.

21. Fontaine, Grassy, Doctors; Merindol, Bontemps, Surgeons; Joint Report on Louis Gaufridi, March 10, 1611, quoted in Summers (page 72-73).

22. Summers, p. 73.

23. John Milton, Areopagitica 40 (R. Jebb, ed., AMS Press, 1971)(1918), cited in, Goldberg.

24. Olson, Richard, The Emergence of the Social Sciences, 1642- 1792, Twayne Publishers (1993), p. 18-20.

36. Goldberg.

37. Edmund Burke, Reflections on the Revolution in France (1790).

38. Felt, Salem, The court consisted of seven Judges, Stoughton [clergy], Chief Justice, Nathaniel Saltonstal, replaced by Janthan Curwin [unknown], John Richards [merchant], Bartholomew Gedney [physician], Wait Winthrop [physician], Samuel Sewall [clergy] and Peter Sargeant [merchant].

39. An example of this is the Alar public scare in 1993 when the public became aware of a growth additive called Alar, and associated it with cancer. Alar was added to apple trees to make the apples more aesthetically appealing to consumers. Without conclusive scientific evidence, the public demanded Congress ban the use of Alar and the apple industry was sent into a tailspin. Later studies indicated that Alar was not carcinogenic.

40. David Levin, ed., Theodore Morrison, preface, What Happened in Salem? Documents Pertaining to 17th Century Witchcraft Trials 7 (1952), also see fn.1, the laws of gravitation were set forth in 1687 in Sir Isaac Newton's Principia.

41. Salem, Massachusettes, Visitor Center display.

32. James Thomson, A Poem Sacred to the Memory of Sir Isaac Newton (London: J. Millan, 1727). 3rd ed. E-10 5269 Fisher Rare Book Library (Toronto).

33. 1 Holmes 255 (1630), Washburn, p. 14.

34. Henry Washburn, Sketches of the Judicial History of Massachusetts — from 1630 to the Revolution in 1775 15 (1840).

35. Bailyn, Bernard; Dallek, Robert; David, David Brion; Donald, David Herbert; Thomas, John L., Wood, Gordon S., The Great Republic — A History of the American People, 4th ed., Lexington, Massachusetts: D. C. Heath and Company (1992), p. 139.

In this essay excerpt, Prof. Jill Lepore, explores the historical context for Frye, in Frye v. United States (D.C. 1923) that reveals much more about the state of the science and the legal-psychology expert who was not allowed to testify as an expert in the case, than the short opinion that is the legacy of Frye.

Frye was an alleged murderer named James Alphonso Frye. People who cite the case usually know no more about him than his last name. They know even less about the expert called by his defense. That expert was Marston. Marston's name is not mentioned in the opinions of either the trial or the appellate court. Nor, generally, does his name appear in textbook discussions of Frye, in the case law that has followed in its wake, or in the considerable legal scholarship on the subject of expert testimony. Marston is missing from Frye because the law of evidence, case law, the case method, and the conventions of legal scholarship—together, and relentlessly—hide facts. This Essay Marston-izes Frye, finding facts long hidden to cast light not only on this particular case but also on the standards of evidence used by lawyers, scientists, and historians. It uses a landmark ruling about whether scientific evidence is admissible in court to illustrate how the law renders historical evidence invisible. The law of evidence began in earnest in the early modern era; the history of evidence remains largely unwritten. Before the eighteenth century, the written rules of evidence were few.

In 1794, Edmund Burke said that they were "comprised in so small a compass that a parrot he had known might get them by rote in one half-hour and repeat them in five minutes." But even as Burke was writing, treatises at once examining and codifying exclusionary rules had already begun to proliferate. This sort of work reached a new height at the beginning of the twentieth century with the publication of John Wigmore's magisterial, four-volume A Treatise on the System of Evidence in Trials at Common Law. Wigmore's study of the law of evidence remains a towering influence in the "New Evidence Scholarship," which emerged in the 1980s, following the adoption of the Federal Rules of Evidence in 1975. The law of evidence is vast; the history of evidence is scant. This is to some degree surprising, because in the last decades of the twentieth century, literary scholars, intellectual historians, and historians of the law and of science became fascinated by epistemological questions about the means by which ideas about evidence police the boundaries between disciplines—a fascination that produced invaluable interdisciplinary work on subjects like the history of truth, the rise of empiricism, and the fall of objectivity. But this line of inquiry has a natural limit: scholars who are engaged in a debate about whether facts exist tend not to be especially interested in digging them up. For all the fascination with questions of evidence, very few scholars have investigated the nitty-gritty, stigmata-to-DNA history of the means by which, at different points in time, and across realms of knowledge, some things count as proof and others don't.. . .

In November 1920, on the Saturday after Thanksgiving, Robert Wade Brown, a doctor, had been shot point blank in the front hall of his house while friends were assembled to celebrate Howard University's football game victory. Brown was the president of the National Life Insurance Company and the richest black man in Washington, the kind of man Booker T. Washington had dinner with when he visited the city. Brown's murder had stunned Washington's black community and had been reported all over the country. As a writer for the Chicago Defender put it, "Such was the news that met the ears of awed Race citizens of the nation's capital as they stood in little groups, here and there, and heard related with bated breath the tale of the tragedy on the gloomy Sunday morning after the night of destruction." The case proved a mystery. Brown's family and his company together offered a thousand-dollar reward for information leading to the killer. For months, nothing came of it. Then, on March 10, 1922, ten days before American University's semester began, twenty-two-year-old James Alphonso Frye was charged with killing Brown and indicted for first-degree murder.

. . .

On July 19, the first day Frye testified, Marston went to court and tested his apparatus, apparently in the hallway (the test, which was photographed, was reported in the Washington Post). Preparing to introduce Marston as a witness, Mattingly and Wood submitted Marston's publications, including his dissertation, to the judge. That night, Marston and some of his students held a meeting at American University. They decided to found an American Psycho-Legal Society. Mars- ton and Wigmore were to be honorary co-presidents. (The society's aim was to burnish Marston's credentials, promote and publicize his research, and raise $15,000 to equip his laboratory. It lasted no more than a few months.)

The next day, the courtroom was full to overflowing, in anticipation of Marston's testimony. With Marston on the witness stand, but before he had a chance to speak, McCoy challenged Mattingly's evidence.

Mr. MATTINGLY. If your honor please, at this time I had intended to offer in evidence the testimony of Dr. William M. Marston as an expert in deception.

The COURT. His testimony on what[?]

Mr. MATTINGLY. Testimony as to the truth or falsity of certain statements of the defendant which were made at a particular time.

The COURT. Made at what time?

Mr. MATTINGLY. The tenth of June of this year.

The COURT. We are not concerned with the truth or falsity of any statements on the 10th of June. He has been testifying on the 19th and 20th of July, and that is the only thing we are interested in.

Mr. MATTINGLY. There has been a great amount of testimony offered, your honor, as to what was said by Frye at various times, both prior to and since his arrest. The testimony which is offered is not offered as evidence of what Frye did say; it is not offered for its effect upon the jury in that way, but it is offered as the opinion of an expert as to whether what he did say was the truth or not. I submit that that is competent.

Mr. BILBREY. If your Honor please —

The COURT. You do not need to argue it. If you object to it, I will sustain the objection.

Mr. BILBREY. I do not want to object, but I think that properly to make the offer the witness ought to be put on the stand and sworn and asked questions.

The COURT. No; I do not think they need to go through that. They offer to show that somebody, as an expert in veracity, has made up his mind that Frye on the tenth day of June either told the truth or did not tell it. Of course I do not know what the witness would say; but, as I say, the witness was here on the stand, and it is for the jury to determine whether or not on the nineteenth and twentieth of July he was telling the truth.

Mr. MATTINGLY. Very well, your honor. That is very true, your honor. But as expert testimony is not this proper as competent evidence to go before the jury to ascertain what the Doctor's opinion is at this time?

The COURT. It is not a question of opinion; it is a question of fact.

Mr. MATTINGLY. Subject to the opinion of an expert, though, your honor.

The COURT. Oh, well we get to be more or less experts ourselves, and so do the jury, upon the question of whether anybody is telling the truth or not. That is what the jury is for.

Mr. MATTINGLY. It depends, just as with a finger-print expert or an alienist, upon whether or not we have specialized in that particular field.

The COURT. The only question is whether the witness on the stand told the truth.

Mr. WOOD. I submit, your honor, that the opinion of the expert is still left up to the jury as a question of fact for their consideration in the case.

Mr. MATTINGLY. Take the instance of an alienist, your honor, when he is put on the stand. He testifies as to an examination at some time prior to the trial. He is permitted to state what the nature of the examination was, what he asked the subject, what the subject[']s replies were, the reasons upon which he bases his conclusion, and the conclusion. I can not see the distinction which you draw between that instance and the present one.

The COURT. Well, I will give you this distinction. Fifty years ago if anybody had said that the human voice spoken in Washington could be heard in Chicago he would have been thought crazy. Since that time we all know that such is the fact, and we do not bring experimental matters into court, but when it is established that scientific development has reached such a point as to become a matter of common knowledge as to its results we allow the results to be shown in court.

Mr. MATTINGLY. It seems to me that your Honor is undertaking to say, without hearing what we have to say on the subject, whether or not this is a matter of common knowledge.

The COURT. Well, if you want to take your analogy, when the expert goes on the stand he testifies whether or not at the time he is testifying the person under inquiry is of sound or unsound mind. What the jury is interested to determine in this case is not whether Frye told the truth last month but whether he told it here yesterday and to-day.

Mr. MATTINGLY. We have proof to offer on this point, that it is a scientifically proven fact that certain results will be accomplished under certain conditions. It seems to me that the very least your honor can do is to permit us to attempt to qualify the expert. I think we are entitled to it as a matter of law.

The COURT. To testify as to whether Frye told the truth last month? Mr. MATTINGLY. That is the proffer, your Honor.

The COURT. You are making an offer to show that Frye told the truth last month.

Mr. MATTINGLY. That is only one of several offers we have to make, your Honor.

The COURT. Go ahead and make them all.

Mr. MATTINGLY. I say that, first, we have a right to attempt to qualify the expert.

The COURT. First, then, I say you have not, if what you are trying to do is to qualify him to prove that Frye told the truth last month.

Mr. MATTINGLY. We wish to note an exception to that ruling, sir.

The COURT. Very well.
Mr. MATTINGLY. The next offer which we wish to make is to offer to have the defendant submit to a deception test, under conditions to be prescribed by the court, based upon his direct and cross examination in this case.

The COURT. It is too late. You ought to have had the test made at the time he was testifying, if you wanted it at all.

Mr. MATTINGLY. I wish to note an exception to that ruling. The third offer which we have to make is that we will offer the blood-pressure record which was made contemporaneously with the examination at the jail on the tenth of June in evidence as a basis for hypothetical questions on that record.

The COURT. The offer will not be acted upon favorably.

Mr. MATTINGLY. I wish to note an exception to that ruling. The fourth offer is that we offer to put the expert on the stand for the purpose of testifying as to the deception or nondeception of the defendant during the examination, which was made at the jail on the tenth of June, as bearing on the issue of the crime, that is, the guilt or innocence of the defendant.

The COURT. The same ruling.

Mr. MATTINGLY. And an exception. Now, the fifth offer is an offer to qualify Dr. Marston as an expert in deception, for whatever purpose his testimony may be available.

The COURT. The same ruling.

Mr. MATTINGLY. You refuse to permit us to attempt to qualify him?

The COURT. Yes.

Mr. MATTINGLY. This offer to attempt to qualify, of course, is for the purpose of showing that this is not merely theory, that it is generally known among experts of this class, that it is not untried, that it has been in practical use, that it is not new, and that it is available.

The COURT. The same ruling.

Mr. MATTINGLY. I wish to note an exception to that ruling. With that the defense closes its case, if your Honor please.

Mr. BILBREY. Call Detective Jackson. [Detective John Jackson took the stand.]

Mr. MATTINGLY. If your Honor please, before this witness begins to testify, may I inquire whether your honor would permit a systolic blood-pressure test to be taken during an examination of the witness on the stand?

The COURT. Officer Jackson?

Mr. MATTINGLY. Or anyone?

The COURT. No, indeed.

Mr. MATTINGLY. Well, of Officer Jackson.

The COURT. If we are going to have a systolic test, you will have to test every witness who testifies in the case. If there is any science about it, we might as well apply the science to every witness. Mind you, I do not know anything about the test at all. I had certain pamphlets submitted to me yesterday to look at, of some Dr. Marston—I believe his thesis when he got his Ph. D. degree. I am going to read them when I come back from my vacation. I see enough in them to know that so far the science has not sufficiently developed detection of deception by blood pressure to make it a useable instrument in a court of law. It would be entirely foreign to our practice to have such tests made out of court and not applied certainly to every witness who goes on the witness stand.

Mr. MATTINGLY. Your Honor, of course, in looking over those papers, did not assume that Dr. Marston was the only authority on the subject?

The COURT. Oh, no, indeed. I take his as an authority. You know how much I got out of them when I tell you that it did not take me five minutes to look at what I did look at. So my opinion about anything on that point is not worth the breath that utters it, except that I did see some tests. I happened to read one test that was made, and I believe it was stated—I could not make out whether it was when a man was on probation after conviction or on the witness stand before conviction. I could not tell that. He was on probation, and it was claimed that this test had been established either that the man—it must be that the man had lied about his case. The judge did something or other—I don't know what it was—but subsequent to the time the test was made it was found that the man had been guilty of some similar crime. Now, did the judge act upon the test, or did he act upon his additional information as to the perpetration of some other similar crime. As far as that test is concerned, Dr. Marston will admit that it was not scientific as far as his instrument was concerned, because, as he understands, as a scientist, he has to exclude everything except the constants before he can make a deduction. If there are a lot of variables, all he can say is that on the whole this is probably so. When it is developed to the perfection of the telephone and the telegraph and wireless and a few other things we will consider it. I shall be dead by that time, probably, and it will bother some other judge, not me.

Mr. MATTINGLY. Of course, your Honor understands that at no time in the history of the country has there ever been an offer of the introduction of this test into evidence during the course of the trial, and therefore it is not in the least surprising that you do not find anything which would completely parallel the offer which is made here. But that fact alone is no reason for excluding it.

The COURT. No, indeed. Somebody has to make the first experiment.

Mr. MATTINGLY. The first experiment, it happens, was made more than nine years ago.

The COURT. I mean in court; somebody has got to try it first.

Mr. MATTINGLY. Precisely. There has to be a beginning to everything. We had the same opposition that your honor is raising to this test in the instance of the finger-print system of identification. That was fought for years and years.

The COURT. But as soon as enough of them were developed photographically so that it could be seen that, like the leaves on the trees, the finger prints of no two different individuals were alike, then, of course, the court said, "All right; let us go ahead." And as soon as it is demonstrated that there is an infallible instrument for ascertaining whether a person is speaking the truth or not, and the instances are so multiplied that there can not be any mistake about the matter, then I presume that some court will begin by allowing the testimony. But I miss my guess if they ever allow it to be done out of court and in the absence of the jury which is to pass upon the matter.

Mr. MATTINGLY. That would be simply a question of the veracity of the expert, of course.

The COURT. No, indeed. The jurors will look at a witness when he is testifying. You will not find a case which passes upon the question whether a court of appeals will reverse a judge below in deciding the case but what refers to the fact that the judge has the opportunity to see the witness and observe his demeanor on the witness stand. It is the same thing with the jury, and that is the advantage of the jury. It sees the witness; it sizes him up.

Mr. MATTINGLY. Of course, the defect in that argument is that this test has proved and will continue to prove the fallibility of the visual perceptions in the matter of deception. They are absolutely fallible; there is no doubt about that. Your honor may be a fine judge as to whether a man is telling the truth or not, but there is absolutely no certainty about it. You may be certain, but whether, as a matter of fact, he is telling the truth or not your opinion means absolutely nothing, nor does mine.

The COURT. I never undertake to be certain, because I have been wrong so often; but I do say that we make use of that thing which God Almighty has implanted in us, the power of observation. Some people, for instance, say that God Almighty made all of man's features except the mouth, and a man makes his own mouth. Now, the jury sits here and watches it—and there is a good deal of truth in that statement. But there is no use taking time on that.

Mr. MATTINGLY. Just one moment more, if your Honor please. You seem to place a good deal of stress upon the fact that the finger-print expert's testimony was not admitted until a sufficient number of finger prints had been developed photographically and observed and tabulated and card indexed, and so on. But if you take the instance of the Bertillon measurements, there is absolutely nothing visual there; it is simply a recordation of the measurements of the human body. And in an even greater degree there is absolutely nothing visual as a basis for the decision of an alienist, which is the nearest parallel to this test which there is. Of course, alienists were also fought to the last ditch at the time they were first attempted to be introduced.

The COURT. Absolutely.

Mr. MATTINGLY. That is always the way with anything new.

The COURT. I suppose it depends upon whether you are before a conservative judge or a young one who is willing to take chances. I have gotten too old and too much inured to certain general principles in regard to the trial of cases to depart from them rashly. Of course anything may happen. It may be that cases will be tried in the absence of defendants with a mere record of whether he is telling the truth about certain things brought in by an expert; I do not know, but so far the jury looks at the witnesses, hears what they have to say, compares their statements with other statements, and so forth, and then does what human beings out of Court do when they determine whether or not a man is telling the truth.

Mr. MATTINGLY. Of course, this test is not offered as an absolute proof of whether or not the defendant was telling the truth or is telling the truth or did tell the truth when he was on the stand. It is simply offered as any other expert testimony would be, the weight to be fixed by the jury. It is not conclusive, it is not binding upon them. Of course, I see your honor's ruling will be the same, and our case is closed.

The COURT. Yes; I may try a case next year after I read these books. I may decide differently next year, but not now. And THEREUPON, the defense announced its case closed. WHEREUPON the Government called various witnesses in rebuttal to further maintain the issues on its part joined. And thereupon the Government rested.

. . .

VII. The Twilight Zone

Initially, the appeal prepared by Frye's attorneys consisted almost entirely of arguments on behalf of Marston's work. "The question whether a witness is testifying or has testified truthfully or falsely is a scientific question which requires the aid of the study and experience of the scientific man to accurately determine," Mattingly and Wood argued in their brief. Men come to judge this question by certain arbitrary standards in the course of their dealings with others, and the decision may hinge upon the look in the eyes, the expression on the face, the nervous condition of the witness, the rosy flush which suffuses his countenance, or upon any one of many other evidences which may or may not be taken to indicate truth or deception. We say that there is no standard and no logical or reasonable basis for the determination of this question in general in the absence

---

Frye test. "That the Frye test was displaced by the Rules of Evidence does not mean, however, that the Rules themselves place no limits on the admissibility of purportedly scientific evidence. Nor is the trial judge disabled from screening such evidence. To the contrary, under the rules the trial judge must ensure that any and all scientific testimony or evidence admitted is not only relevant, but reliable." 509 U.S. at 589.

Frye v. United States
293 F. 1013 (D.C.. Cir 1923)

Opinion by: Associate Justice Van Orsdel.

Appellant, defendant below, was convicted of the crime of murder in the second degree, and from the judgment prosecutes this appeal. A single assignment of error is presented for our consideration. In the course of the trial counsel for defendant offered an expert witness to testify to the result of a deception test made upon defendant. The test is described as the systolic blood pressure deception test. It is asserted that blood pressure is influenced by change in the emotions of the witness, and that the systolic blood pressure rises are brought about by nervous impulses sent to the sympathetic branch of the autonomic nervous system.

Scientific experiments, it is claimed, have demonstrated that fear, rage, and pain always produce a rise of systolic blood pressure, and that conscious deception or falsehood, concealment of facts, or guilt of crime, accompanied by fear of detection when the person is under examination, raises the systolic blood pressure in a curve, which corresponds exactly to the struggle going on in the subject's mind, between fear and attempted control of that fear, as the examination touches the vital points in respect of which he is attempting to deceive the examiner. In other words, the theory seems to be that truth is spontaneous, and comes without conscious effort, while the utterance of a falsehood requires a conscious effort, which is reflected in the blood pressure. The rise thus produced is easily detected and distinguished from the rise produced by mere fear of the examination itself. In the former instance, the pressure rises higher than in the latter, and is more pronounced as the examination proceeds, while in the latter case, if the subject is telling the truth, the pressure registers highest at the beginning of the examination, and gradually diminishes as the examination proceeds. Prior to the trial defendant was subjected to this deception test, and counsel offered the scientist who conducted the test as an expert to testify to the results obtained. The offer was objected to by counsel for the government, and the court sustained the objection. Counsel for defendant then offered to have the proffered witness conduct a test in the presence of the jury.

This also was denied.

Counsel for defendant, in their able presentation of the novel question involved, correctly state in their brief that no cases directly in point have been found. The broad ground, however, upon which they plant their case, is succinctly stated in their brief as follows: "The rule is that the opinions of experts or skilled witnesses are admissible in evidence in those cases in which the matter of inquiry is such that inexperienced persons are unlikely to prove capable of forming a correct judgment upon it, for the reason that the subject-matter so far partakes of a science, art, or trade as to require a previous habit or experience or study in it, in order to acquire a knowledge of it. When the question involved does not lie within the range of common experience or common knowledge, but requires special experience or special knowledge, then the opinions of witnesses skilled in that particular science, art, or trade to which the question relates are admissible in evidence."

Numerous cases are cited in support of this rule. Just when a scientific principle or discovery crosses the line between the experimental and demonstrable stages is difficult to define. Somewhere in this twilight zone the evidential force of the principle must be recognized, and while courts will go a long way in admitting expert testimony deduced from a well-recognized scientific principle or discovery, the thing from which the deduction is made must be sufficiently established to have gained general acceptance in the particular field in which it belongs. We think the systolic blood pressure deception test has not yet gained such standing and scientific recognition among physiological and psychological authorities as would justify the courts in admitting expert testimony deduced from the discovery, development, and experiments thus far made.

The judgment is affirmed.

7.1.2   Scientific Evidence – Foundation cases, Part 2

The standard established in Frye was the standard for scientific evidence for the next seventy years. In 1975, the U.S. Supreme Court established the Federal Rules of Evidence, and included rules applicable specifically to scientific evidence. The Federal Rules of Evidence which are relevant to the admissibility and reliability of scientific evidence are as follows:

FRE Rule 702. Testimony by Experts. If scientific, technical, or other specialized knowledge will assist the trier of fact to understand the evidence or to determine a fact in issue, a witness qualified as an expert by knowledge, skill, experience, training, or education, may testify thereto in the form of an opinion or otherwise.

FRE Rule 703. Bases of Opinion Testimony by Experts. The facts or dat in the particular case upon which an expert bases an opinoin or inference may be those perceived by or made known to the expert at or before the hearing. If of a type

Id., at 1130, quoting United States v. Solomon, 753 F.2d 1522, 1526 (CA9 1985).

The court emphasized that other Courts of Appeals considering the risks of Bendectin had refused to admit reanalyses of epidemiological studies that had been neither published nor subjected to peer review. 951 F.2d at 1130-1131. Those courts had found unpublished reanalyses "particularly problematic in light of the massive weight of the original published studies supporting [respondent's] position, all of which had undergone full scrutiny from the scientific community." Id., at 1130.

Contending that reanalysis is generally accepted by the scientific community only when it is subjected to verification and scrutiny by others in the field, the Court of Appeals rejected petitioners' reanalyses as "unpublished, not subjected to the normal peer review process and generated solely for use in litigation." Id., at 1131. The court concluded that petitioners' evidence provided an insufficient foundation to allow admission of expert testimony that Bendectin caused their injuries and, accordingly, that petitioners could not satisfy their burden of proving causation at trial.

We granted certiorari, 506 U.S. 914 (1992), in light of sharp divisions among the courts regarding the proper standard for the admission of expert testimony. . . .

II A

In the 70 years since its formulation in the Frye case, the "general acceptance" test has been the dominant standard for determining the admissibility of novel scientific evidence at trial. Although under increasing attack of late, the rule continues to be followed by a majority of courts, including the Ninth Circuit. . .

The Frye test has its origin in a short and citation-free 1923 decision concerning the admissibility of evidence derived from a systolic blood pressure deception test, a crude precursor to the polygraph machine. In what has become a famous (perhaps infamous) passage, the then Court of Appeals for the District of Columbia described the device and its operation and declared:. . .

"Just when a scientific principle or discovery crosses the line between the experimental and demonstrable stages is difficult to define. Somewhere in this twilight zone the evidential force of the principle must be recognized, and while courts will go a long way in admitting expert testimony deduced from a well-recognized scientific principle or discovery, the thing from which the deduction is made must be sufficiently established to have gained general acceptance in the particular field in which it belongs." 54 App. D.C. at 47, 293 F. at 1014 (emphasis added).

Because the deception test had "not yet gained such standing and scientific recognition among physiological and psychological authorities as would justify the courts in admitting expert testimony deduced from the discovery, development, and experiments thus far made," evidence of its results was ruled inadmissible. Ibid. The merits of the Frye test have been much debated, and scholarship on its proper scope and application is legion. Petitioners' primary attack, however, is not on the content but on the continuing authority of the rule. They contend that the Frye test was superseded by the adoption of the Federal Rules of Evidence.   We agree.

"All relevant evidence is admissible, except as otherwise provided by the Constitution of the United States, by Act of Congress, by these rules, or by other rules prescribed by the Supreme Court pursuant to statutory authority. Evidence which is not relevant is not admissible."

"Relevant evidence" is defined as that which has "any tendency to make the existence of any fact that is of consequence to the determination of the action more probable or less probable than it would be without the evidence." Rule 401. The Rules' basic standard of relevance thus is a liberal one. Frye, of course, predated the Rules by half a century. In United States v. Abel, 469 U.S. 45, 83 L. Ed. 2d 450, 105 S. Ct. 465 (1984), we considered the pertinence of background common law in interpreting the Rules of Evidence. We noted that the Rules occupy the field, id., at 49, but, quoting Professor Cleary, the Reporter, explained that the common law nevertheless could serve as an aid to their application:

"'In principle, under the Federal Rules no common law of evidence remains. "All relevant evidence is admissible, except as otherwise provided . . . ." In reality, of course, the body of common law knowledge continues to exist, though in the somewhat altered form of a source of guidance in the exercise of delegated powers.'" Id., at 51-52.

. . .

Here there is a specific Rule that speaks to the contested issue. Rule 702, governing expert testimony, provides: "If scientific, technical, or other specialized knowledge will assist the trier of fact to understand the evidence or to determine a fact in issue, a witness qualified as an expert by knowledge, skill, experience, training, or education, may testify thereto in the form of an opinion or otherwise."

Nothing in the text of this Rule establishes "general acceptance" as an absolute prerequisite to admissibility. Nor does respondent present any clear indication that Rule 702 or the Rules as a whole were intended to incorporate a "general acceptance" standard. The drafting history makes no mention of Frye, and a rigid "general acceptance" requirement would be at odds with the "liberal thrust" of the Federal Rules and their "general approach of relaxing the traditional barriers to 'opinion' testimony." Given the Rules' permissive backdrop and their inclusion of a specific rule on expert testimony that does not mention "general acceptance," the assertion that the Rules somehow assimilated Frye is unconvincing. Frye made "general acceptance" the exclusive test for admitting expert scientific testimony. That austere standard, absent from, and incompatible with, the Federal Rules of Evidence, should not be applied in federal trials. B That the Frye test was displaced by the Rules of Evidence does not mean, however, that the Rules themselves place no limits on the admissibility of purportedly scientific evidence. . . .Nor is the trial judge disabled from screening such evidence. To the contrary, under the Rules the trial judge must ensure that any and all scientific testimony or evidence admitted is not only relevant, but reliable.

The primary locus of this obligation is Rule 702, which clearly contemplates some degree of regulation of the subjects and theories about which an expert may testify. "If scientific, technical, or other specialized knowledge will assist the trier of fact to understand the evidence or to determine a fact in issue" an expert "may testify thereto." (Emphasis added.) The subject of an expert's testimony must be "scientific . . . knowledge." The adjective "scientific" implies a grounding in the methods and procedures of science. Similarly, the word "knowledge" connotes more than subjective belief or unsupported speculation.

The term "applies to any body of known facts or to any body of ideas inferred from such facts or accepted as truths on good grounds." Webster's Third New International Dictionary 1252 (1986). Of course, it would be unreasonable to conclude that the subject of scientific testimony must be "known" to a certainty; arguably, there are no certainties in science. See, e.g., Brief for Nicolaas Bloembergen et al. as Amici Curiae 9 ("Indeed, scientists do not assert that they know what is immutably 'true' -- they are committed to searching for new, temporary, theories to explain, as best they can, phenomena"); Brief for American Association for the Advancement of Science et al. as Amici Curiae 7-8 ("Science is not an encyclopedic body of knowledge about the universe.

Instead, it represents a process for proposing and refining theoretical explanations about the world that are subject to further testing and refinement" (emphasis in original)). But, in order to qualify as "scientific knowledge," an inference or assertion must be derived by the scientific method. Proposed testimony must be supported by appropriate validation -- i.e., "good grounds," based on what is known. In short, the requirement that an expert's testimony pertain to "scientific knowledge" establishes a standard of evidentiary reliability.

Rule 702 further requires that the evidence or testimony "assist the trier of fact to understand the evidence or to determine a fact in issue." This condition goes primarily to relevance. . . .The consideration has been aptly described by Judge Becker as one of "fit." "Fit" is not always obvious, and scientific validity for one purpose is not necessarily scientific validity for other, unrelated purposes. . .

The study of the phases of the moon, for example, may provide valid scientific "knowledge" about whether a certain night was dark, and if darkness is a fact in issue, the knowledge will assist the trier of fact. However (absent creditable grounds supporting such a link), evidence that the moon was full on a certain night will not assist the trier of fact in determining whether an individual was unusually likely to have behaved irrationally on that night. Rule 702's "helpfulness" standard requires a valid scientific connection to the pertinent inquiry as a precondition to admissibility.

That these requirements are embodied in Rule 702 is not surprising. Unlike an ordinary witness, see Rule 701, an expert is permitted wide latitude to offer opinions, including those that are not based on firsthand knowledge or observation. See Rules 702 and 703. Presumably, this relaxation of the usual requirement of firsthand knowledge -- a rule which represents "a 'most pervasive manifestation' of the common law insistence upon 'the most reliable sources of information,'" Advisory Committee's Notes on Fed. Rule Evid. 602, 28 U.S.C. App., p. 755 (citation omitted) -- is premised on an assumption that the expert's opinion will have a reliable basis in the knowledge and experience of his discipline. C Faced with a proffer of expert scientific testimony, then, the trial judge must determine at the outset, pursuant to Rule 104(a), . . whether the expert is proposing to testify to (1) scientific knowledge that (2) will assist the trier of fact to understand or determine a fact in issue. This entails a preliminary assessment of whether the reasoning or methodology underlying the testimony is scientifically valid and of whether that reasoning or methodology properly can be applied to the facts in issue.

We are confident that federal judges possess the capacity to undertake this review. Many factors will bear on the inquiry, and we do not presume to set out a definitive checklist or test. But some general observations are appropriate.

Ordinarily, a key question to be answered in determining whether a theory or technique is scientific knowledge that will assist the trier of fact will be whether it can be (and has been) tested. "Scientific methodology today is based on generating hypotheses and testing them to see if they can be falsified; indeed, this methodology is what distinguishes science from other fields of human inquiry." See also C. Hempel, Philosophy of Natural Science 49 (1966) ("The statements constituting a scientific explanation must be capable of empirical test"); K. Popper, Conjectures and Refutations: The Growth of Scientific Knowledge 37 (5th ed. 1989) ("The criterion of the scientific status of a theory is its falsifiability, or refutability, or testability") (emphasis deleted). Another pertinent consideration is whether the theory or technique has been subjected to peer review and publication. Publication (which is but one element of peer review) is not a sine qua non of admissibility; it does not necessarily correlate with reliability, see S. Jasanoff, The Fifth Branch: Science Advisors as Policymakers 61-76 (1990), and in some instances well-grounded but innovative theories will not have been published, see Horrobin, The Philosophical Basis of Peer Review and the Suppression of Innovation, 263 JAMA 1438 (1990). Some propositions, moreover, are too particular, too new, or of too limited interest to be published. But submission to the scrutiny of the scientific community is a component of "good science," in part because it increases the likelihood that substantive flaws in methodology will be detected. See J. Ziman, Reliable Knowledge: An Exploration of the Grounds for Belief in Science 130-133 (1978); Relman & Angell, How Good Is Peer Review?, 321 New Eng. J. Med. 827 (1989). The fact of publication (or lack thereof) in a peer reviewed journal thus will be a relevant, though not dispositive, consideration in assessing the scientific validity of a particular technique or methodology on which an opinion is premised.

Additionally, in the case of a particular scientific technique, the court ordinarily should consider the known or potential rate of error, see, e.g., United

States v. Smith, 869 F.2d 348, 353-354 (CA7 1989) (surveying studies of the error rate of spectrographic voice identification technique), and the existence and maintenance of standards controlling the technique's operation, see United States v. Williams, 583 F.2d 1194, 1198 (CA2 1978) (noting professional organization's standard governing spectrographic analysis), cert. denied, 439 U.S. 1117, 59 L. Ed. 2d 77, 99 S. Ct. 1025 (1979).

Finally, "general acceptance" can yet have a bearing on the inquiry. A "reliability assessment does not require, although it does permit, explicit identification of a relevant scientific community and an express determination of a particular degree of acceptance within that community." United States v. Downing, 753 F.2d at 1238. See also 3 Weinstein & Berger P702[03], pp. 702-41 to 702-42. Widespread acceptance can be an important factor in ruling particular evidence admissible, and "a known technique which has been able to attract only minimal support within the community," Downing, 753 F.2d at 1238, may properly be viewed with skepticism.

The inquiry envisioned by Rule 702 is, we emphasize, a flexible one. . . .Its overarching subject is the scientific validity -- and thus the evidentiary relevance and reliability -- of the principles that underlie a proposed submission. The focus, of course, must be solely on principles and methodology, not on the conclusions that they generate. Throughout, a judge assessing a proffer of expert scientific testimony under Rule 702 should also be mindful of other applicable rules. Rule 703 provides that expert opinions based on otherwise inadmissible hearsay are to be admitted only if the facts or data are "of a type reasonably relied upon by experts in the particular field in forming opinions or inferences upon the subject." Rule 706 allows the court at its discretion to procure the assistance of an expert of its own choosing.

Finally, Rule 403 permits the exclusion of relevant evidence "if its probative value is substantially outweighed by the danger of unfair prejudice, confusion of the issues, or misleading the jury . . . ." Judge Weinstein has explained: "Expert evidence can be both powerful and quite misleading because of the difficulty in evaluating it. Because of this risk, the judge in weighing possible prejudice against probative force under Rule 403 of the present rules exercises more control over experts than over lay witnesses." Weinstein, 138 F.R.D. at 632. III

We conclude by briefly addressing what appear to be two underlying concerns of the parties and amici in this case. Respondent expresses apprehension that abandonment of "general acceptance" as the exclusive requirement for admission will result in a "free-for-all" in which befuddled juries are confounded by absurd and irrational pseudoscientific assertions. In this regard respondent seems to us to be overly pessimistic about the capabilities of the jury and of the adversary system generally. Vigorous cross-examination, presentation of contrary evidence, and careful instruction on the burden of proof are the traditional and appropriate means of attacking shaky but admissible evidence. . . . Additionally, in the event the trial court concludes that the scintilla of evidence presented supporting a position is insufficient to allow a reasonable juror to conclude that the position more likely than not is true, the court remains free to direct a judgment, Fed. Rule Civ. Proc. 50(a), and likewise to grant summary judgment, Fed. Rule Civ. Proc. 56. Cf., e.g., Turpin v. Merrell Dow Pharmaceuticals, Inc., 959 F.2d 1349 (CA6) (holding that scientific evidence that provided foundation for expert testimony, viewed in the light most favorable to plaintiffs, was not sufficient to allow a jury to find it more probable than not that defendant caused plaintiff's injury), cert. denied, 506 U.S. 826, 121 L. Ed. 2d 47, 113 S. Ct. 84 (1992); Brock v. Merrell Dow Pharmaceuticals, Inc., 874 F.2d 307 (CA5 1989) (reversing judgment entered on jury verdict for plaintiffs because evidence regarding causation was insufficient), modified, 884 F.2d 166 (CA5 1989), cert. denied, 494 U.S. 1046 (1990); Green 680-681. These conventional devices, rather than wholesale exclusion under an uncompromising "general acceptance" test, are the appropriate safeguards where the basis of scientific testimony meets the standards of Rule 702. Petitioners and, to a greater extent, their amici exhibit a different concern. They suggest that recognition of a screening role for the judge that allows for the exclusion of "invalid" evidence will sanction a stifling and repressive scientific orthodoxy and will be inimical to the search for truth. See, e.g., Brief for Ronald Bayer et al. as Amici Curiae. It is true that open debate is an essential part of both legal and scientific analyses. Yet there are important differences between the quest for truth in the courtroom and the quest for truth in the laboratory. Scientific conclusions are subject to perpetual revision. Law, on the other hand, must resolve disputes finally and quickly. The scientific project is advanced by broad and wide-ranging consideration of a multitude of hypotheses, for those that are incorrect will eventually be shown to be so, and that in itself is an advance. Conjectures that are probably wrong are of little use, however, in the project of reaching a quick, final, and binding legal judgment -- often of great consequence -- about a particular set of events in the past.

We recognize that, in practice, a gatekeeping role for the judge, no matter how flexible, inevitably on occasion will prevent the jury from learning of authentic insights and innovations. That, nevertheless, is the balance that is struck by Rules of Evidence designed not for the exhaustive search for cosmic understanding but for the particularized resolution of legal disputes. . . .

IV To summarize: "General acceptance" is not a necessary precondition to the admissibility of scientific evidence under the Federal Rules of Evidence, but the Rules of Evidence -- especially Rule 702 -- do assign to the trial judge the task of ensuring that an expert's testimony both rests on a reliable foundation and is relevant to the task at hand. Pertinent evidence based on scientifically valid principles will satisfy those demands. The inquiries of the District Court and the Court of Appeals focused almost exclusively on "general acceptance," as gauged by publication and the decisions of other courts.

Accordingly, the judgment of the Court of Appeals is vacated, and the case is remanded for further proceedings consistent with this opinion. It is so ordered.

Concur by REHNQUIST (In Part) ; and dissent by Rehnquist (in Part)Dissent by CHIEF JUSTICE REHNQUIST, with whom JUSTICE STEVENS joins, concurring in part and dissenting in part.

. . . The petition for certiorari in this case presents . . . first, whether the rule of Frye v. United States, 54 App. D.C. 46, 293 F. 1013 (1923), remains good law after the enactment of the Federal Rules of Evidence; and second, if Frye remains valid, whether it requires expert scientific testimony to have been subjected to a peer review process in order to be admissible. The Court concludes, correctly in my view, that the Frye rule did not survive the enactment of the Federal Rules of Evidence . . . .

Daubert was the case that interpreted how the Federal Rules of Evidence with regard to scientific evidence should be applied, twenty years after the establishment of the Federal Rules of Evidence. It remains the most important landmark case in modern scientific evidence cases. In the usual evidence course, the story stops with the complex task for students of sorting through the criteria for scientific evidence in the U.S Supreme Court opinion. However, in considering how emerging technologies may be considered, the remand to the Circuit Court will next be examined. Did the Circuit Court, which was reversed, re-confirm its confirmation of the District Court's granting of summary judgment for the defendants? Or did the Circuit Court in following the directions of the opinion from the U.S. Supreme Court, come to a different decision and remand the case back to the District Court to reconsider admitting the testimony?

Daubert v. Merrell Dow Pharmaceuticals, Inc. (on remand)
43 F.3d 1311 (9th Cir. 1995)

Kozinski, Circuit Judge.

On remand from the United States Supreme Court, we undertake "the task of ensuring that an expert's testimony both rests on a reliable foundation and is relevant to the task at hand." Daubert v. Merrell Dow Pharmaceuticals, Inc. (1993).

I.

A. BACKGROUND

Two minors brought suit against Merrell Dow Pharmaceuticals, claiming they suffered limb reduction birth defects because their mothers had taken Bendectin, a drug prescribed for morning sickness to about 17.5 million pregnant women in the United States between 1957 and 1982. This appeal deals with an evidentiary question: whether certain expert scientific testimony is admissible to prove that Bendectin caused the plaintiffs' birth defects.

For the most part, we don't know how birth defects come about. We do know they occur in 2-3% of births, whether or not the expectant mother has taken Bendectin. See Jose F. Cordero & Godfrey P. Oakley, Jr., Drug Exposure During Pregnancy: Some Epidemiologic Considerations, 26 Clinical Obstetrics & Gynecology 418, 424-25 (June 1983). Limb defects are even rarer, occurring in fewer than one birth out of every 1000. But scientists simply do not know how teratogens (chemicals known to cause limb reduction defects) do their damage: They cannot reconstruct the biological chain of events that leads from an expectants mother's ingestion of a teratogenic substance to the stunted development of a baby's limbs. Nor do they know what it is about teratogens that causes them to have this effect. No doubt, someday we will have this knowledge, and then we will be able to tell precisely whether and how Bendectin (or any other suspected teratogen) interferes with limb development; in the current state of scientific knowledge, however, we are ignorant.

Not knowing the mechanism whereby a particular agent causes a particular effect is not always fatal to a plaintiff's claim. Causation can be proved even when we don't know precisely how the damage occurred, if there is sufficiently compelling proof that the agent must have caused the damage somehow. One method of proving causation in these circumstances is to use statistical evidence. If 50 people who eat at a restaurant one evening come down with food poisoning during the night, we can infer that the restaurant's food probably contained something unwholesome, even if none of the dishes is available for analysis. This inference is based on the fact that, in our health-conscious society, it is highly unlikely that 50 people who have nothing in common except that they ate at the same restaurant would get food poisoning from independent sources.

It is by such means that plaintiffs here seek to establish that Bendectin is responsible for their injuries. They rely on the testimony of three groups of scientific experts. One group proposes to testify that there is a statistical link between the ingestion of Bendectin during pregnancy and limb reduction defects. These experts have not themselves conducted epidemiological (human statistical) studies on the effects of Bendectin; rather, they have reanalyzed studies published by other scientists, none of whom reported a statistical association between Bendectin and birth defects. Other experts proffered by plaintiffs propose to testify that Bendectin causes limb reduction defects in humans because it causes such defects in laboratory animals. A third group of experts sees a link between Bendectin and birth defects because Bendectin has a chemical structure that is similar to other drugs suspected of causing birth defects.

The opinions proffered by plaintiffs' experts do not, to understate the point, reflect the consensus within the scientific community. The FDA—an agency not known for its promiscuity in approving drugs—continues to approve Bendectin for use by pregnant women because "available data do not demonstrate an association between birth defects and Bendectin." U.S. Department of Health and Human Services News, No. P80-45 (Oct. 7, 1980). Every published study here and abroad—and there have been many—concludes that Bendectin is not a teratogen. In fact, apart from the small but determined group of scientists testifying on behalf of the Bendectin plaintiffs in this and many other cases, there doesn't appear to be a single scientist who has concluded that Bendectin causes limb reduction defects.

It is largely because the opinions proffered by plaintiffs' experts run counter to the substantial consensus in the scientific community that we affirmed the district court's grant of summary judgment the last time the case appeared before us. The standard for admissibility of expert testimony in this circuit at the time was the so-called Frye test: Scientific evidence was admissible if it was based on a scientific technique generally accepted as reliable within the scientific community. We found that the district court properly applied this standard, and affirmed. The Supreme Court reversed, holding that Frye was superseded by Federal Rule of Evidence 702, and remanded for us to consider the admissibility of plaintiffs' expert testimony under this new standard. . . .

II.

A. BRAVE NEW WORLD

Federal judges ruling on the admissibility of expert scientific testimony face a far more complex and daunting task in a post-Daubert world than before. The judge's task under Frye is relatively simple: to determine whether the method employed by the experts is generally accepted in the scientific community. Under Daubert, we must engage in a difficult, two-part analysis. First, we must determine nothing less than whether the experts' testimony reflects "scientific knowledge," whether their findings are "derived by the scientific method," and whether their work product amounts to "good science." Second, we must ensure that the proposed expert testimony is "relevant to the task at hand," i.e., that it logically advances a material aspect of the proposing party's case. The Supreme Court referred to this second prong of the analysis as the "fit" requirement.

The first prong of Daubert puts federal judges in an uncomfortable position. The question of admissibility only arises if it is first established that the individuals whose testimony is being proffered are experts in a particular scientific field; here, for example, the Supreme Court waxed eloquent on the impressive qualifications of plaintiffs' experts. Yet something doesn't become "scientific knowledge" just because it's uttered by a scientist; nor can an expert's self-serving assertion that his conclusions were "derived by the scientific method" be deemed conclusive, else the Supreme Court's opinion could have ended with footnote two. As we read the Supreme Court's teaching in Daubert, therefore, though we are largely untrained in science and certainly no match for any of the witnesses whose testimony we are reviewing, it is our responsibility to determine whether those experts' proposed testimony amounts to "scientific knowledge," constitutes "good science," and was "derived by the scientific method."

The task before us is more daunting still when the dispute concerns matters at the very cutting edge of scientific research, where fact meets theory and certainty dissolves into probability. As the record in this case illustrates, scientists often have vigorous and sincere disagreements as to what research methodology is proper, what should be accepted as sufficient proof for the existence of a "fact," and whether information derived by a particular method can tell us anything useful about the subject under study.

Our responsibility, then, unless we badly misread the Supreme Court's opinion, is to resolve disputes among respected, well-credentialed scientists about matters squarely within their expertise, in areas where there is no scientific consensus as to what is and what is not "good science," and occasionally to reject such expert testimony because it was not "derived by the scientific method." Mindful of our position in the hierarchy of the federal judiciary, we take a deep breath and proceed with this heady task.

B. DEUS EX MACHINA

The Supreme Court's opinion in Daubert focuses closely on the language of Fed. R. Evid. 702, which permits opinion testimony by experts as to matters amounting to "scientific . . . knowledge." The Court recognized, however, that knowledge in this context does not mean absolute certainty. Rather, the Court said, "in order to qualify as 'scientific knowledge,' an inference or assertion must be derived by the scientific method." Elsewhere in its opinion, the Court noted that Rule 702 is satisfied where the proffered testimony is "based on scientifically valid principles." Our task, then, is to analyze not what the experts say, but what basis they have for saying it.

Which raises the question: How do we figure out whether scientists have derived their findings through the scientific method or whether their testimony is based on scientifically valid principles? Each expert proffered by the plaintiffs assures us that he has "utiliz[ed] the type of data that is generally and reasonably relied upon by scientists" in the relevant field, and that he has "utilized the methods and methodology that would generally and reasonably be accepted" by people who deal in these matters. The Court held, however, that federal judges perform a "gatekeeping role," to do so they must satisfy themselves that scientific evidence meets a certain standard of reliability before it is admitted. This means that the expert's bald assurance of validity is not enough. Rather, the party presenting the expert must show that the expert's findings are based on sound science, and this will require some objective, independent validation of the expert's methodology.

While declining to set forth a "definitive checklist or test," the Court did list several factors federal judges can consider in determining whether to admit expert scientific testimony under Fed. R. Evid. 702: whether the theory or technique employed by the expert is generally accepted in the scientific community; whether it's been subjected to peer review and publication; whether it can be and has been tested; and whether the known or potential rate of error is acceptable.3 We read these factors as illustrative rather than exhaustive; similarly, we do not deem each of them to be equally applicable (or applicable at all) in every case. Rather, we read the Supreme Court as instructing us to determine whether the analysis undergirding the experts' testimony falls within the range of accepted standards governing how scientists conduct their research and reach their conclusions.

One very significant fact to be considered is whether the experts are proposing to testify about matters growing naturally and directly out of research they have conducted independent of the litigation, or whether they have developed their opinions expressly for purposes of testifying. That an expert testifies for money does not necessarily cast doubt on the reliability of his testimony, as few experts appear in court merely as an eleemosynary gesture. But in determining whether proposed expert testimony amounts to good science, we may not ignore the fact that a scientist's normal workplace is the lab or the field, not the courtroom or the lawyer's office.

That an expert testifies based on research he has conducted independent of the litigation provides important, objective proof that the research comports with the dictates of good science.

See Peter Huber, Galileo's Revenge: Junk Science in the Courtroom 206-09 (1991) (describing how the prevalent practice of expert-shopping leads to bad science). For one thing, experts whose findings flow from existing research are less likely to have been biased toward a particular conclusion by the promise of remuneration; when an expert prepares reports and findings before being hired as a witness, that record will limit the degree to which he can tailor his testimony to serve a party's interests. Then, too, independent research carries its own indicia of reliability, as it is conducted, so to speak, in the usual course of business and must normally satisfy a variety of standards to attract funding and institutional support. Finally, there is usually a limited number of scientists actively conducting research on the very subject that is germane to a particular case, which provides a natural constraint on parties' ability to shop for experts who will come to the desired conclusion. That the testimony proffered by an expert is based directly on legitimate, preexisting research unrelated to the litigation provides the most persuasive basis for concluding that the opinions he expresses were "derived by the scientific method."

We have examined carefully the affidavits proffered by plaintiffs' experts, as well as the testimony from prior trials that plaintiffs have introduced in support of that testimony, and find that none of the experts based his testimony on preexisting or independent research. While plaintiffs' scientists are all experts in their respective fields, none claims to have studied the effect of Bendectin on limb reduction defects before being hired to testify in this or related cases.

If the proffered expert testimony is not based on independent research, the party proffering it must come forward with other objective, verifiable evidence that the testimony is based on "scientifically valid principles." One means of showing this is by proof that the research and analysis supporting the proffered conclusions have been subjected to normal scientific scrutiny through peer review and publication. Huber, Galileo's Revenge at 209 (suggesting that "[t]he ultimate test of [a scientific expert's] integrity is her readiness to publish and be damned").

Peer review and publication do not, of course, guarantee that the conclusions reached are correct; much published scientific research is greeted with intense skepticism and is not borne out by further research. But the test under Daubert is not the correctness of the expert's conclusions but the soundness of his methodology. That the research is accepted for publication in a reputable scientific journal after being subjected to the usual rigors of peer review is a significant indication that it is taken seriously by other scientists, i.e., that it means at least the minimal criteria of good science. . . . If nothing else, peer review and publication "increase the likelihood that substantive flaws in methodology with be detected."

Bendectin litigation has been pending in the courts for over a decade, yet the only review the plaintiffs' experts' work has received has been by judges and juries, and the only place their theories and studies have been published is in the pages of federal and state reporters. None of the plaintiffs' experts has published his work on Bendectin in a scientific journal or solicited formal review by his colleagues. Despite the many years the controversy has been brewing, no one in the scientific community—except defendant's experts—has deemed these studies worthy of verification, refutation or even comment. It's as if there were a tacit understanding within the scientific community that what's going on here is not science at all, but litigation.

Establishing that an expert's proffered testimony grows out of pre-litigation research or that the expert's research has been subjected to peer review are the two principal ways the proponent of expert testimony can show that the evidence satisfies the first prong of Rule 702. [10] Where such evidence is unavailable, the proponent of expert scientific testimony may attempt to satisfy its burden through the testimony of its own experts. For such a showing to be sufficient, the experts must explain precisely how they went about reaching their conclusions and point to some objective source—a learned treatise, the policy statement of a professional association, a published article in a reputable scientific journal or the like—to show that they have followed the scientific method, as it is practiced by (at least) a recognized minority of scientists in their field. See United States v. Rincom, 28 F.3d 921, 924 (9th Cir. 1994) (research must be described "in sufficient detail that the district court [can] determine if the research was scientifically valid").[11]

Plaintiffs have made no such showing. As noted above, plaintiffs rely entirely on the experts' unadorned assertions that the methodology

---

10. This showing would not, of course, be conclusive. Proffering scientific testimony and making an initial showing that it was derived by the scientific method enables a party to establish a prima facie case as to admissibility under

Rule 702. The opposing party would then be entitled to challenge that showing. This it could do by presenting evidence (including expert testimony) that the proposing party's expert employed unsound methodology or failed to assiduously follow an otherwise sound protocol. Where the opposing party thus raises a material dispute as to the admissibility of expert scientific evidence, the district court must hold an in limine hearing (a so-called Daubert hearing) to consider the conflicting evidence and make findings about the soundness and reliability of the methodology employed by the scientific experts. . . .

11. This underscores the difference between Daubert and Frye. Under Frye, the party proffering scientific evidence had to show it was based on the method generally accepted in the scientific community. The focus under Daubert is on the reliability of the methodology, and in addressing that question the court and the parties are not limited to what is generally accepted; methods accepted by a minority in the scientific community may well be sufficient. However, the party proffering the evidence must explain the expert's methodology and demonstrate in some objectively verifiable way that the expert has both chosen a reliable scientific method and followed it faithfully. Of course, the fact that one party's experts use a methodology accepted by only a minority of scientists would be a proper basis for impeachment at trial they employed comports with standard scientific procedures. In support of these assertions, plaintiffs offer only the trial and deposition testimony of these experts in other cases. While these materials indicate that plaintiffs' experts have relied on animal studies, chemical structure analyses and epidemiological data, they neither explain the methodology the experts followed to reach their conclusions nor point to any external source to validate that methodology. We've been presented with only the experts' qualifications, their conclusions and their assurances of reliability. Under Daubert, that's not enough.

This is especially true of Dr. Palmer—the only expert willing to testify "that Bendectin did cause the limb defects in each of the children." In support of this conclusion, Dr. Palmer asserts only that Bendectin is a teratogen and that he has examined the plaintiffs' medical records, which apparently reveal the timing of their mothers' ingestion of the drug. Dr. Palmer offers no tested or testable theory to explain how, from this limited information, he was able to eliminate all other potential causes of birth defects, nor does he explain how he alone can state as a fact that Bendectin caused plaintiffs' injuries. We therefore agree with the Sixth Circuit's observation that "Dr. Palmer does not testify on the basis of the collective view of his scientific discipline, nor does he take issue with his peers and explain the grounds for his differences. Indeed, no understandable scientific basis is stated. Personal opinion, not science, is testifying here." For this reason, Dr. Palmer's testimony is inadmissible as a matter of law under Rule 702.

The failure to make any objective showing as to admissibility under the first prong of Rule 702 would also fatally undermine the testimony of plaintiffs' other experts, but for the peculiar posture of this case. Plaintiffs submitted their experts' affidavits while Frye was the law of the circuit and, although they've not requested an opportunity to augment their experts' affidavits in light of Daubert, the interests of justice would be disserved by precluding plaintiffs from doing so. Given the opportunity to augment their original showing of admissibility, plaintiffs might be able to show that the methodology adopted by some of their experts is based on sound scientific principles. For instance, plaintiffs' epidemiologists might validate their reanalyses by explaining why they chose only certain of the data that was available, or the experts relying on animal studies might point to some authority for extrapolating human causation from teratogenicity in animals.

Were this the only question before us, we would be inclined to remand to give plaintiffs an opportunity to submit additional proof that the scientific testimony they proffer was "derived by the scientific method." Daubert, however, establishes two prongs to the Rule 702 admissibility inquiry. We therefore consider whether the testimony satisfies the second prong of Rule 702: Would plaintiffs' proffered scientific evidence "assist the trier of fact to . . . determine a fact in issue"? Fed. R. Evid. 702.

C. NO VISIBLE MEANS OF SUPPORT

In elucidating the second requirement of Rule 702, Daubert stressed the importance of the "fit" between the testimony and an issue in the case: "Rule 702's 'helpfulness' standard requires a valid scientific connection to the pertinent inquiry as a precondition to admissibility." Here, the pertinent inquiry is causation. In assessing whether the proffered expert testimony "will assist the trier of fact" in resolving this issue, we must look to the governing substantive standard, which in this case is supplied by California tort law.

Plantiffs do not attempt to show causation directly; instead, they rely on experts who present circumstantial proof of causation. Plaintiffs' experts testify that Bendectin is a teratogen because it causes birth defects when it is tested on animals, because it is similar in chemical structure to other suspected teratogens, and because statistical studies show that Bendectin use increases the risk of birth defects. Modern tort law permits such proof, but plaintiffs must nevertheless carry their traditional burden; they must prove that their injuries were the result of the accused cause and not some independent factor. In the case of birth defects, carrying this burden is made more difficult because we know that some defects— including limb reduction defects—occur even when expectant mothers do not take Bendectin, and that most birth defects occur for no known reason.

California tort law requires plaintiffs to show not merely that Bendectin increased the likelihood of injury, but that it more likely than not caused their injuries. See Jones v. Ortho Pharmaceutical Corp., 163 Cal. App. 3d 396, 403, 209 Cal. Rptr. 456 (1985). In terms of statistical proof, this means that plaintiffs must establish not just that their mothers' ingestion of Bendectin increased somewhat the likelihood of birth defects, but that it more than doubled it—only then can it be said that Bendectin is more likely than not the source of their injury. Because the background rate of limb reduction defects is one per thousand births, plaintiffs must show that among children of mothers who took Bendectin the incidence of such defects was more than two per thousand.

None of plaintiffs' epidemiological experts claims that ingestion of Bendectin during pregnancy more than doubles the risk of birth defects. To evaluate the relationship between Bendectin and limb reduction defects, an epidemiologist would take a sample of the population and compare the frequency of birth defects in children whose mothers took Bendectin with the frequency of defects in children whose mothers did not. The ratio derived from this comparison would be an estimate of the "relative risk" associated with Bendectin. See generally Joseph L. Fleiss, Statistical Methods for Rates and Proportions (2d ed. 1981). For an epidemiological study to show causation under a preponderance standard, "the relative risk of limb reduction defects arising from the epidemiological data . . . will, at a minimum, have to exceed '2'." That is, the study must show that children whose mothers took Bendectin are more than twice as likely to develop limb reduction birth defects as children whose mothers did not. While plaintiffs' epidemiologists make vague assertions that there is a statistically significant relationship between Bendectin and birth defects, none states that the relative risk is greater than two. These studies thus would not be helpful, and indeed would only serve to confuse the jury, if offered to prove rather than refute causation. A relative risk of less than two may suggest teratogenicity, but it actually tends to disprove legal causation, as it shows that Bendectin does not double the likelihood of birth defects.

With the exception of Dr. Palmer, whose testimony is inadmissible under the first prong of the Rule 702 analysis, the remaining experts proffered by plaintiffs were equally unprepared to testify that Bendectin caused plaintiffs' injuries; they were willing to testify only that Bendectin is "capable of causing" birth defects. Plaintiffs argue "these scientists use the words 'capable of causing' meaning that it does cause. This is an ambiguity of language. . . . If something is capable of causing damage in humans, it does." But what plaintiffs must prove is not that Bendectin causes some birth defects, but that it caused their birth defects. To show this, plaintiffs' experts would have had to testify either that Bendectin actually caused plaintiffs' injuries (which they could not say) or that Bendectin more than doubled the likelihood of limb reduction birth defects (which they did not say).

As the district court properly found below, "the strongest inference to be drawn for plaintiffs based on the epidemiological evidence is that Bendectin could possibly have caused plaintiffs' injuries." The same is true of the other testimony derived from animal studies and chemical structure analyses—these experts "testify to a possibility rather than a probability." Plaintiffs do not quantify this possibility, or otherwise indicate how their conclusions about causation should be weighted, even though the substantive legal standard has always required proof of causation by a preponderance of the evidence. Unlike these experts' explanation of their methodology, this is not a shortcoming that could be corrected on remand; plaintiffs' experts could augment their affidavits with independent proof that their methods were sound, but to augment the substantive testimony as to causation would require the experts to change their conclusions altogether. Any such tailoring of the experts' conclusions would, at this stage of the proceedings, fatally undermine any attempt to show that these findings were "derived by the scientific method." Plaintiffs' experts must, therefore, stand by the conclusions they originally proffered, rendering their testimony inadmissible under the second prong of Fed. R. Evid. 702.

Conclusion
The district court's grant of summary judgment is affirmed.

Two years after *Daubert*, the remand decision was issued and the result remained the same. The application of the principles of *Daubert* in this case are instructive in how the court responded to the necessity of going beyond the Frye test and applying the Rule 702 criteria as articulated by the U.S. Supreme Court.

Two years later, the next decision from the U.S. Supreme Court in 1997, dealt with a number of problems with the scientific evidence, each of which presented an opportunity to the U.S. Supreme Court to further articulate the principles of Daubert. The case is *General Electric v. Joiner*.

7.1.3   Scientific Evidence –Foundation cases, Part 3

General Electric Company v. Joiner
522 U.S. 136 (1997)

CHIEF JUSTICE Rehnquist delivered the opinion of the Court.

We granted certiorari in this case to determine what standard an appellate court should apply in reviewing a trial court's decision to admit or exclude expert testimony under Daubert v. Merrell Dow Pharmaceuticals, Inc., 509 U.S. 579, 125 L. Ed. 2d 469, 113 S. Ct. 2786 (1993). We hold that abuse of discretion is the appropriate standard. We apply this standard and conclude that the District Court in this case did not abuse its discretion when it excluded certain proffered expert testimony.

Respondent Robert Joiner began work as an electrician in the Water & Light Department of Thomasville, Georgia (City) in 1973. This job required him to work with and around the City's electrical transformers, which used a mineral-based dielectric fluid as a coolant. Joiner often had to stick his hands and arms into the fluid to make repairs. The fluid would sometimes splash onto him, occasionally getting into his eyes and mouth. In 1983 the City discovered that the fluid in some of the transformers was contaminated with polychlorinated biphenyls (PCBs). PCBs are widely considered to be hazardous to human health.

Congress, with limited exceptions, banned the production and sale of PCBs in 1978. Joiner was diagnosed with small cell lung cancer in 1991. He sued petitioners in Georgia state court the following year. Petitioner Monsanto manufactured PCBs from 1935 to 1977; petitioners General Electric and Westinghouse Electric manufactured transformers and dielectric fluid. In his complaint Joiner linked his development of cancer to his exposure to PCBs and their derivatives, polychlorinated dibenzofurans (furans) and polychlorinated dibenzodioxins (dioxins). Joiner had been a smoker for approximately eight years, his parents had both been smokers, and there was a history of lung cancer in his family. He was thus perhaps already at a heightened risk of developing lung cancer eventually. The suit alleged that his exposure to PCBs "promoted" his cancer; had it not been for his exposure to these substances, his cancer would not have developed for many years, if at all. Petitioners removed the case to federal court. Once there, they moved for summary judgment. They contended that (1) there was no evidence that Joiner suffered significant exposure to PCBs, furans, or dioxins, and (2) there was no admissible scientific evidence that PCBs promoted Joiner's cancer. Joiner responded that there were numerous disputed factual issues that required resolution by a jury. He relied largely on the testimony of expert witnesses. In depositions, his experts had testified that PCBs alone can promote cancer and that furans and dioxins can also promote cancer. They opined that since Joiner had been exposed to PCBs, furans, and dioxins, such exposure was likely responsible for Joiner's cancer.

The District Court ruled that there was a genuine issue of material fact as to whether Joiner had been exposed to PCBs. But it nevertheless granted summary judgment for petitioners because (1) there was no genuine issue as to whether Joiner had been exposed to furans and dioxins, and (2) the testimony of Joiner's experts had failed to show that there was a link between exposure to PCBs and small cell lung cancer. The court believed that the testimony of respondent's experts to the contrary did not rise above "subjective belief or unsupported speculation." 864 F. Supp. 1310, 1326 (ND Ga. 1994). Their testimony was therefore inadmissible.

The Court of Appeals for the Eleventh Circuit reversed. 78 F.3d 524 (1996). It held that "because the Federal Rules of Evidence governing expert testimony display a preference for admissibility, we apply a particularly stringent standard of review to the trial judge's exclusion of expert testimony." . Applying that standard, the Court of Appeals held that the District Court had erred in excluding the testimony of Joiner's expert witnesses. The District Court had made two fundamental errors. First, it excluded the experts' testimony because it "drew different conclusions from the research than did each of the experts." The Court of Appeals opined that a district court should limit its role to determining the "legal reliability of proffered expert testimony, leaving the jury to decide the correctness of competing expert opinions." Second, the District Court had held that there was no genuine issue of material fact as to whether Joiner had been exposed to furans and dioxins. This was also incorrect, said the Court of

Appeals, because testimony in the record supported the proposition that there had been such exposure.

We granted petitioners' petition for a writ of certiorari, 520 U.S. (1997), and we now reverse. . . .

III

We believe that a proper application of the correct standard of review here indicates that the District Court did not abuse its discretion. Joiner's theory of liability was that his exposure to PCBs and their derivatives "promoted" his development of small cell lung cancer. In support of that theory he proffered the deposition testimony of expert witnesses. Dr. Arnold Schecter testified that he believed it "more likely than not that Mr. Joiner's lung cancer was causally linked to cigarette smoking and PCB exposure." Dr. Daniel Teitelbaum testified that Joiner's "lung cancer was caused by or contributed to in a significant degree by the materials with which he worked." Petitioners contended that the statements of Joiner's experts regarding causation were nothing more than speculation. Petitioners criticized the testimony of the experts in that it was "not supported by epidemiological studies . . . [and was] based exclusively on isolated studies of laboratory animals." Joiner responded by claiming that his experts had identified "relevant animal studies which support their opinions." He also directed the court's attention to four epidemiological studies . . .on which his experts had relied. The District Court agreed with petitioners that the animal studies on which respondent's experts relied did not support his contention that exposure to PCBs had contributed to his cancer. The studies involved infant mice that had developed cancer after being exposed to PCBs. The infant mice in the studies had had massive doses of PCBs injected directly into their peritoneums or stomachs. Joiner was an adult human being whose alleged exposure to PCBs was far less than the exposure in the animal studies. The PCBs were injected into the mice in a highly concentrated form. The fluid with which Joiner had come into contact generally had a much smaller PCB concentration of between 0-500 parts per million. The cancer that these mice developed was alveologenic adenomas; Joiner had developed small-cell carcinomas. No study demonstrated that adult mice developed cancer after being exposed to PCBs. One of the experts admitted that no study had demonstrated that PCBs lead to cancer in any other species. Respondent failed to reply to this criticism. Rather than explaining how and why the experts could have extrapolated their opinions from these seemingly far-removed animal studies, respondent chose "to proceed as if the only issue [was] whether animal studies can ever be a proper foundation for an expert's opinion." Joiner, 864 F. Supp. at 1324. Of course, whether animal studies can ever be a proper foundation for an expert's opinion was not the issue. The issue was whether these experts' opinions were sufficiently supported by the animal studies on which they purported to rely. The studies were so dissimilar to the facts presented in this litigation that it was not an abuse of discretion for the District Court to have rejected the experts' reliance on them. The District Court also concluded that the four epidemiological studies on which respondent relied were not a sufficient basis for the experts' opinions.

The first such study involved workers at an Italian capacitor plant who had been exposed to PCBs. Bertazzi, Riboldi, Pesatori, Radice, & Zocchetti, Cancer Mortality of Capacitor Manufacturing Workers, 11 American Journal of Industrial Medicine 165 (1987). The authors noted that lung cancer deaths among ex-employees at the plant were higher than might have been expected, but concluded that "there were apparently no grounds for associating lung cancer deaths (although increased above expectations) and exposure in the plant." Given that Bertazzi et al. were unwilling to say that PCB exposure had caused cancer among the workers they examined, their study did not support the experts' conclusion that Joiner's exposure to PCBs caused his cancer.

The second study followed employees who had worked at Monsanto's PCB production plant. J. Zack & D. Munsch, Mortality of PCB Workers at the Monsanto Plant in Sauget, Illinois (Dec. 14, 1979)(unpublished report), 3 Rec., Doc. No. 11. The authors of this study found that the incidence of lung cancer deaths among these workers was somewhat higher than would ordinarily be expected. The increase, however, was not statistically significant and the authors of the study did not suggest a link between the increase in lung cancer deaths and the exposure to PCBs. The third and fourth studies were likewise of no help.

The third involved workers at a Norwegian cable manufacturing company who had been exposed to mineral oil. Ronneberg, Andersen, Skyberg, Mortality and Incidence of Cancer Among Oil-Exposed Workers in a Norwegian Cable Manufacturing Company, 45 British Journal of Industrial Medicine 595 (1988). A statistically significant increase in lung cancer deaths had been observed in these workers. The study, however, (1) made no mention of PCBs and (2) was expressly limited to the type of mineral oil involved in that study, and thus did not support these experts' opinions.

The fourth and final study involved a PCB-exposed group in Japan that had seen a statistically significant increase in lung cancer deaths. Kuratsune, Nakamura, Ikeda, & Hirohata, Analysis of Deaths Seen Among Patients with Yusho – A Preliminary Report, 16 Chemosphere, Nos. 8/9, 2085 (1987). The subjects of this study, however, had been exposed to numerous potential carcinogens, including toxic rice oil that they had ingested. Respondent points to Daubert's language that the "focus, of course, must be solely on principles and methodology, not on the conclusions that they generate." 509 U.S. at 595. He claims that because the District Court's disagreement was with the conclusion that the experts drew from the studies, the District Court committed legal error and was properly reversed by the Court of Appeals. But conclusions and methodology are not entirely distinct from one another. Trained experts commonly extrapolate from existing data. But nothing in either Daubert or the Federal Rules of Evidence requires a district court to admit opinion evidence which is connected to existing data only by the ipse dixit of the expert. A court may conclude that there is simply too great an analytical gap between the data and the opinion proffered. See Turpin v. Merrell Dow Pharmaceuticals, Inc., 959 F.2d 1349, 1360 (CA 6), cert. denied, 506 U.S. 826, 121 L. Ed. 2d 47, 113 S. Ct. 84 (1992).

That is what the District Court did here, and we hold that it did not abuse its discretion in so doing. We hold, therefore, that abuse of discretion is the proper standard by which to review a district court's decision to admit or exclude scientific evidence. We further hold that, because it was within the District Court's discretion to conclude that the studies upon which the experts relied were not sufficient, whether individually or in combination, to support their conclusions that Joiner's exposure to PCBs contributed to his cancer, the District Court did not abuse its discretion in excluding their testimony. These conclusions, however, do not dispose of this entire case. Respondent's original contention was that his exposure to PCBs, furans, and dioxins contributed to his cancer. The District Court ruled that there was a genuine issue of material fact as to whether Joiner had been exposed to PCBs, but concluded that there was no genuine issue as to whether he had been exposed to furans and dioxins. The District Court accordingly never explicitly considered if there was admissible evidence on the question whether Joiner's alleged exposure to furans and dioxins contributed to his cancer.

The Court of Appeals reversed the District Court's conclusion that there had been no exposure to furans and dioxins. Petitioners did not challenge this determination in their petition to this Court. Whether Joiner was exposed to furans and dioxins, and whether if there was such exposure, the opinions of Joiner's experts would then be admissible, remain open questions. We accordingly reverse the judgment of the Court of Appeals and remand this case for proceedings consistent with this opinion.

It is so ordered.

Concurrence by Justice Breyer.

The Court's opinion, which I join, emphasizes Daubert's statement that a trial judge, acting as "gatekeeper," must "'ensure that any and all scientific testimony or evidence admitted is not only relevant, but reliable.'" Ante, at 5 (quoting Daubert v. Merrell Dow Pharmaceuticals, Inc., 509 U.S. 579, 589, 125 L. Ed. 2d 469, 113 S. Ct. 2786 (1993)). This requirement will sometimes ask judges to make subtle and sophisticated determinations about scientific methodology and its relation to the conclusions an expert witness seeks to offer -- particularly when a case arises in an area where the science itself is tentative or uncertain, or where testimony about general risk levels in human beings or animals is offered to prove individual causation. Yet, as amici have pointed out, judges are not scientists and do not have the scientific training that can facilitate the making of such decisions. See, e.g., Brief for Trial Lawyers for Public Justice as Amicus Curiae 15; Brief for The New England Journal of Medicine et al. as Amici Curiae 2 ("Judges . . . are generally not trained scientists "). Of course, neither the difficulty of the task nor any comparative lack of expertise can excuse the judge from exercising the "gatekeeper" duties that the Federal Rules impose -- determining, for example, whether particular expert testimony is reliable and "will assist the trier of fact," Fed. Rule Evid. 702, or whether the "probative value" of testimony is substantially outweighed by risks of prejudice, confusion or waste of time. Fed. Rule Evid. 403. To the contrary, when law and science intersect, those duties often must be exercised with special care. . . . It is, thus, essential in this science-related area that the courts administer the Federal Rules of Evidence in order to achieve the "ends" that the Rules themselves set forth, not only so that proceedings may be "justly determined," but also so "that the truth may be ascertained." Fed. Rule Evid. 102. I therefore want specially to note that, as cases presenting significant science-related issues have increased in number, see Judicial Conference of the United States, Report of the Federal Courts Study Committee 97 (Apr. 2, 1990) ("Economic, statistical, technological, and natural and social scientific data are becoming increasingly important in both routine and complex litigation"), judges have increasingly found in the Rules of Evidence and Civil Procedure ways to help them overcome the inherent difficulty of making determinations about complicated scientific or otherwise technical evidence. Among these techniques are an increased use of Rule 16's pretrial conference authority to narrow the scientific issues in dispute, pretrial hearings where potential experts are subject to examination by the court, and the appointment of special masters and specially trained law clerks. . . .

In the present case, the New England Journal of Medicine has filed an amici brief "in support of neither petitioners nor respondents" in which the Journal writes:

"[A] judge could better fulfill this gatekeeper function if he or she had help from scientists. Judges should be strongly encouraged to make greater use of their inherent authority . . . to appoint experts . . . . Reputable experts could be recommended to courts by established scientific organizations, such as the National Academy of Sciences or the American Association for the Advancement of Science."

Brief for The New England Journal of Medicine 18-19; cf. Fed. Rule Evid. 706 (court may "on its own motion or on the motion of any party" appoint an expert to serve on behalf of the court, and this expert may be selected as "agreed upon by the parties" or chosen by the court); see also Weinstein, supra, at 116 (a court should sometimes "go beyond the experts proffered by the parties" and "utilize its powers to appoint independent experts under Rule 706 of the Federal Rules of Evidence"). Given this kind of offer of cooperative effort, from the scientific to the legal community, and given the various Rules-authorized methods for facilitating the courts' task, it seems to me that Daubert's gatekeeping requirement will not prove inordinately difficult to implement; and that it will help secure the basic objectives of the Federal Rules of Evidence; which are, to repeat, the ascertainment of truth and the just determination of proceedings.

Dissent by Justice Stevens, concurring in part and dissenting in part:

The question that we granted certiorari to decide is whether the Court of Appeals applied the correct standard of review. That question is fully answered in Parts I and II of the Court's opinion. Part III answers the quite different question whether the District Court properly held that the testimony of plaintiff 's expert witnesses was inadmissible. Because I am not sure that the parties have adequately briefed that question, or that the Court has adequately explained why the Court of Appeals' disposition was erroneous, I do not join Part III. Moreover, because a proper answer to that question requires a study of the record that can be performed more efficiently by the Court of Appeals than by the nine members of this Court, I would remand the case to that court for application of the proper standard of review. One aspect of the record will illustrate my concern. As the Court of Appeals pointed out, Joiner's experts relied on "the studies of at least thirteen different researchers, and referred to several reports of the World Health Organization that address the question of whether PCBs cause cancer." 78 F.3d 524, 533 (CA11 1996). Only one of those studies is in the record, and only six of them were discussed in the District Court opinion. Whether a fair appraisal of either the methodology or the conclusions of Joiner's experts can be made on the basis of such an incomplete record is a question that I do not feel prepared to answer. It does seem clear, however, that the Court has not adequately explained why its holding is consistent with Federal Rule of Evidence 702,. . . as interpreted in Daubert v. Merrell Dow Pharmaceuticals, Inc., 509 U.S. 579, 125 L. Ed. 2d 469, 113 S. Ct. 2786 (1993). . . . In general, scientific testimony that is both relevant and reliable must be admitted and testimony that is irrelevant or unreliable must be excluded. Id., at 597. In this case, the District Court relied on both grounds for exclusion. The relevance ruling was straightforward. The District Court correctly reasoned that an expert opinion that exposure to PCBs, "furans" and "dioxins" together may cause lung cancer would be irrelevant unless the plaintiff had been exposed to those substances. Having already found that there was no evidence of exposure to furans and dioxins, 864 F. Supp. 1310, 1318-1319 (ND Ga. 1994), it necessarily followed that this expert opinion testimony was inadmissible. Correctly applying Daubert, the District Court explained that the experts' testimony "manifestly does not fit the facts of this case, and is therefore inadmissible." 864 F. Supp. at 1322. Of course, if the evidence raised a genuine issue of fact on the question of Joiner's exposure to furans and dioxins – as the Court of Appeals held that it did -- then this basis for the ruling on admissibility was erroneous, but not because the district judge either abused her discretion or misapplied the law. The reliability ruling was more complex and arguably is not faithful to the statement in Daubert that "the focus, of course, must be solely on principles and methodology, not on the conclusions that they generate." 509 U.S. at 595. Joiner's experts used a "weight of the evidence" methodology to assess whether Joiner's exposure to transformer fluids promoted his lung cancer. . . .They did not suggest that any one study provided adequate support for their conclusions, but instead relied on all the studies taken together (along with their interviews of Joiner and their review of his medical records). The District Court, however, examined the studies one by one and concluded that none was sufficient to show a link between PCBs and lung cancer. 864 F. Supp. at 1324-1326. The focus of the opinion was on the separate studies and the conclusions of the experts, not on the experts' methodology. ("Defendants . . . persuade the court that Plaintiffs' expert testimony would not be admissible . . . by attacking the conclusions that Plaintiffs' experts draw from the studies they cite"). The Court of Appeals' discussion of admissibility is faithful to the dictum in Daubert that the reliability inquiry must focus on methodology, not conclusions. Thus, even though I fully agree with both the District Court's and this Court's explanation of why each of the studies on which the experts relied was by itself unpersuasive, a critical question remains unanswered: When qualified experts have reached relevant conclusions on the basis of an acceptable methodology, why are their opinions inadmissible?. . .

7.2.1   Scientific Evidence –Foundation cases, Part 3

The only question that we granted certiorari to decide is whether a trial judge "[m]ay . . . consider the four factors set out by this Court in Daubert v. Merrill Dow Pharmaceuticals, Inc., 509 U. S. 579 (1993), in a Rule 702 analysis of admissibility of an engineering expert's testimony."

Kumho Tire Company v. Carmichael
526 U.S. 137 (1999)

JUSTICE BREYER delivered the opinion of the Court.

In Daubert v. Merrell Dow Pharmaceuticals, Inc., 509 U.S. 579, 125 L. Ed. 2d 469, 113 S. Ct. 2786 (1993), this Court focused upon the admissibility of scientific expert testimony. It pointed out that such testimony is admissible only if it is both relevant and reliable. And it held that the Federal Rules of Evidence "assign to the trial judge the task of ensuring that an expert's testimony both rests on a reliable foundation and is relevant to the task at hand." Id. at 597. The Court also discussed certain more specific factors, such as testing, peer review, error rates, and "acceptability" in the relevant scientific community, some or all of which might prove helpful in determining the reliability of a particular scientific "theory or technique." Id. at 593-594. This case requires us to decide how Daubert applies to the testimony of engineers and other experts who are not scientists.

We conclude that Daubert's general holding -- setting forth the trial judge's general "gatekeeping" obligation -- applies not only to testimony based on "scientific" knowledge, but also to testimony based on "technical" and "other specialized" knowledge. See Fed. Rule Evid. 702. We also conclude that a trial court may consider one or more of the more specific factors that Daubert mentioned when doing so will help determine that testimony's reliability. But, as the Court stated in Daubert, the test of reliability is "flexible," and Daubert's list of specific factors neither necessarily nor exclusively applies to all experts or in every case.   Rather, the law grants a district court the same broad latitude when it decides how to determine reliability as it enjoys in respect to its ultimate reliability determination.

See General Electric Co. v. Joiner, 522 U.S. 136, 143, 139 L. Ed. 2d 508, 118 S. Ct. 512 (1997) (courts of appeals are to apply "abuse of discretion" standard when reviewing district court's reliability determination). Applying these standards, we determine that the District Court's decision in this case -- not to admit certain expert testimony -- was within its discretion and therefore lawful.

On July 6, 1993, the right rear tire of a minivan driven by Patrick Carmichael blew out. In the accident that followed, one of the passengers died, and others were severely injured. In October 1993, the Carmichaels brought this diversity suit against the tire's maker and its distributor, whom we refer to collectively as Kumho Tire, claiming that the tire was defective. The plaintiffs rested their case in significant part upon deposition testimony provided by an expert in tire failure analysis, Dennis Carlson, Jr., who intended to testify in support of their conclusion. Carlson's depositions relied upon certain features of tire technology that are not in dispute. A steel-belted radial tire like the Carmichaels' is made up of a "carcass" containing many layers of flexible cords, called "plies," along which (between the cords and the outer tread) are laid steel strips called "belts." Steel wire loops, called "beads," hold the cords together at the plies' bottom edges. An outer layer, called the "tread," encases the carcass, and the entire tire is bound together in rubber, through the application of heat and various chemicals. . . .The bead of the tire sits upon a "bead seat," which is part of the wheel assembly. That assembly contains a "rim flange," which extends over the bead and rests against the side of the tire.

Carlson's testimony also accepted certain background facts about the tire in question. He assumed that before the blowout the tire had traveled far. (The tire was made in 1988 and had been installed some time before the Carmichaels bought the used minivan in March 1993; the Carmichaels had driven the van approximately 7,000 additional miles in the two months they had owned it.) Carlson noted that the tire's tread depth, which was 11/32 of an inch when new, had been worn down to depths that ranged from 3/32 of an inch along some parts of the tire, to nothing at all along others. He conceded that the tire tread had at least two punctures which had been inadequately repaired.

Despite the tire's age and history, Carlson concluded that a defect in its manufacture or design caused the blow-out. He rested this conclusion in part upon three premises which, for present purposes, we must assume are not in dispute: First, a tire's carcass should stay bound to the inner side of the tread for a significant period of time after its tread depth has worn away. . . . Second, the tread of the tire at issue had separated from its inner steel-belted carcass prior to the accident. . . . Third, this "separation" caused the blowout. . . . Carlson's conclusion that a defect caused the separation, however, rested upon certain other propositions, several of which the defendants strongly dispute. First, Carlson said that if a separation is not caused by a certain kind of tire misuse called "overdeflection" (which consists of underinflating the tire or causing it to carry too much weight, thereby generating heat that can undo the chemical tread/carcass bond), then, ordinarily, its cause is a tire defect. . . . Second, he said that if a tire has been subject to sufficient overdeflection to cause a separation, it should reveal certain physical symptoms. These symptoms include (a) tread wear on the tire's shoulder that is greater than the tread wear along the tire's center; (b) signs of a "bead groove," where the beads have been pushed too hard against the bead seat on the inside of the tire's rim; (c) sidewalls of the tire with physical signs of deterioration, such as discoloration; and/or (d) marks on the tire's rim flange. Third, Carlson said that where he does not find at least two of the four physical signs just mentioned (and presumably where there is no reason to suspect a less common cause of separation), he concludes that a manufacturing or design defect caused the separation. . . . Carlson added that he had inspected the tire in question. He conceded that the tire to a limited degree showed greater wear on the shoulder than in the center, some signs of "bead groove," some discoloration, a few marks on the rim flange, and inadequately filled puncture holes (which can also cause heat that might lead to separation). . . . in each instance, he testified that the symptoms were not significant, and he explained why he believed that they did not reveal overdeflection. For example, the extra shoulder wear, he said, appeared primarily on one shoulder, whereas an overdeflected tire would reveal equally abnormal wear on both shoulders. . . . Carlson concluded that the tire did not bear at least two of the four overdeflection symptoms, nor was there any less obvious cause of separation; and since neither overdeflection nor the punctures caused the blowout, a defect must have done so.

Kumho Tire moved the District Court to exclude Carlson's testimony on the ground that his methodology failed Rule 702's reliability requirement. The court agreed with Kumho that it should act as a Daubert-type reliability "gatekeeper," even though one might consider Carlson's testimony as "technical," rather than "scientific." . . . The court then examined Carlson's methodology in light of the reliability-related factors that Daubert mentioned, such as a theory's testability, whether it "has been a subject of peer review or publication," the "known or potential rate of error," and the "degree of acceptance . . . within the relevant scientific community." 923 F. Supp. at 1520 (citing Daubert, 509 U.S. 579 at 592-594).

The District Court found that all those factors argued against the reliability of Carlson's methods, and it granted the motion to exclude the testimony (as well as the defendants' accompanying motion for summary judgment). The plaintiffs, arguing that the court's application of the Daubert factors was too "inflexible," asked for reconsideration. And the Court granted that motion. . . . After reconsidering the matter, the court agreed with the plaintiffs that Daubert should be applied flexibly, that its four factors were simply illustrative, and that other factors could argue in favor of admissibility. It conceded that there may be widespread acceptance of a "visual-inspection method" for some relevant purposes. But the court found insufficient indications of the reliability of "the component of Carlson's tire failure analysis which most concerned the Court, namely, the methodology employed by the expert in analyzing the data obtained in the visual inspection, and the scientific basis, if any, for such an analysis."

It consequently affirmed its earlier order declaring Carlson's testimony inadmissable and granting the defendants' motion for summary judgment. The Eleventh Circuit reversed. . . . It "reviewed . . . de novo" the "district court's legal decision to apply Daubert.". . . It noted that "the Supreme Court in Daubert explicitly limited its holding to cover only the 'scientific context,'" adding that "a Daubert analysis" applies only where an expert relies "on the application of scientific principles," rather than "on skill- or experience-based observation." . . . It concluded that Carlson's testimony, which it viewed as relying on experience, "falls outside the scope of Daubert," that "the district court erred as a matter of law by applying Daubert in this case," and that the case must be remanded for further (non-Daubert-type) consideration under Rule 702. . . .

Kumho Tire petitioned for certiorari, asking us to determine whether a trial court "may" consider Daubert's specific "factors" when determining the "admissibility of an engineering expert's testimony." Pet. for Cert. We granted certiorari in light of uncertainty among the lower courts about whether, or how, Daubert applies to expert testimony that might be characterized as based not upon "scientific" knowledge, but rather upon "technical" or "other specialized" knowledge. Fed. Rule Evid. 702. . . .

II

A

In Daubert, this Court held that Federal Rule of Evidence 702 imposes a special obligation upon a trial judge to "ensure that any and all scientific testimony . . . is not only relevant, but reliable." 509 U.S. at 589. The initial question before us is whether this basic gatekeeping obligation applies only to "scientific" testimony or to all expert testimony. We, like the parties, believe that it applies to all expert . . . For one thing, Rule 702 itself says: "If scientific, technical, or other specialized knowledge will assist the trier of fact to understand the evidence or to determine a fact in issue, a witness qualified as an expert by knowledge, skill, experience, training, or education, may testify thereto in the form of an opinion or otherwise."

This language makes no relevant distinction between "scientific" knowledge and "technical" or "other specialized" knowledge. It makes clear that any such knowledge might become the subject of expert testimony. In Daubert, the Court specified that it is the Rule's word "knowledge," not the words (like "scientific") that modify that word, that "establishes a standard of evidentiary reliability.". . . Hence, as a matter of language, the Rule applies its reliability standard to all "scientific," "technical," or "other specialized" matters within its scope. We concede that the Court in Daubert referred only to "scientific" knowledge. But as the Court there said, it referred to "scientific" testimony "because that was the nature of the expertise" at issue. . . . Neither is the evidentiary rationale that underlay the Court's basic Daubert "gatekeeping" determination limited to "scientific" knowledge.

Daubert pointed out that Federal Rules 702 and 703 grant expert witnesses testimonial latitude unavailable to other witnesses on the "assumption that the expert's opinion will have a reliable basis in the knowledge and experience of his discipline." (pointing out that experts may testify to opinions, including those that are not based on firsthand knowledge or observation). The Rules grant that latitude to all experts, not just to "scientific" ones.

Finally, it would prove difficult, if not impossible, for judges to administer evidentiary rules under which a gatekeeping obligation depended upon a distinction between "scientific" knowledge and "technical" or "other specialized" knowledge. There is no clear line that divides the one from the others. Disciplines such as engineering rest upon scientific knowledge. Pure scientific theory itself may depend for its development upon observation and properly engineered machinery. And conceptual efforts to distinguish the two are unlikely to produce clear legal lines capable of application in particular cases. Neither is there a convincing need to make such distinctions. Experts of all kinds tie observations to conclusions through the use of what Judge Learned Hand called "general truths derived from . . . specialized experience." . . . And whether the specific expert testimony focuses upon specialized observations, the specialized translation of those observations into theory, a specialized theory itself, or the application of such a theory in a particular case, the expert's testimony often will rest "upon an experience confessedly foreign in kind to [the jury's] own." The trial judge's effort to assure that the specialized testimony is reliable and relevant can help the jury evaluate that foreign experience, whether the testimony reflects scientific, technical, or other specialized knowledge.

We conclude that Daubert's general principles apply to the expert matters described in Rule 702. The Rule, in respect to all such matters, "establishes a standard of evidentiary reliability." 509 U.S. at 590. It "requires a valid . . . connection to the pertinent inquiry as a precondition to admissibility." Id. at 592. And where such testimony's factual basis, data, principles, methods, or their application are called sufficiently into question, see Part III, infra, the trial judge must determine whether the testimony has "a reliable basis in the knowledge and experience of [the relevant] discipline." 509 U.S. at 592. B The petitioners ask more specifically whether a trial judge determining the "admissibility of an engineering expert's testimony" may consider several more specific factors that Daubert said might "bear on" a judge's gate-keeping determination. These factors include: -- Whether a "theory or technique . . . can be (and has been) tested"; -- Whether it "has been subjected to peer review and publication"; -- Whether, in respect to a particular technique, there is a high "known or potential rate of error" and whether there are "standards controlling the technique's operation"; and -- Whether the theory or technique enjoys "general acceptance" within a "relevant scientific community." 509 U.S. at 592-594.

Emphasizing the word "may" in the question, we answer that question yes. Engineering testimony rests upon scientific foundations, the reliability of which will be at issue in some cases. . . . In other cases, the relevant reliability concerns may focus upon personal knowledge or experience. As the Solicitor General points out, there are many different kinds of experts, and many different kinds of expertise. . . .We agree with the Solicitor General that "the factors identified in Daubert may or may not be pertinent in assessing reliability, depending on the nature of the issue, the expert's particular expertise, and the subject of his testimony." The conclusion, in our view, is that we can neither rule out, nor rule in, for all cases and for all time the applicability of the factors mentioned in Daubert, nor can we now do so for subsets of cases categorized by category of expert or by kind of evidence.

Too much depends upon the particular circumstances of the particular case at issue. Daubert itself is not to the contrary. It made clear that its list of factors was meant to be helpful, not definitive. Indeed, those factors do not all necessarily apply even in every instance in which the reliability of scientific testimony is challenged. It might not be surprising in a particular case, for example, that a claim made by a scientific witness has never been the subject of peer review, for the particular application at issue may never previously have interested any scientist. Nor, on the other hand, does the presence of Daubert's general acceptance factor help show that an expert's testimony is reliable where the discipline itself lacks reliability, as, for example, do theories grounded in any so-called generally accepted principles of astrology or necromancy. At the same time, and contrary to the Court of Appeals' view, some of Daubert's questions can help to evaluate the reliability even of experience-based testimony. In certain cases, it will be appropriate for the trial judge to ask, for example, how often an engineering expert's experience-based methodology has produced erroneous results, or whether such a method is generally accepted in the relevant engineering community. Likewise, it will at times be useful to ask even of a witness whose expertise is based purely on experience, say, a perfume tester able to distinguish among 140 odors at a sniff, whether his preparation is of a kind that others in the field would recognize as acceptable. We must therefore disagree with the Eleventh Circuit's holding that a trial judge may ask questions of the sort Daubert mentioned only where an expert "relies on the application of scientific principles," but not where an expert relies "on skill- or experience-based observation." . . .

We do not believe that Rule 702 creates a schematism that segregates expertise by type while mapping certain kinds of questions to certain kinds of experts. Life and the legal cases that it generates are too complex to warrant so definitive a match. To say this is not to deny the importance of Daubert's gatekeeping requirement. The objective of that requirement is to ensure the reliability and relevancy of expert testimony. It is to make certain that an expert, whether basing testimony upon professional studies or personal experience, employs in the courtroom the same level of intellectual rigor that characterizes the practice of an expert in the relevant field.

Nor do we deny that, as stated in Daubert, the particular questions that it mentioned will often be appropriate for use in determining the reliability of challenged expert testimony. Rather, we conclude that the trial judge must have considerable leeway in deciding in a particular case how to go about determining whether particular expert testimony is reliable.

That is to say, a trial court should consider the specific factors identified in Daubert where they are reasonable measures of the reliability of expert testimony.

C

The trial court must have the same kind of latitude in deciding how to test an expert's reliability, and to decide whether or when special briefing or other proceedings are needed to investigate reliability, as it enjoys when it decides whether that expert's relevant testimony is reliable. Our opinion in Joiner makes clear that a court of appeals is to apply an abuse-of-discretion standard when it "reviews a trial court's decision to admit or exclude expert testimony." 522 U.S. at 138-139.

That standard applies as much to the trial court's decisions about how to determine reliability as to its ultimate conclusion. Otherwise, the trial judge would lack the discretionary authority needed both to avoid unnecessary "reliability" proceedings in ordinary cases where the reliability of an expert's methods is properly taken for granted, and to require appropriate proceedings in the less usual or more complex cases where cause for questioning the expert's reliability arises. Indeed, the Rules seek to avoid "unjustifiable expense and delay" as part of their search for "truth" and the "just determination" of proceedings. Fed. Rule Evid. 102. Thus, whether Daubert's specific factors are, or are not, reasonable measures of reliability in a particular case is a matter that the law grants the trial judge broad latitude to determine. . . . And the Eleventh Circuit erred insofar as it held to the contrary. III We further explain the way in which a trial judge "may" consider Daubert's factors by applying these considerations to the case at hand, a matter that has been briefed exhaustively by the parties and their 19 amici.

. . . In our view, the doubts that triggered the District Court's initial inquiry here were reasonable, as was the court's ultimate conclusion. For one thing, and contrary to respondents' suggestion, the specific issue before the court was not the reasonableness in general of a tire expert's use of a visual and tactile inspection to determine whether overdeflection had caused the tire's tread to separate from its steel-belted carcass.

Rather, it was the reasonableness of using such an approach, along with Carlson's particular method of analyzing the data thereby obtained, to draw a conclusion regarding the particular matter to which the expert testimony was directly relevant. That matter concerned the likelihood that a defect in the tire at issue caused its tread to separate from its carcass. The tire in question, the expert conceded, had traveled far enough so that some of the tread had been worn bald; it should have been taken out of service; it had been repaired (inadequately) for punctures; and it bore some of the very marks that the expert said indicated, not a defect, but abuse through overdeflection. The relevant issue was whether the expert could reliably determine the cause of this tire's separation. Nor was the basis for Carlson's conclusion simply the general theory that, in the absence of evidence of abuse, a defect will normally have caused a tire's separation. Rather, the expert employed a more specific theory to establish the existence (or absence) of such abuse.

Carlson testified precisely that in the absence of at least two of four signs of abuse (proportionately greater tread wear on the shoulder; signs of grooves caused by the beads; discolored sidewalls; marks on the rim flange) he concludes that a defect caused the separation. And his analysis depended upon acceptance of a further implicit proposition, namely, that his visual and tactile inspection could determine that the tire before him had not been abused despite some evidence of the presence of the very signs for which he looked (and two punctures).

For another thing, the transcripts of Carlson's depositions support both the trial court's initial uncertainty and its final conclusion. Those transcripts cast considerable doubt upon the reliability of both the explicit theory (about the need for two signs of abuse) and the implicit proposition (about the significance of visual inspection in this case).

Among other things, the expert could not say whether the tire had traveled more than 10, or 20, or 30, or 40, or 50 thousand miles, adding that 6,000 miles was "about how far" he could "say with any certainty." Id. at 265. The court could reasonably have wondered about the reliability of a method of visual and tactile inspection sufficiently precise to ascertain with some certainty the abuse-related significance of minute shoulder/center relative tread wear differences, but insufficiently precise to tell "with any certainty" from the tread wear whether a tire had traveled less than 10,000 or more than 50,000 miles.

And these concerns might have been augmented by Carlson's repeated reliance on the "subjectiveness" of his mode of analysis in response to questions seeking specific information regarding how he could differentiate between a tire that actually had been overdeflected and a tire that merely looked as though it had been. Id. at 222, 224-225, 285-286. They would have been further augmented by the fact that Carlson said he had inspected the tire itself for the first time the morning of his first deposition, and then only for a few hours. (His initial conclusions were based on photographs.)

Moreover, prior to his first deposition, Carlson had issued a signed report in which he concluded that the tire had "not been . . . overloaded or underinflated," not because of the absence of "two of four" signs of abuse, but simply because "the rim flange impressions . . . were normal." Id. at 335-336. That report also said that the "tread depth remaining was 3/32 inch," id. at 336, though the opposing expert's (apparently undisputed) measurements indicate that the tread depth taken at various positions around the tire actually ranged from .5/32 of an inch to 4/32 of an inch, with the tire apparently showing greater wear along both shoulders than along the center. Further, in respect to one sign of abuse, bead grooving, the expert seemed to deny the sufficiency of his own simple visual-inspection methodology. He testified that most tires have some bead groove pattern, that where there is reason to suspect an abnormal bead groove he would ideally "look at a lot of [similar] tires" to know the grooving's significance, and that he had not looked at many tires similar to the one at issue.

. . .   Finally, the court, after looking for a defense of Carlson's methodology as applied in these circumstances, found no convincing defense. Rather, it found (1) that "none" of the Daubert factors, including that of "general acceptance" in the relevant expert community, indicated that Carlson's testimony was reliable, 923 F. Supp. at 1521; (2) that its own analysis "revealed no countervailing factors operating in favor of admissibility which could outweigh those identified in Daubert," App. to Pet. for Cert. 4c; and (3) that the "parties identified no such factors in their briefs," ibid. For these three reasons taken together, it concluded that Carlson's testimony was unreliable. Respondents now argue to us, as they did to the District Court, that a method of tire failure analysis that employs a visual/tactile inspection is a reliable method, and they point both to its use by other experts and to Carlson's long experience working for Michelin as sufficient indication that that is so. But no one denies that an expert might draw a conclusion from a set of observations based on extensive and specialized experience. Nor does anyone deny that, as a general matter, tire abuse may often be identified by qualified experts through visual or tactile inspection of the tire. . . .The particular issue in this case concerned the use of Carlson's two-factor test and his related use of visual/tactile inspection to draw conclusions on the basis of what seemed small observational differences. We have found no indication in the record that other experts in the industry use Carlson's two-factor test or that tire experts such as Carlson normally make the very fine distinctions about, say, the symmetry of comparatively greater shoulder tread wear that were necessary, on Carlson's own theory, to support his conclusions. Nor, despite the prevalence of tire testing, does anyone refer to any articles or papers that validate Carlson's approach. Indeed, no one has argued that Carlson himself, were he still working for Michelin, would have concluded in a report to his employer that a similar tire was similarly defective on grounds identical to those upon which he rested his conclusion here.

Of course, Carlson himself claimed that his method was accurate, but, as we pointed out in Joiner, "nothing in either Daubert or the Federal Rules of Evidence requires a district court to admit opinion evidence that is connected to existing data only by the ipse dixit of the expert." 522 U.S. at 146. Respondents additionally argue that the District Court too rigidly applied Daubert's criteria.

They read its opinion to hold that a failure to satisfy any one of those criteria automatically renders expert testimony inadmissible.

The District Court's initial opinion might have been vulnerable to a form of this argument. There, the court, after rejecting respondents' claim that Carlson's testimony was "exempted from Daubert-style scrutiny" because it was "technical analysis" rather than "scientific evidence," simply added that "none of the four admissibility criteria outlined by the Daubert court are satisfied." 923 F. Supp. at 1522. Subsequently, however, the court granted respondents' motion for reconsideration. It then explicitly recognized that the relevant reliability inquiry "should be 'flexible,'" that its "'overarching subject [should be] . . . validity' and reliability," and that "Daubert was intended neither to be exhaustive nor to apply in every case." App. to Pet. for Cert. 4c (quoting Daubert, 509 U.S. at 594-595). And the court ultimately based its decision upon Carlson's failure to satisfy either Daubert's factors or any other set of reasonable reliability criteria. In light of the record as developed by the parties, that conclusion was within the District Court's lawful discretion. In sum, Rule 702 grants the district judge the discretionary authority, reviewable for its abuse, to determine reliability in light of the particular facts and circumstances of the particular case.

The District Court did not abuse its discretionary authority in this case. Hence, the judgment of the Court of Appeals is Reversed.

Concur by Justice Scalia, with whom JUSTICE O'CONNOR and JUSTICE THOMAS join, concurring.

I join the opinion of the Court, which makes clear that the discretion it endorses- trial-court discretion in choosing the manner of testing expert reliability- is not discretion to abandon the gatekeeping function. I think it worth adding that it is not discretion to perform the function inadequately. Rather, it is discretion to choose among reasonable means of excluding expertise that is false and science that is junky. Though, as the Court makes clear today, the Daubert factors are not holy writ, in a particular case the failure to apply one or another of them may be unreasonable, and hence an abuse of discretion.

7.2.2   Scientific Evidence—Emerging Technologies and Novel Scientific Evidence

Federal judges ruling on the admissibility of expert scientific testimony face a far more complex and daunting task in a post-Daubert world than before.

> ---Judge Kozinski,
> Daubert v. Merrell Dow Pharmaceuticals, Inc. (on remand)
> 43 F.3d 1311 (9th Cir. 1995)

The following excerpt from a law review essay, reflecting on novel scientific evidence after Daubert, is a general look at admission of scientific evidence. The cases that are considered landmark cases were all landmark cases because they considered novel scientific evidence, which is the primary concern of admission of scientific evidence – to insure it is relevant, reliable, does not prejudice the jury if it fails to assist the trier of fact, and to ensure that it follows scientific methodology.

A Review of the Admissibility of Novel Scientific Evidence[15]
J. Ken Thompson

I. Introduction

The appropriate standard for the admission of novel scientific evidence, usually presented in the form of expert testimony,' has long been a source of controversy. This result should come as no surprise in a judicial system with evidentiary rules grounded in ancient common law doctrines, which has been forced to deal with evidentiary issues arising in an age of technology. However, jurisdictions employing modem codified rules of evidence have also encountered difficulty in establishing a uniform standard of admissibility for novel scientific evidence.

For the purpose of this discussion, novel scientific evidence may be defined as evidence derived from an innovative theory or technique which is therefore inappropriate for validation through judicial notice. Since novel scientific evidence is an inappropriate subject for judicial notice in a majority of cases, a trial court must make an independent determination of the admissibility of such evidence in subsequent proceedings. This requirement of independent admissibility, coupled with what one commentator has described as the "realization that lay jurors expect scientific proof," translates into increasing amounts of judicial resources being consumed by determinations relating to the admissibility of scientific evidence. Thus, the importance of the admissibility of novel scientific evidence cannot be overstated.

I. Scientific Evidence Generally

Although they differ as to the appropriate standard of admissibility for novel scientific evidence, all jurisdictions adhere to the notion that the proponent of the evidence must establish its reliability. In the legal sense of the word, "reliability" refers to (1) the validity of the theory upon which the scientific evidence is based, (2) the validity of the technique used in the application of that theory, and (3) the proper application of the theory and technique on the particular occasion in question. In this context, "validity" refers to the ability of the theory or technique, or both, to accurately measure what it is designed to measure.' °

Thus, the instrumentality from which the scientific evidence is adduced "must implement (reliably) a true (valid) theory."" The courts' preoccupation with the reliability of scientific evidence, in general, reflects a recognition that such evidence has an inherent potential for unduly influencing a jury. According to one

---

[15] 17 Am. J. Trial Advoc. 741 (1993-1994).

court, "scientific proof may in some instances assume a posture of mystic infallibility in the eyes of a jury of laymen." The fear that scientific evidence contains the propensity to unduly influence juries has found some support in early empirical studies involving polygraph evidence. However, more recent empirical studies, also involving polygraph evidence, tend to indicate that juries are not overly influenced by scientific evidence, but may actually evaluate scientific evidence in much the same manner as other testimonial evidence.' A further cause for concern with the use of scientific evidence at trial involves the possibility that some scientific evidence may be based upon fraudulent research.
. . .

VI. Conclusion

Although the Frye (general acceptance) standard began as a means to achieve a noble purpose, primarily excluding specious scientific evidence, the standard has more recently been found to be "too rigid and unworkable." With the advent of modem codified rules of evidence, such as the Federal Rules of Evidence, and with the questionability of some of Frye's underlying assumptions, namely that jurors are inherently incapable of properly assessing scientific evidence, the general acceptance standard's days appear to be numbered. Thus, as more states follow the trend toward adopting codified rules of evidence modeled after the federal rules, whose liberal thrust and specific treatment of expert testimony arguably create a standard inconsistent with Frye, the further erosion of the general acceptance standard in state courts appears likely.

However, such a long standing rule of evidence is not easily discarded, as demonstrated by the conflicting opinions of the federal courts subsequent to the adoption of the Federal Rules of Evidence. In part, seemingly, a lack of legislative history accompanying the Federal Rules of Evidence on the issue of novel scientific evidence contributed to the confusion in this area. Thus, as more states encounter the issue after Daubert, proponents and opponents of the decision alike should look to their legislatures for guidance in an area of the law where there remains no clear answer to the problems inherent in the methodology of science.

The First Recorded Influence

An early meeting of science and law occurring long before the 1600s is commonly known among scientists, but one that should be equally shared with lawyers. The popular story is that of Archimedes's famous announcement of his discovery of the principle of specific gravity around 230 B.C. in Syracuse. Archimedes was said to have been floating his bar of soap in his bathtub, when he suddenly realized that the displacement of water reflected the density of the soap. It was at this point, that he ran into the streets of Syracuse, shouting "Eureka!" — still in bathtub attire. This is where the story ends for scientists. However, the rest of the story is of interest to lawyers. It seems that his discovery was the result of a forensics problem that had been posed by King Heiro. Archimedes had been contemplating a way in which to determine the amount of gold in the King's crown. It seems that the King had become suspicious of his goldsmith and had accused him of fraudulently adulterating the gold of the crown, and had subsequently sought Archimedes' help in solving the problem,1 which led to Archimedes' scientific discovery. And so began the recorded influence of science on law.

Much has been published about the influence of science on law in the twentieth century, but very little about the influence of science on law in the seventeenth, eighteenth and nineteenth centuries. The increased interest in the twentieth century influences of science reflects the great explosion of knowledge in the physical sciences during the 1950s and 60s, in the biological sciences in the 1980s and 90s, and particularly the influence of science on law making and on court proceedings.

The year 1603 however is identified as the beginning point of the institutional influence of science on law, based on the establishment of the first professional scientific society. The period identified in this paper ends in 1863 in America with the establishment of the U.S. National Academy of Sciences, and the beginning of what is understood to be the period of modern science.

Setting the stage for this development was the Copernican era. One of the most famous of the scientists of his time, Copernicus was actually by profession a lawyer, having received his doctorate of canon law from the University of Ferarra, Italy in 1503.

The first federal court case to use novel scientific evidence with the modern science of "bacteriology" was **Missouri v. Illinois** (1906) heard by Justice Oliver Wendell Holmes. His insight into the use of new technologies in the years to come, make this case a landmark in federal cases using novel scientific evidence.

The first case to be heard by the U.S. Supreme Court to utilize sociological evidence was **Brown v. Board of Education** (1954). This case is significant for many jurisprudential reasons, but it is also a significant scientific evidence case. The studies presented in the case were persuasive in the findings that the "separate but equal" doctrine" was damaging to African-American children that was devastating.

Silicon Breast Implants cases

[Excerpt from the AMA Journal of Ethics (formerly Virtual Mentor), Kristin E. Schleiter, JD, LLM, *Silicon Breast Implant Litigation*, May 2010, Volume 12, Number 5: 389-394.][16]

An Ethics Warning for Physicians
Lawsuits alleging harm from silicone gel breast implants were successful largely because of the support of a group of "silicone doctors" who approved women for inclusion in the class of plaintiffs. These doctors claimed to trace a

---

[16] http://journalofethics.ama-assn.org/2010/05/hlaw1-1005.html .

broad range of symptoms (chronic fatigue, insomnia, depression, headaches, and muscle or joint pain) to silicone poisoning. Doctors received referrals in bulk from plaintiffs' attorneys, who were known to fly them around the country to see patients and offer their law offices as exam rooms. In some cases, plaintiffs' lawyers paid the doctors' medical bills (a practice barred by some states); in other cases, doctors agreed to defer payment of their patients' bills until after the lawsuit was settled (a practice bioethicist Art Caplan called "somewhere between slimy, skuzzy and sleazy").

One doctor who treated more than 4,700 women with implants, most between 1993 and 1995, reported that lawyers had referred over 90 percent of his patients. He had found that 93 percent of the women had been harmed by silicone gel breast implants. This doctor's privileges had been suspended by at least one hospital after it concluded that he had failed to visit implant patients as frequently as hospital guidelines required and had not adequately documented their treatment.

Medical experts also questioned whether the "powerful drugs and painful, expensive tests administered by some of these doctors" were appropriate. Because no consensus existed for how to treat the symptoms described, some doctors prescribed treatments such as "intravenous gamma globulin, ordinarily used in rare clotting disorders; plasmapheresis, sometimes used in rare immune disorders; and the cancer drug Cytoxan". At the time, such treatments cost as much as $40,000 and carried the risk of serious side effects.

The silicone breast implant litigation of the nineties is notable for way in which judges and juries overlooked an astonishing lack of scientific evidence, while plaintiffs and their attorneys raked in millions. The hysteria and hype that the lawsuits generated caused some medical device companies to go bankrupt or leave the implant market altogether. More recently, doctors' roles in asbestos litigation have prompted the U.S. Chamber of Commerce to call for an investigation into their conduct (and that of lawyers) in the "explosion of meritless and abusive asbestos claims". While physicians have an affirmative duty to "assist in the administration of justice," those who are involved in litigation must testify honestly, without the influence of financial compensation, and with the interests of patients in mind.

———————————

The rules and case law of scientific evidence are important to considering emerging technologies. The fact that an emerging technology is "novel" does not mean that it cannot be admitted. Increasingly sophisticated technology will allow greater tools to be used in scientific evidence and so it is important to professionals to use available technology even if it is challenging for a court when the technology is "novel."

Chapter 11

Space Law

7.2.3 Space Law-Overview

 "We go into space because whatever mankind must undertake, free men must fully share. I believe that this [n]ation should commit itself to achieving the goal, before this decade is out, of landing a man on the [M]oon and returning him safely to earth.[17]"

> ---President Kennedy, May 25, 1961,
> addressing a joint session of Congress

A Brief History of Space Law

The history of Space Law began with the first articulation of the term by Emile Laude, a Belgian lawyer in 1910, who wrote:

> *Are we to say that we can foresee the juridical solution that our descendants will have to give to all the questions raised by the use of the layer of unbreatheable gas and the layer of ether that bathe our planet? . . .A new law will govern new juridical relations. This will no longer be the Aerial Law. What will it be? It may be hazardous to predict it, for the term Ether itself only hides our ignorance and we dare no propose the term Ethereal Law. But certainly it is a question of the Law of Space.*

> *The term LAW OF SPACE will thus be the generic term; the Law of Space will be to Aerial Law as Private Law is to Civil Law andCommercial Law.[18]*

The next noted mention was by a Russian lawyer in 1926, V.A. Zarzar of the Soviet Aviation Ministry. In a paper circulated at a conference in Moscow, he introduced the idea of

---

[17] U.S. Code Cong. & Adm. News, 87th Cong., 1st Sess., Vol. 1 at 1149, 1157 (1961), President Kennedy statement to a joint session of Congress the same year that the U.S.S.R. sent the first human, Yuri Gagarin, into space.
[18] The comment was translated from the French in NASA Technical Memorandum NASA TM-77513, Wash, DC 1984. Quoted in *Origins of International Space Law* at
http://www.iislweb.org/docs/Origins_International_Space_Law.pdf .

interplanetary travel and the division between zones of aviation and the "upper zone". He wrote,"[T]he theory of zones . . . involves the fact that the atmosphere is divided into two concentric layers of which the lower is subject to national control, and the second which is international, so that the upper zone of air travel is free." He went on to discuss the topic of sovereignty in air space and and the development of "interplanetary communications" and "interplanetary transport law".

What is called the world's first major work of substance in the field of Space Law emerged in Germany, Dr. Vladimire Mandl, from Czechoslovakia, who wrote a treatise on space law which was published in 1932.[19] It was not until 1944, that the first book was published in English on the topic of "Rockets".[20]

Generally, there was a consensus in the world that sovereignty must prevail with regard to overflights in air space; but among these writers, they conceded that the type of travel in the air space above usual flight altitudes and speeds would be so different that flights would be beyond the control of subjacent states. Thus, they theorized, these flights in this air space would be free of and unrestrained by considerations of sovereignty over the airspace. Dissenters cited concerns of security of the states below.

In 1948, the U.S. Department of State approached the countries abutting Antarctica to propose a treaty that would making claiming the territory impossible for the common good of scientific research shared by all of the nations. The concept had application to space.[21]

From 1939-1945, during World War II, the government funded rocketry research by the United States, Germany and the USSR advanced the state of rocketry science more than any other period of time. This led to the bombardment of London by the Germans.

In 1949, a British engineer wrote a letter chastising the United States for a U.S. scientist, Dr. Goddard, for proposing to launch a missile at the moon, that upon contact would cause an explosion that could be seen from earth. His argument against this was that "the Moon is not their [U.S.] property. . . it is the common heritage of man."[22]

An American lawyer, Haley, observed that the emergence of new cooperation at the end of World War II for the International Astronautical Federation, just formed, had a mission to "convert the rocket from an engine of war to a peaceful vehicle of interplanetary exploration."[23]

The theory of sovereignty was revised by Nicolas Matesco, Canadian, who researched the legal *maxim cujus soli usque ad coelom et ad sidera*,[24] and concluded it did not originate in Roman law but originated in Jewish Law found in an ancient Talmud and brought to Great

---

[19] Ibid.

[20] Ibid.

[21] Ibid. at 18.

[22] Ibid.

[23] Haley, A.G., "International Cooperaiton in Rocketry and Astronautics," Jet Propulsion, Nov. 1955.

[24] "Whose is the soil, his it is up to the sky", or "He who possesses the land possesses also that which is above it," or "He who owns the soil owns everthing avoe (and below) from heaven (to hell)" and "he who owns the land owns up to the sky." See Yehuda Abramovitch, "The Maxim "cujus est solum ejus usque ad coelom" as applied in Aviation, 8 McGill Law Journal 248- 269 (195_) at http://www.lawjournal.mcgill.ca/userfiles/other/8509457-abramovitch.pdf .

Britain right after the Normand Conquest in 1066.[25] This line of inquiry is not likely to resolve the question of sovereignty but writers continued to explore this theory for decades.

For the United States, the launching of Sputnik, the U.S.S.R. satellite in 1957 and the launch of the first human into space in 1961, was an embarrassment that triggered the most ambitious science program ever pursued by the United States. It also triggered the development of a modern theory of Space Law, where passing through the sovereign territory of a nation, was no longer a principle of law. Matthew J. Kleiman explains it:

> If this rule extended to outer space, the Soviet Union would have violated
> international law by launching Sputnik into an orbit that passed over many
> countries, including the United States, without permission. Nevertheless,
> President Eisenhower, knowing that the United States was interested in
> eventually overflying Soviet airspace with its own spy satellites, tacitly accepted
> the Soviet Union's right to operate a satellite in orbit over U.S. territory. It was
> thus established that the rules that governed spacecraft would differ from those
> that governed aircraft, and the field of space law was born.[26]

Here is a timeline with the landmarks which help describe the history of space law in the United States.

A Timeline of U.S. Space Law

1957, Oct. 4. the USSR launched the first artificial satellite, Sputnik,
      triggering a "space race" spurred by USSR Premier Khurshchev's remark, "We will bury you."
1957 the U.S. launched Explorer I
1958 the United Nations General Assembly voted to create a permanent
      Committee on the Peaceful Uses of Outer Space (COPUOS)
1958, the U.S. passed the National Aeronautics and Space Act of 1958, 42 U.S.C.
      §§2451-2477 (1958).
1961, April 12, Yuri Gagarin had become the first human in space.
1961, May 25, President John F. Kennedy addressed a special joint session of
      Congress to outline the historic start of the U.S. space program.
1967 Treaty on Principles Governing the Activities of States in the Exploration and
      Use of Outer Space, including the Moon and Other Celestial Bodies (the "Outer Space
      Treaty")
1982 Space Command in the U.S. was launched.
1983 Star Wars was announced
1986 Principles Relating to Remote Sensing of the Earth from Outer Space, the
1992 Principles Relevant to the Use of Nuclear Power Sources In Outer Space,
1996 Declaration on International Cooperation in the Exploration and Use of Outer Space for the
      benefit and in the Interest of All States, Taking into Particular Account the Needs of
      Developing Countries.

---

[25] Yehuda Abramovitch, "The Maxim "cujus est solum ejus usque ad coelom" as applied in Aviation, 8 McGill Law Journal 248- 269 (195_) at http://www.lawjournal.mcgill.ca/userfiles/other/8509457-abramovitch.pdf .
[26] Matthew J. Kleiman, "Space Law 101: An Introduction to Space Law" for the American Bar Association at http://www.americanbar.org/groups/young_lawyers/publications/the_101_201_practice_series/space_law_101_an_introduction_to_space_law.html .

1983 Star Wars was announced

In 1983, Pres. Reagan declared that the U.S.S.R. was capable of launching nuclear missiles against the U.S., and he was announcing the start of the Strategic Defense Initiative, aimed at building a satellite-controlled, "missile shield" that could intercept incoming nuclear projectiles. The new weapons system was called "Star Wars" following the epic success of the movie by the same name in 1977, although no one in the Administration ever made a formal connection to the movie.

1986 Principles Relating to Remote Sensing of the Earth from Outer Space, the 1992 Principles Relevant to the Use of Nuclear Power Sources In Outer Space, and the 1996 Declaration on International Cooperation in the Exploration and Use of Outer Space for the benefit and in the Interest of All States, Taking into Particular Account the Needs of Developing Countries.

About Space Law

Timothy M. Ravich, wrote:

Practitioners unfamiliar with space law may dismiss the subject matter as a species of science fiction, a fantastical, imaginative, and precedentless topic that exists outside the sphere of regular business and legal discourse. Among nonlawyers, too, there is scant first-hand knowledge about outer space as fewer than 500 humans have traveled there. Despite that fact, space law is a substantive area of the law that consists of a discrete set of international treaties,1 resolutions, statutes, regulations, and court opinions that address aerospace activities, among other contexts, in terms of contract, tort, property, patent, and even tax law.[27]

Existing National Policy: Lost in Space

America's current space policy is adrift. The space shuttle fleet that has flown since 1981 is scheduled to retire in 2010, creating an operational "gap" that will leave the country that won the "space race" without an independent means of human spaceflight until completion of the next generation of rockets, at earliest, in approximately 2015. Thousands of residents of Florida's "Space Coast" who contribute to the aerospace industry are losing jobs as a direct result.12 Meanwhile, putting aside the suspicious outer space programs of North Korea and Iran, other nations, including Brazil, China, and India. . .

. . .in 2004, President Bush proposed a "Vision for Space Exploration" involving a return to the Moon and to Mars and worlds beyond. The federal government proposed the "Constellation" program and production of the Ares and Orion rockets and crew launch vehicles toward those destinations. Not only have those programs been put on hold in the current economic climate, but "a big lesson of the race to the Moon was that it was a dead end" in any

---

[27] Timothy M. Ravich, "2010: Space Law in the Sunshine State," 84-OCT Fla. B.J. 24, September/October, 2010 at http://www.americanbar.org/groups/young_lawyers/publications/the_101_201_practice_series/space_law_101_an_introduction_to_space_law.html .

event. Moreover, a "Review of U.S. Human Space Flight Plans Committee" convened by President Barak Obama in late 2009 concluded that, given current budgetary constraints, the United States space program is on an "unsustainable trajectory" and will not be able to engage in human exploration beyond low earth orbit for the foreseeable future.

The Trump Administration announced a bold new space policy almost immediately. noting the increasing activity by China and Russia in space, and that they were positioning themselves for potential threats to our national security. By November 2019, the first observation of a weapons test by Russia was observed,[28] A program to take humans to Mars, first returning to the Moon, again; and the establishment of the Space Force as a co-equal branch of the military are both landmark achievements in national space policy.

The term "space law" refers to the body of international and national laws and customs that govern human activities in outer space. For the last half century, most outer space operations have been conducted by government agencies. Now, however, we stand at the precipice of a new era in spaceflight. With the retirement of the Space Shuttle, private companies are preparing to assume many of the missions traditionally undertaken by governments and to open outer space to the general public.[29]

With these changes, space law will face many new challenges. This article will provide an introduction to space law and some of the issues that the space law community will need to address in the next decade and beyond.

The Outer Space Legal Landscape

The foundational instrument of the outer space legal regime is the 1967 Treaty on Principles Governing the Activities of States in the Exploration and Use of Outer Space, including the Moon and Other Celestial Bodies (the "Outer Space Treaty"). The Outer Space Treaty established a series of broad principles that have been elaborated upon and implemented in a series of subsequent international treaties and national laws. These principles include:

· The exploration and use of outer space shall be carried on for the benefit and in the interests of all mankind;

· Outer space and celestial bodies are free for exploration and use by all States;

· Outer space and celestial bodies are not subject to national appropriation;

---

[28] W.J. Hennigan, "America Really Does Have a Space Force," TIME at https://time.com/5869987/spaceforce/ (July 23, 2020).
[29] Matthew J. Kleiman, Space Law 101: An Introduction to Space Law, for the American Bar Association at

·   No Weapons of Mass Destruction are permitted in outer space;

·   The Moon and other celestial bodies shall be used exclusively for peaceful purposes;

·   States shall be responsible for their national activities in outer space, whether carried on by governmental or non-governmental entities;

·   The activities of non-governmental entities in outer space shall require the authorization and continuing supervision by the appropriate State;

·   States shall retain jurisdiction and control over their space objects   and any personnel thereon;

·   States shall be liable for damage caused by their space objects; and

·   States shall avoid the harmful contamination of outer space.

The Outer Space Treaty was followed by (i) the 1968 Agreement on the Rescue of Astronauts, the Return of Astronauts and the Return of Objects Launched into Outer Space, (ii) the 1972 Convention on International Liability for Damage Caused by Space Objects, (iii) the 1975 Convention on Registration of Objects Launched into Outer Space, and (iv) the 1979 Agreement Governing the Activities of States on the Moon and Other Celestial Bodies, which is now considered dormant because it has not been ratified by any of the major space powers.

In addition to the major treaties, the U.N. General Assembly has adopted several resolutions that are generally followed by the international community on a non-binding basis. These include the 1982 Principles Governing the Use by States of Artificial Earth Satellites for International Direct Television Broadcasting, the 1986 Principles Relating to Remote Sensing of the Earth from Outer Space, the 1992 Principles Relevant to the Use of Nuclear Power Sources In Outer Space, and the 1996 Declaration on International Cooperation in the Exploration and Use of Outer Space for the Benefit and in the Interest of All States, Taking into Particular Account the Needs of Developing Countries. The International Telecommunications Union plays an important role in space operations by assigning positions and frequencies for satellites in geostationary orbit, where most telecommunications satellites are located. The U.N. Committee on the Peaceful Uses of Outer Space administers the major space treaties and advises the international community on space policy matters.

In the United States, each government agency that operates spacecraft is responsible for complying with U.S. law and international treaty obligations. The Federal Aviation Administration (FAA) regulates non-government spaceports and the launch and reentry of private spacecraft under the Commercial Space Launch Act, as amended by the 2004 Commercial Space Launch Amendments Act. Various other federal laws, such as the 1992 Land Remote Sensing Policy Act and International Traffic in Arms Regulations, state contract and tort laws, and decades of commercial practice in the telecommunications, remote sensing and launch services industries also affect government and private space operations.

. . . .

7.3.1
TREATIES

The treaties commonly referred to as the "five United Nations treaties on outer space" are as follows:

The "Outer Space Treaty"
Treaty on Principles Governing the Activities of States in the Exploration and Use of Outer Space, including the Moon and Other Celestial Bodies
Adopted by the General Assembly in its resolution 2222 (XXI), opened for signature on 27 January 1967, entered into force on 10 October 1967

The "Rescue Agreement"
Agreement on the Rescue of Astronauts, the Return of Astronauts and the Return of Objects Launched into Outer Space
Adopted by the General Assembly in its resolution 2345 (XXII), opened for signature on 22 April 1968, entered into force on 3 December 1968

The "Liability Convention"
Convention on International Liability for Damage Caused by Space Objects
Adopted by the General Assembly in its resolution 2777 (XXVI), opened for signature on 29 March 1972, entered into force on 1 September 1972

The "Registration Convention"
Convention on Registration of Objects Launched into Outer Space
Adopted by the General Assembly in its resolution 3235 (XXIX), opened for signature on 14 January 1975, entered into force on 15 September 1976

The "Moon Agreement"
Agreement Governing the Activities of States on the Moon and Other Celestial Bodies
Adopted by the General Assembly in its resolution 34/68, opened for signature on 18 December 1979, entered into force on 11 July 1984.

These five treaties deal with issues such as the non-appropriation of outer space by any one country, arms control, the freedom of exploration, liability for damage caused by space objects, the safety and rescue of spacecraft and astronauts, the prevention of harmful interference with space activities and the environment, the notification and registration of space activities, scientific investigation and the exploitation of natural resources in outer space and the settlement of disputes.

Each of the treaties stresses the notion that outer space, the activities carried out in outer space and whatever benefits might be accrued from outer space should be devoted to enhancing the well-being of all countries and humankind, with an emphasis on promoting international cooperation.

U.S. Domestic Space Law

[Excerpt from the following article.]
ONE HALF CENTURY AND COUNTING: THE EVOLUTION OF U.S. NATIONAL SPACE LAW AND THREE LONG-TERM EMERGING ISSUES
Joanne Irene Gabrynowicz
4 Harv. L. & Pol'y Rev. 405 (Summer 2010)
Copyright (c) 2010 the President and Fellows of Harvard College; Joanne Irene Gabrynowicz

[L]aws and institutions must go hand in hand with the progress of the human mind. As that becomes more developed, more enlightened, as new discoveries are made, new truths discovered and manners and opinions change, with the change of circumstances, institutions must advance also to keep pace with the times.
-- Thomas Jefferson1

Introduction
A hallmark of United States national space law is that it tends to follow the development of space technology and geopolitical events. Technology that develops into applications tends to catalyze law that addresses the commercialization of the technology. After the successful launch of Sputnik I on October 4, 1957, the United States addressed the legal void that then existed for space activities by promulgating its own national law and encouraging the global community to establish space law at the international level. This resulted in the 1958 National Aeronautics and Space Act at the national level and in a treaty regime at the international level including, among others, the Outer Space Treaty. Since then, U.S. national space law has continued to develop, catalyzed in large part by technological and geopolitical advances. The historical significance of the early origins of U.S. space law is quite remarkable when one considers that even nations that have been major space farers for decades, like France and Japan, did not pass national space laws until 2008.

. . .

I. 1958-2008
A. 1958 and 1962: Institutional and Legal Space Infrastructure
1. The 1958 National Aeronautics and Space Act
 Early space activities were catalyzed by geopolitical events. They were not identified as a stand-alone policy goal. It was the successful launch of Sputnik I that sent the United States on a search for a dramatic and effective demonstration to prove that U.S. technology was superior to the Soviet Union's. Sputnik I, the world's first artificial satellite, shocked the world. Sputnik, (Russian for "traveling companion") was the size of a basketball and weighed 183 pounds.4 The fear caused by Sputnik I may be hard to understand in today's internet era. But for the World War II-weary world, it represented the potential for atom bombs to rain down unexpectedly from space anywhere on Earth. For the United States, it also

represented the first credible potential attack on national territory since the War of 1812. This threat prompted the U.S. Congress to create a legal and institutional infra *407 structure that would enable the United States to respond to Sputnik. As a result, it passed, and President Eisenhower signed, the National Aeronautics and Space Act of 1958 (NAS Act).5

The new law established the means to respond to the threat Sputnik represented: the U.S. civil space program. It also established the institution responsible for executing the response, the National Aeronautics and Space Administration (NASA). NASA began developing a program for human space exploration on October 1, 1958, almost exactly one year after Sputnik I was launched.6 Three years later, in 1961, the Kennedy Administration gave NASA its first mission: to land, within a decade, a human on the Moon and return him safely. Since then, both the nation's space activities and the law that authorizes them have continued to evolve as required by politics and technology.

Over the years, the NAS Act has become an amalgam of many bodies of law including contract, tort, international, insurance and indemnification, and intellectual property, among others. It also addresses a wide variety of subjects ranging from the philosophical and scientific (such as determining the extent of life in the universe7) to space-specific activities (like the International Space Station8) to the terrestrially pragmatic (like appropriations9). More recently, the mechanisms of the Act have expanded to include innovations like awards and competitive prizes to stimulate research and development.10

However, in the beginning a number of basic, major decisions had to be made. Two of the most important issues were the purpose of the newly established space program and the appropriate relationship between the civil and military programs. Regarding the first decision, the purpose described in the NAS Act tracks the diplomatic strategy taken by the United States in the United Nations to develop new law to prevent the U.S.-U.S.S.R. rivalry from extending into space.11 Therefore Congress declared that "it is the policy of the United States that activities in space should be devoted to peaceful purposes for the benefit of all mankind."12

This language has both precedential and strategic significance. The legal term of art "peaceful purposes" emerged almost simultaneously in the NAS Act and in the historic UN General Assembly resolutions relating to outer space that became the foundation for the eventual space law treaty regime.13 Regarding strategy, when Sputnik I orbited the Earth, policymakers *408 and lawmakers believed space could only be used for war making. According to Eilene Galloway, the congressional researcher recruited by then-Senator Lyndon B. Johnson to help create U.S. space law,14 it was only when scientists told lawmakers that space could also be used for "purposes other than war: communications, weather, medicine" and "instead of fear of war, we could be motivated by the hope for peace"15 that space law was able to move space activities in an entirely new direction. Lawmakers codified this delicate balance between fear and hope when they declared that space activities should be devoted to peaceful purposes rather than declaring that they shall be. Without knowing the full extent of the Soviet Union's space capabilities, Congress gave itself room to address the unknown as it unfolded by advocating rather than requiring "peaceful purposes."

Congress addressed the second basic question, the appropriate relationship between the civil and military space programs, when it declared: Aeronautical and space activities . . . shall be the responsibility of, and shall be directed by, a civilian agency . . . except activities peculiar to or primarily associated with development of weapons systems, military operations, or the defense of the United States . . . shall be the responsibility of, and shall be directed by, the Department of Defense.16

The characteristics of this relationship were strongly influenced by the former Supreme Allied Commander, President Dwight D. Eisenhower. He was determined that the U.S. space program should be the opposite of the overtly militaristic Soviet program and that it would not create a national deficit.17 Therefore, Eisenhower resisted popular sentiment and military pressure and endeavored to place the national space program under civil control. By executive order, Eisenhower transferred all space-related civilian personnel, property, and funds not primarily related to military operations and weapon system development from the Department of Defense (DoD) to NASA.18

The civil-military relationship has ebbed and flowed over the years, with the relative closeness of purpose waxing and waning as political forces *409 changed. It continues to be a source of tension for both NASA and DoD.19 Nonetheless, NASA remains a civil agency committed to civil missions.

2. The 1962 Commercial Communications Satellite Act

The Communications Satellite Act of 1962 (Comsat Act)20 began as a Cold War tool and contained a strategy that became the legal foundation for the United States' and the world's most lucrative space-based industry: telecommunications. The Act embodied both Cold War political and humanitarian motives. It was intended to influence what President John F. Kennedy called "emerging democracies" by providing for services for less economically developed countries.

The Comsat Act authorized U.S. participation in the development and operation of Intelsat, an international communications satellite organization and system.21 Intelsat members agreed to make effective and equitable use of space communications satellites. Under this agreement the electromagnetic spectrum was considered to be a scarce resource that should be made available to all nations on a global and nondiscriminatory basis. Intelsat would provide a legal, administrative, and technological system under which participating countries could access portions of the spectrum for use within their nations. As a condition of membership, member nations agreed not to compete with Intelsat, making it a legal global monopoly.

Satellite communications quickly became an enormous commercial success, and technology enabled more efficient use of both the electromagnetic spectrum and the slots in geosynchronous orbit where the communications satellites are placed. In the 1990s, political pressure to break up national and international communications monopolies and to increase the role of the private sector led to the substantial restructuring of Intelsat from 2000 to 2005.22 Controversy currently exists over whether this new form is a viable and equitable one.23 Satellite communications have spawned a dynamic and complex body of law at the national and international level, a discussion of which is beyond the scope of this Article. Suffice it to say, like all other U.S. space-based activities and law, it began in the Cold War and has transformed to meet the needs of the globalization era.

B. 1980s: Commerce

Once the legislative and executive branches determined the relative roles of NASA and DoD, the civil space program proceeded to make history with the Mercury, Gemini, and Apollo programs. Together, on July 20, 1969, they resulted in the epic landing of the first humans on another celestial body, the Moon. The post-Apollo program continued with Skylab, the Apollo-Soyuz Test Program, and the Space Shuttle, which was declared operational in 1982. All of these missions relied on the U.S. private sector to provide the government with goods and services on a contractual basis.

Around this time, the Reagan Administration ushered in an era driven by the conviction that the private sector could conduct many government activities more efficiently and more appropriately than the public sector. Further, the mature technology could now be subjected to market forces, and the private sector could use those forces to make space technology and its products available to public, nongovernmental customers. The Reagan Administration began to seek proposals for transferring various space assets and activities out of the government and into the private sector.24 These proposals led to laws that were passed on the premise that launch and remote sensing technologies had matured to a point where government participation was no longer, or nearly no longer, needed.

Congress, in an attempt to gain control of a process begun by the executive branch, also began to seek opportunities to commercialize or privatize space activities. In 1984, Congress amended the Declaration of Policy and Purpose section of the NAS Act to state: "Congress declares that the general welfare of the United States requires that [NASA] . . . seek and encourage, to the maximum extent possible, the fullest commercial use of space."25 Thus, commercial space joined civil and military space to become the third legally recognized sector of U.S. space activities.

In addition to this expanded statement of policy and purpose, the same Congress, through the same committees, also passed the 1984 Commercial Space Launch Act (Launch Act)26 and the Land Remote-Sensing Commercialization Act of 1984 (Commercialization Act).27 It was not long, however, before both laws were amended to reflect changes driven by intertwined politics, economics, and technology.

C. 1980s and 1990s: Applications--Launch and Remote Sensing Technology
1. Launch Law

Congress had two main objectives when it passed the Launch Act in 1984: to encourage, facilitate, and promote commercial space launches by the private sector; and to develop licensing requirements through consultation with other government agencies.28 It also made a single federal agency, the Department of Transportation (DoT), responsible for regulating the industry. The Launch Act and subsequent regulations addressed three substantive areas: licensing and regulation, liability insurance requirements, and access to government launch facilities by private launch companies.

Before the passage of the Launch Act, it was U.S. national policy that all civil, military, and commercial payloads would be launched by the Shuttle. There were a variety of reasons for this policy, but essentially the Nixon Administration expected the Shuttle program to attract the important electoral votes of California, Florida, and Texas--states that are home to large space centers.29 National policymakers intended to make the Shuttle an all-purpose space transportation vehicle with a successful record of delivering payloads to orbit. This policy effectively made it illegal to employ single-use rockets, known as expendable launch vehicles (ELVs). So the Launch Act was intended to permit the use of ELVs on a commercial basis. However, the tragic loss of the Challenger in 1986 caused the Reagan Administration to reconsider U.S. national launch policy and to prohibit NASA from launching commercial payloads. The new policy later became law in the NASA Authorization Act for U.S. federal fiscal year 1991.30 This law limits the Shuttle to activities that require either a human presence or unique capabilities that only the Shuttle can provide.

The separation of civil, military, and commercial launches and an increased emphasis on commercialization has resulted in a series of changes in space transportation law since 1986. In these years, launches may have become more common commercial activities, but they still involve immensely expensive technology, high-powered explosives, and range-safety requirements. A launch gone wrong has the potential to cause extremely large amounts of human injury and property damage. Further, all launch facilities in the United States are government built, funded, maintained, and operated. Private sector launches occur from Cape Canaveral in Florida, Vandenberg Air Force Base in California (DoD), and the Kennedy Space Flight Center in Florida (NASA). Therefore, a major feature of recent legislative changes *412 has been the articulation of the relationship between the public and private sectors as it relates to the risks inherent in launch activities.

The fact that the U.S. private sector must rely on government facilities to provide its launch services and products is part of an ongoing trans-Atlantic debate between U.S. companies and their European counterparts. This issue will be discussed in greater detail below, but in short, U.S. aerospace companies continue to cite the commercial activities of foreign governments and their use of industrial policy as reasons for continuing the favorable U.S. government-industry risk-sharing regime contained in U.S. launch law. Since most western industrialized nations, including Canada and Japan, follow a European model for aerospace funding systems and policies, it is reasonable to expect that Congress will extend the U.S. risk-sharing regime each time it is up for review.

In 1988, Congress substantially amended the Launch Act to further define the commercial launch legal regime.31 The 1988 Amendments authorized the U.S. government to indemnify commercial space transportation for third-party liability and required the industry to obtain insurance up to a "maximum probable loss" standard for each launch. These and other industry-government risk sharing provisions were in effect through 1993 and were subsequently extended through 2004. The 2004 Commercial Space Launch Amendments Act,32 discussed below, also required that DoT study whether or not the indemnification of commercial expendable launch vehicles ought to be continued. Over the decade, Congress twice extended indemnification for third-party liability, first until 2009, and currently through 2012.33

In the 1990s, the Shuttle became NASA's most expensive activity and threatened to consume NASA's budget.34 As a result, Shuttle operations were privatized in 1996 with a ten-year Space Program Operations Contract between NASA and United Space Alliance (USA), a limited liability company currently owned equally by the Boeing Company and the Lockheed Martin Space Operations Company.35 NASA and USA entered into a second contract in 2006, which establishes USA as NASA's primary industry partner in human space operations, including for the Shuttle and the International Space Station (ISS).36

The most recent major change in the law occurred in 2004 with the passage of the Commercial Space Launch Amendments Act of 2004.37 This *413 law reflects a belief in a commercial market for "space tourism": flights into suborbital space for individuals willing to pay $200,000 or more for one trip. The 2004 law authorizes private and commercial passengers to engage in space travel and establishes the licensing of private sector spacecraft to bring paying passengers on suborbital flights.

2. Remote Sensing Law

Remote sensing is the imaging of the Earth and its atmosphere from a distance. The first civil remote sensing satellite, Landsat 1, was launched in 1972. Since then, there have been four distinct phases of U.S. remote sensing law.38 In all of these phases, the core issue that has driven the law's development is the proper institutionalization of a technology that was funded with tax dollars and developed by the government, but which also has clear benefits for both the public and private sectors. For weather satellites, this determination has been clear: they are a public good that shall not be subject to commercialization.39 However, for land-imaging satellites, the determination has been tortured and dynamic for three main reasons: human nature, an institutional lag between Cold War and globalization era policies, and technological development in the transition from the industrial age to the information age.40

Regarding human nature, land is where humans live, work, play, and address all kinds of conflicts. Imaging the land therefore raises privacy, security, and economic issues that are less problematic when imaging oceans and the atmosphere. These aspects of land imaging encouraged Congress to ask in many sessions whether the institutional home for land imaging was more appropriately public or private, national or international.

In the 1970s, familiar Cold War rationales encouraged the United States to embark upon civil remote sensing.41 Just like with the Apollo program, the United States aimed to use its space technology to persuade nations to align with it in the then-bipolar world. Policymakers focused on the actual satellites, and they gave little thought to how the data would be stored, processed, and used.

Finally, the ability to understand and use image-processing technology lagged far behind the ability to understand, launch, and orbit a remote sensing satellite. Building and launching satellites is an industrial age "metal-bending" activity with which the U.S. aerospace industry had decades of experience. The seemingly more esoteric requirements of developing, marketing, and maintaining information-based technological products were beyond its ken. Initially, satellite-building companies bid for remote-sensing *414 commercialization contracts as a means of selling satellites to the federal government. They thought only in terms of selling raw data, not information products. It was not until the 1990s when information-age industries could make dramatically increased computing power commercially available at concomitantly decreased costs that ground-based image processing began to look viable outside of government agencies.

The events that followed were analogous to a football game in which the opposing sides try to gain control of the ball before the end of a quarter. In this analogy, the teams were public federal agencies and private companies, and the ball was congressional authorization to process and make available to the public land satellite imagery and data. Each side asserted that it was the most appropriate entity to do so. Which side got the ball depended on the latest iteration of software technology and the last team who influenced Congress before the quarter, that is, session, ended.

From 1972 to 1984 no specific regulatory regime existed despite numerous attempts by Congress to enact a remote sensing law. Then, in 1984, the Commercialization Act42 was passed to commercialize the Landsat system, a federally funded series of Earth-observing satellites that had been in operation since 1972. This law provided for a three-phase process that began by privatizing the then-existing system through a government contract with a private company that would operate it. The second and third phases envisioned a privately built and funded system that would sell data to the federal government at first, but eventually would become a robust commercial environment with a number of thriving competitive companies that did not need government assistance. Because of the reasons discussed above, reality never progressed beyond the first phase. Therefore, driven by failed Landsat commercialization, the high cost of its data, and the reprioritization of national scientific goals, the 1984 law was replaced with the 1992 Land Remote Sensing Policy Act (Policy Act).

The Policy Act recognizes that Landsat data has value to researchers, educators, and nonprofit public interest entities. It returned the Landsat system to the public sector and set a minimum standard of making its unenhanced data available to U.S. government-supported researchers and agencies. The long-term objective goal was to make Landsat data fully available to all users at the cost of fulfilling user requests. This goal was achieved and surpassed when, in 2005, Landsat data was made available to all at no cost. Thus, the Policy Act recognizes the commercial value of land remote sensing, but also acknowledges that commercialization of the Landsat program is unachievable within the foreseeable future and therefore is an inappropriate near-term national goal. Currently, medium-resolution Landsat data primarily benefits research concerning forestry, land management, and climate change--primarily public sector activities.

Attempts are underway to commercialize declassified high-resolution satellite technology that once was used only in government intelligence satellites. Two federally licensed private system operators currently use this technology, but they rely heavily on the federal government as an anchor client, each having a $500 million government contract. A new generation of follow-on satellites is in development, and at least one company claims it will be "independent of any formal U.S. Government commitment as an anchor customer."46 The success of these companies will largely depend on their ability to diversify their clientele and on continuing national security sensitivities.

D. 2000s: Regulatory Refinement
The first decade of the 2000s has been a time of regulatory refinement across all areas of U.S. national space law. To be sure, regulations have existed from space law's inception. However, private space activities and the United States' participation in some international activities have resulted in more detailed and revised regulations in the 2000s due to agencies' growing experience and the lengthy, politically charged regulatory process. This section briefly addresses regulations for remote sensing, commercial human spaceflight, and U.S. participation in the ISS.

1. Remote Sensing
The U.S. Commerce Department's National Oceanic and Atmospheric Administration is responsible for licensing and regulating private remote-sensing

systems. The first regulations were issued in 2000 and revised in 2006.48 They are comprehensive and address all aspects of ground-based and space-based activities, including license terms and conditions, annual operational auditing and recordkeeping, a monitoring and compliance program, and notification of foreign agreements. Two issues concerning these regulations have attracted the most interest from observers. First, who can acquire the data generated by these systems? Second, can the government prevent a licensed operator from acquiring or distributing data in the first place?

As to the first issue, the Commercialization Act required that a policy called nondiscriminatory access be applied to both public and private operators. Nondiscriminatory access, like the rest of remote-sensing law, has a long and complex history. It was originally a U.S. foreign policy intended to address the fears of economic and military espionage felt by nations whose territories could be imaged. Therefore, the Commercialization Act required that all data from Landsat and from federally licensed operators be made available to all who requested it; no one could be denied. However, the Policy Act modified the nondiscriminatory access policy, and now private operators are only required to make their data available to nations that request the imagery of their own territory.50 Private operators can deny their data to anyone else for business reasons and any national security, foreign policy, or other reasons that are contained in the terms of their licenses. The nondiscriminatory access policy still applies in varying degrees to all data, depending on the amount of government funding involved.

The answer to observers' second question is yes: the government can prevent a licensed operator from acquiring or distributing data. This issue is addressed in a 2000 interagency Memorandum of Understanding Concerning the Licensing of Private Remote Sensing Satellite Systems.51 Normal commercial operations can be interrupted for national security or other national interests through a complex decision-making process called "shutter control," which may require a final determination by the President. Although the President did not become involved, after September 11, 2001, the federal government and a licensee entered into an exclusive contract that temporarily limited public access to imagery of Afghanistan and surrounding areas. At the time, many observers in the space community said that this agreement avoided regulatory shutter control, so they dubbed the agreement "checkbook shutter control." Observers on the left accepted this new term because they believed that regulatory shutter control undermined the important principle of government transparency. Observers on the right accepted the term because they thought the regulation unduly interfered with private sector business interests. Both said regulatory shutter control never happened.

However, a close reading of the regulation shows that both sides are wrong: regulatory shutter control was successfully implemented and all but a few images were released to the public as soon as possible, giving rise to a presumption of openness. The regulation specifically provides that in order to limit licensees' activities for national security reasons, licensees "shall, on request, provide unenhanced restricted images on a commercial basis exclusively to the U.S. Government." The result was an appropriate balance of the practical issues of national security and the presumptions of a free market and government transparency in an open society. In an era of sharply divided ideological politics, it is not surprising that disputes like this have made their way to space issues. Unfortunately, in this case, the balanced execution of law in a difficult situation that is likely to occur again has been lost in the fray.

2. Commercial Human Space Flight

Only three nations have successfully placed humans in space, all of whom have had the legal and professional status of "astronaut." Astronauts are specifically selected and trained to achieve scientific, engineering, or political space goals. Like all professionals working for their national governments, they are also paid employees. But many people who cannot become astronauts have dreamt of traveling into space. This desire, coupled with increased attempts to commercialize other space technology applications, has encouraged some entrepreneurs to pursue businesses that can bring people into space on a commercial, for-profit basis.

Space tourism, as it is colloquially called, currently consists of a number of activities. They range from $7,000 rides on a modified Boeing 727 that performs parabolic arcs to create a weightless environment, to $20 million orbital trips.55 Suborbital flights, though yet to occur, are the most well-known type of space tourism and are offered by a number of companies. Virgin Galactic, perhaps the most flamboyant of the companies, joined forces with Burt Rutan and Scaled Composites to "form a new aerospace production company to build a fleet of commercial sub-orbital spaceships and launch aircraft." In comparison, orbital opportunities are rare and require brokered agreements with government-funded facilities like the ISS. Russia has been the most active nation in this kind of tourist trip, but it recently announced that it would not be providing such opportunities for the foreseeable future because of ISS transportation needs.

Against this exciting and dynamic backdrop remains the fact that "[d]espite tantalizing commercial possibilities, the long-term technological and commercial viability of commercial human space flight . . . remains to be seen. Among the factors contributing to the industry's ultimate success or failure will be the application of laws and the formulation of regulations governing the carriage of human beings into space."

Federal regulations written after the passage of the Commercial Space Launch Act Amendments of 2004 require commercial suborbital flight operators to make several written informational disclosures in order to obtain the informed consent of customers, called "space flight participants" (SFPs). "[SFPs] are excluded from indemnification eligibility under the 2004 Space Act and are not entitled to the benefits of liability insurance coverage." And, because commercial suborbital human spaceflight technology lacks an established track record, it is still unclear what information operators must give SFPs so that they are "informed." What is clear, however, is that SFPs, not operators, bear the risks and must be so informed. "There is no doubt that Congress and the federal oversight agency are trying to establish a 'risk shifting' regime as between the SFP and the operator if adequate information is delivered from the operator to the SFP." Further, because of SFPs' likely deep pockets, "it is not unreasonable to expect that a wealthy space flight participant would be named as a defendant in the event of damage claims brought by an injured third party." Given this risk-shifting regime, it is crucial that suborbital space flight operators obtain the SFPs' informed consent--whatever that may be.

Finally, an interesting and important point about space tourism concerns the science upon which the commercial human spaceflight law is based. Current laws and regulations address only suborbital flight, that is trips during which ships leave Earth, go beyond air space to a very high altitude, and then return to Earth, but do not enter into an orbit around Earth. Based on distinctions in physics between the "lift" and "thrust" needed to accomplish such a trip, the law classifies commercial space tourism ships as rockets, not aircraft. It may be expected that as the industry matures, there will be some questions raised about this definition and whether the industry should be regulated by international aviation law and institutions rather than national space law. However, for the foreseeable future the U.S. commercial space flight industry will be regulated by national space law.

3. International Space Station Code of Conduct

The laws governing the complex activities at the ISS demonstrate the interplay between national and international space law. The ISS generally is governed by international law as described in the ISS Intergovernmental Agreement (IGA). However, policy decisions regarding participation in ISS activities are made at the national level by the individual partner countries, including the United States. As a more specific example, the IGA includes a Code of Conduct for the ISS crew that was developed and approved by the partner countries. However, each partner retains jurisdiction and control over its personnel and station elements and therefore implements the Code at its own national level. In the United States, the Code has become part of the terms and conditions of the U.S. astronauts' employment and applies to all NASA-provided persons, including federal employees, members of the armed services, U.S. citizens who are not federal employees, and foreign nationals. In this way, national and international laws are intricately intertwined.

II.

2009: Codification--The Bridge From the 20th to the 21st Century

As the above discussion describes in an abridged manner, a substantial amount of U.S. national space law has been enacted over the past half century. All of it was passed after 1926, the year that United States Code was organized. Therefore, the Code contains no separate space law title. When each statute was written, it was placed in a Code title deemed relevant to the particular activities covered by the statute. Some of the provisions are in Title 15--Commerce and Trade, some in title 42--Public Health and Welfare, and some in Title 49--Transportation.

In 2009, the Office of Law Revision Counsel provided the U.S. House of Representatives Committee on the Judiciary with a proposed bill to improve the structure of U.S. national space law. The bill gathers and restates the laws regarding the national and commercial space programs in a new Title 51--National and Commercial Space Programs, but does not modify the existing laws in any other way. It restates existing law according to the policy, intent, and purpose of the original statutes and improves the law's organizational structure while removing ambiguities and contradictions.

Codification of U.S. national space law is significant for two reasons. First, it demonstrates the maturity of a body of law that was distinctly the product of the twentieth century and the expectation that it will continue to evolve going forward. Codification will also make U.S. national law more accessible to other nations as a model for developing their own space law. Significant segments of U.S. space law, such as shutter control and maximum probable loss, are already the de facto standard for other nations; and scholars in the newly active space nations of the Pacific Rim have also identified U.S. law as a possible model for their emerging space law.

At the time of this article's publication, the codification bill has been passed by the House of Representatives and awaits action by the Senate. . . . . .

7.3.1 Space Law

[Excerpt from Matthew J. Kleiman, Space Law 101: An Introduction to Space Law.]

The Challenges Ahead

The legal regime established by the Outer Space Treaty has been successful in maintaining peace in outer space since the height of the Cold War. However, there are many issues that current space law is not fully equipped to address. The remainder of this article will discuss four of these issues.

Commercial human spaceflight

Humans will soon routinely travel into outer space on spacecraft built and operated by private companies. The first of these flights will be suborbital spaceflights, where the spacecraft launches from and returns to the same spaceport and is in outer space for only a few minutes. By the middle of the decade, private companies are expected to take passengers on orbital spaceflights to the International Space Station (ISS) and privately operated space habitats.

Commercial human spaceflight will raise many complicated legal issues. The FAA is already in the process of establishing licensing and safety criteria for private spacecraft, a process that will continue to evolve as the industry matures. Space companies, legislatures and courts will need to address questions of liability in the event of accidents, the enforceability of liability waivers, insurance requirements, and the sufficiency of informed consent for passengers. Indeed, Florida, New Mexico, Texas, and Virginia have already passed laws limiting the liability of space tourism providers under state tort law.

Space debris

Earth orbit is crowded. As many as 600,000 objects larger than a centimeter (deadly at orbital velocities) are in orbit, and only about 19,000 of those objects can be tracked as of today. Most of these objects are no longer under control and are classified as "space debris." Satellites and the ISS are routinely moved to avoid orbital debris, and occasionally the inhabitants of the ISS are required to take shelter in station's lifeboat as a precautionary measure when an avoidance maneuver is not possible. In 2009, two satellites collided in orbit for the first time. If enough debris accumulates, it will become virtually impossible to operate spacecraft in Earth orbit.

Current space law does not adequately address the space debris problem. Most importantly, liability for damage caused by space debris is unclear. Under the 1972 Liability Convention, countries are liable for damage caused to other spacecraft only if they act negligently. There is no commonly accepted standard for operating spacecraft in a manner to completely avoid the creation of new space debris, so showing that a spacecraft operator acted negligently could be difficult. It may also be impossible to determine who is ultimately responsible for a debris collision since it is difficult to establish with certainty the origin of most space debris. Moreover, because there is no law of salvage in outer space similar to the law of salvage under maritime law, it is technically illegal for one country to remove another country's debris without permission.

Export control reform

Currently, all spacecraft, regardless of whether they were built for military or non-military purposes, are classified as "defense articles" on the United States Munitions List (USML). This classification means that the transfer of space technologies or any information concerning space technologies to any foreign person or country is tightly restricted under the State Department's International Traffic in Arms Regulations (ITAR). These restrictions make it difficult for U.S. space companies to compete in the global space marketplace. In fact, foreign companies sometimes advertise their products as "ITAR-free" as a selling point to other non-U.S. companies.

A more nuanced approach to controlling the export of space technologies will be required for U.S. space companies to maintain their leadership in this industry. For example, non-military spacecraft, such as communication and research satellites, can be moved off of the USML and onto the less restrictive Commercial Control List maintained by the Commerce Department for dual-use technologies.

Flags of convenience in outer space

Under the Outer Space Treaty, each country retains jurisdiction and control over its governmental and non-governmental spacecraft. As privately operated spacecraft become more prevalent, countries will need to determine how much regulation is appropriate to impose on their activities.

Some countries might seek to attract private space companies by maintaining a loose regulatory regime. This might create a "flag of convenience" problem where commercial operators register their spacecraft in these countries to reduce operating costs, just as ship operators often register their vessels in flag of convenience countries, such as Panama and Liberia, to take advantage of lower taxes and lax labor and environmental laws. Spacecraft operating under flags of convenience could create safety hazards for their passengers and other spacecraft.

Conclusion

Commercial human spaceflight, space debris, export control reform and flags of convenience are just a few of the challenges that the space law community will face in the coming years. Other issues, such as property rights to outer space resources, will grow in importance as the commercial spaceflight industry matures. Spaceflight lawyers will be at the forefront of helping the space community to meet these challenges and adapt to the new commercial spaceflight paradigm.

———————————

[Excerpt from Timothy M. Ravich, "2010: Space Law in the Sunshine State," 84-OCT Fla. B.J. 24, September/October, 2010.]

The "Florida Informed Consent for Spaceflight Act"

Florida law is at the forefront of space tourism. Effective October 1, 2008, the Florida Informed Consent for Spaceflight Act, F.S. §331.501 (2010), has regulated spaceflight operators. To avoid liability, private space operators (i.e., "spaceflight entities") must provide a minimum statutory warning statement to outer space passengers:

> WARNING: Under Florida law, there is no liability for an injury to or death of a participant in a spaceflight activity provided by a spaceflight entity if such injury or death results from the inherent

risks of the spaceflight activity. Injuries caused by the inherent
risks of spaceflight activities may include, among others, injury to
land, equipment, persons, and animals, as well as the potential for
you to act in a negligent manner that may contribute to your injury
or death. You are assuming the risk of participating in this
spaceflight activity.

By signing a consent form acknowledging this warning, space tourists in
Florida voluntarily release spaceflight carriers from liability for injury or death
arising from the "inherent risks of spaceflight activities." Of course, a spaceflight
entity cannot escape liability if it commits an act or omission that constitutes
gross negligence or willful or wanton disregard for the safety of the space tourist
that proximately causes injury, damage, or death.36

The convergence of public, private, and commercial space initiatives,
supported by a corresponding (albeit nascent) set of space tourism laws,
evidences an inflexion point in human space activity and potentially greater
accessibility to outer space for the global community. Indeed, to date, the Federal
Aviation Administration has licensed five commercial "spaceports," including
Cape Canaveral. Florida has an outstanding opportunity to lead a new era in
aerospace commerce and the expectation of a commercial space tourism
industry that is comparable to that of commercial aviation is not unreasonable.

"Space Florida"

The creation of "Space Florida" is another important aspect of new space
in Florida. The space, aeronautics, and aviation industries account for nearly
150,000 high-value jobs and more than $7 billion in wages that typically exceed
the state average by 40 percent. Florida Governor Jeb Bush recognized as much
when he created the Commission on the Future of Space and Aeronautics in
Florida in 2005 to "assess and make recommendations on how to strengthen
Florida's role as a leader in space and aeronautics and to maximize the
economic development and job creations opportunities throughout the state."
One year later, in May 2006, the state legislature formally recognized Florida's
unique national role as a platform for global, private aerospace activities by
enacting the Space Florida Act, F.S. §331.302(1) (2010), which declares "the
aerospace industry of this state [to be] integral to the state's long-term success in
diversifying its economy and building a knowledge-based economy that is able to
support the creation of high-valueadded businesses and jobs."

The heart of the Space Florida Act is "Space Florida," an independent
special district created to be the face of state aerospace activities and a single
point of contact for federal and state agencies, the military, universities, and the
private sector.40 Through its president, board of directors, and committees,
Space Florida is charged with attracting, retaining, and growing a healthy space
and aeronautics industry in Florida. Toward these objectives, Space Florida
enjoys significant authorities and economic development powers as a matter of

statutory law. Space Florida has achieved some milestones to date, including preliminary steps to refurbish and commercialize the Kennedy Space Center to house jets that will train would-be space tourists.42 However, significant work remains to be done if Florida is to compete meaningfully with space tourism infrastructures that are developing throughout the United States, including in Alabama, Alaska, California, Colorado, New Mexico, and Texas.

7.3.2 Space Law

U.N. Asteroid Defense, Asteroid Mining
[EXCERPT]
Mining the Final Frontier: Keeping Earth's Asteroid Mining Ventures from Becoming the Next Gold Rush

Matthew Feinman*

INTRODUCTION

"Space: The Final Frontier."

While that phrase has been a call to arms for generations of science fiction fans and space enthusiasts to look up at the night sky in wonder and amazement, it has increasingly become a siren call for private space pioneers. Since man first went to space in 1961, humankind has been pushing the boundaries of experimentation, research, and exploration into the cosmos. Even though Earth's supply of certain rare and precious metals may be

reaching depletion, researchers have found that asteroids are likely to contain vast quantities of these resources.

Today, there are companies attempting to tap into this potential wealth of resources to make them available for use, both on Earth and in space. Before these companies can begin mining, stronger property laws are needed to ensure that the Asteroid Belt of our solar system is not described as the next California Gold Rush and as having the lawlessness associated with it.. . .

Each of these asteroids is projected to weigh roughly two billion tons and "contain 30 million tons of nickel, 1.5 million tons of metal cobalt, and 7,500 tons of platinum." The value of these items, for both private companies and governments around the world could be significant with the dollar value being somewhere in the trillions or higher. With nickel selling for $14,575 per ton, cobalt selling for $26,600 per ton, and platinum at $1,454 per ounce, mining one single asteroid could be more than profitable. The asteroid's resources could easily be used on Earth for the same purposes as on-planet resources, but without having to extract it from the Earth. This is important as all three of these elements can be used in fuel cell technology, as well as in other new, high-tech devices.

B. The Pioneers of the Asteroid Gold Rush: The Companies and Technologies in the Asteroid Mining Industry Two companies have taken early positions in the asteroid mining field, Planetary Resources and Deep Space Industries ("DSI"). Planetary Resources' primary goal is to bring "the natural resources of space within humanity's economic sphere of influence, propelling our future into the 21st century and beyond."

To accomplish this, Planetary Resources currently is developing three pieces of proprietary technology to explore and mine potential asteroids. The first model, a space telescope called the ARKYD-100, can be used to find near-earth asteroids. The second model, called the Interceptor ARKYD—200, studies asteroids that pass between the Earth and the Moon. Finally, the third model, a Rendezvous Prospector, ARKYD-300, is designed to scout distant asteroids and quickly relay back data about its findings.

The vision of DSI, an asteroid mining and harvesting company, is to increase the prosperity of Earth's people by using resources found in space. In addition to asteroid mining, DSI is also experimenting with harvesting solar power by using satellites, which are studying and mining asteroids, to also face the sun twenty-four hours a day. The solar power will allow DSI to keep their technologies working around the clock, without having to rely on external power sources to operate.

DSI currently has five technologies in development to achieve their goals. Two of these inventions will scout ahead and find suitable asteroids to mine, while the final three inventions all have to do with harvesting the asteroids and returning resources to Earth.36 DSI's first invention is the Firefly. The Firefly is a type of probe designed to perform unmanned scouting missions to potentially minable asteroids and to study their properties and compositions. The first Firefly is expected to launch in 2015. The Dragonfly—DSI's second invention and is essentially an upgrade of the Firefly—would be responsible for collecting asteroid materials and returning them to Earth for experimentation, processing, and mineral extraction. In 2016, DSI plans to begin launching Dragonfly satellites to capture and return 50-100 pounds of asteroid material. According to DSI, the availability of fuel while in space will be one of the primary factors that will boost or stall any future manned missions. If DSI can bring carbonaceous asteroids close enough to harvest, the Mars mission shuttles will no longer be as heavy when they launch because they will no longer need to carry all the propellant necessary to get to Mars. The shuttles could simply launch into space, refuel at a DSI facility, and head out towards Mars. The Harvestor, DSI's third invention, will mine for water, metals, and resources for building materials, as well as harvest solar energy. The Microgravity Foundry, DSI's fourth invention, will take asteroid materials and use them as the "ink" for 3-D printing in space, which will then be used to create vital components needed to maintain machinery in space. Finally, DSI's fifth invention, the Propellant Refinery will harvest the water and hydrocarbons found in asteroids and refine them into propellant and usable water. . . . .

III. UNITED NATIONS' LAWS ON SPACE USAGE Once past property laws and customs regarding mining are understood, if we are to go out into space to mine and explore new opportunities, current laws regarding space travel and usage must be analyzed to find any gaps or openings where new regulations can or should be established. The United Nations Office of Outer Space Affairs ("UNOOSA") is responsible for promoting the peaceful use of outer space. UNOOSA is the administrative office for the United Nations' Committee on the Peaceful Uses of Outer Space ("COPUOS"). COPUOS was created as a part of the United Nations General Assembly Resolution 1348 (XIII) in 1958. It was founded to "avoid the extension of present national rivalries into" the new field of space travel, exploration, and usage. Among the treaties, agreements, and conventions COPUOS oversees are the Outer Space Treaty, the Liability Convention, and the Moon Agreement.

A. Outer Space Treaty

The Outer Space Treaty ("OST") was written as an overview of the rules regarding the usage of space, including the Moon and other celestial bodies, to ensure it is shared peacefully and for the benefit of all mankind. The Outer Space Treaty has been fairly well accepted by the international community with 102 Parties and 26 Signatories, out of the total 193 Member States of the UN.

Article II of the OST could hinder the usages of asteroids for mining. Article II states "[o]uter space, including the Moon and other celestial bodies, is not subject to national appropriation by claim of sovereignty, by means of use or occupation, or by any other means." This could mean that, unless the changes advocated for in this Article are put in place, mining claims would not be recognized once companies and governments start to reach asteroids and begin mining.

The countries in which asteroid mining companies are located will be particularly interested in Article VI of the OST. Even though Article VI of the OST is of particular concern to the United States, it may soon be the province of other Western countries, Russia, and China. Article VI reads: "States Parties to the Treaty shall bear international responsibility for national activities in outer space, including the Moon and other celestial bodies, whether such activities are carried on by governmental agencies or by non-governmental entities. . . " It is important to note that once the technology to mine asteroids becomes more widely available and economically feasible, federal governments will probably not want to be held liable for private mining companies' accidents or obligations simply because the private mining company is domiciled within that government's jurisdiction.

———————————

Written Testimony of Joanne Irene Gabrynowicz
Before the Subcommittee on Space of the Committee on Science, Space, and
Technology United States House of Representatives
September 10, 2014

Chairman Palazzo, Ranking Member Edward, Members of the Committee:

Thank you for giving me the opportunity to address H.R. 5063, the American Space Technology for Exploring Resource Opportunities in Deep Space Act (ASTEROIDS). You have provided four questions on specific issues, and I am delighted to respond.

I. "Provide feedback on H.R. 5063, the American Space Technology for Exploring Resource Opportunities in (ASTEROIDS) Deep Space Act."

All of this written testimony is my "feedback" on H.R. 5063. Under this particular question, I will address one issue.

The issue addressed under this section is the need to more clearly identify which Federal agencies will be relevant to private sector asteroid resource exploration and utilization and the specific responsibility of each agency. As written, the only standard used in H.R. 5063 to determine agency jurisdiction is "appropriateness." It does not designate who determines which Federal agency is an "appropriate" agency and for what purpose. Jurisdictional disagreements are the reality of everyday Federal administration and politics. Resolution can be difficult and take a long time.

In general, Federal agencies can use the authority granted to them in Executive Orders and their organic statutes to reach agreements that define the 1 Letter from Rep. Steven Palazzo, Chair, Space Subcommittee of the U.S. House of Representatives Committee on Science, Space and Technology (August 22, 2014) to Joanne Irene Gabrynowicz, Prof. Emerita, on file with author. 2 H.R. 5063, 113th Cong., § 51301, "The President, through the Administration, the Federal Aviation Administration, and other appropriate Federal agencies,..." scope and implementation of their collaborative activities. These can take the form of interagency agreements, memoranda of understanding, etc. However, to be effective and to have the authority necessary to carry out an agreement's terms, the agreement ought to be entered into at a high level. To occur at a high level, there must be practical and political incentives strong enough to bring the agencies to discussions. An example of this is the 2012 Memorandum of Understanding Between the Federal Aviation Administration (FAA) and the National Aeronautics and Space Administration (NASA) for Achievement of Mutual Goals in Human Space Transportation. The Shuttle was retired and responsibility for transportation to the International Space Station (ISS) was shifting from the government to the private sector. The FAA had the authority to regulate; NASA had the human spaceflight expertise; the Nation needed transportation to the ISS. An agreement was reached at the level of associate administrator. It is unclear whether asteroid resource exploration and utilization will command this kind of attention when needed.

Private sector asteroid resource exploration and utilization is an unprecedented enterprise. It will raise novel issues requiring a wide range of entrepreneurial, technical, economic, legal, policy, space situational awareness, and diplomatic expertise. No one agency houses all that will be needed. Absent a clearer statement of which agency is responsible for what kind of regulation, an unpredictable over-regulated environment that relies on ad hoc dispute resolution could be created. It will produce unnecessary risk that is counterproductive to industry.

An interagency structure analogous to the ones that formally govern the Global Positioning System (GPS) and commercial remote sensing5 ought to be considered. These feature a formal agreement among a lead agency and other agencies to work in coordination. Each agency houses a particular expertise relevant to some specific aspect of the industry.

II. "How does current law provide an industry whose purpose is to potentially extract resources from asteroids?"

Current law that addresses an industry whose purpose is to potentially extract resources from an asteroid is an amalgam of space and nonspace laws that address existing commercial activities. United States law regulates launches and reentry; the technology, financing, and behavior of various payloads; as well as related activities, for example, intellectual property and export and import control. Laws were promulgated for specific space-related applications as their technologies matured and were available for commercialization: communications satellites; launch vehicles and services; remote sensing; and, GPS. To the extent that a private asteroid mission uses any of these applications, the laws that govern the applications will also govern the part of an asteroid mission that employs them. For example, an asteroid mission launched or operated by a U.S. citizen will require a launch license from the U.S. Department of Transportation/FAA/Office of Commercial Space Transportation. Depending on its use of communications spectrum and equipment, it will likely also need a license from the Federal Communications Commission. If advertising in space is part of the business plan of an asteroid mission, the advertising must be "nonobtrusive". The Department of Commerce/National Oceanic and Atmospheric Administration is responsible for licensing commercial remote sensing and has already determined that due to the profile of one planned private asteroid mission, it will not require a license. The license requirement could change for other missions with different profiles. 6 Palazzo, supra note 1 at 1. 51 U.S.C § 50901, et. seq. 8 51 U.S.C. § 50902 (9) and § 50911. " '[O]btrusive space advertising' means advertising in outer space that is capable of being recognized by a human being on the surface of the Earth without the aid of a telescope or other technological advice."

There is one Federal Court case regarding an asteroid claim. The plaintiff alleged "ownership" of Asteroid 433/Eros based on a "registration" claim made by him at an online "registry". He asserted that NASA infringed his "property rights" and sought compensation for "parking" and "storage" fees as well as special damages. He sought declaratory judgment for five causes of action based on the Fifth, Ninth, and Tenth Amendments to the United States Constitution. The plaintiff did not raise the issue of whether natural or juridical persons could claim asteroids. The case was dismissed by the District Court and lost on appeal. The Court held that the plaintiff/appellant did not present a claim for which the District Court may provide relief. Despite this relevant body of law there are "gaps" in the law that will have to be raised by private sector asteroid resource exploration and utilization. Some of them are known. Some are not. This will be addressed in the next section.

III. "What are the greatest challenges to legislating and regulating an industry of this nature?"

One of the greatest known challenges to legislating and regulating an industry of this nature is establishing uniform licensing and regulations of the activities on-orbit and at the asteroid. This is often referred to as "on-orbit authority."

Space, itself, is a global commons and is governed by international law. However, as a State-Party to the Outer Space Treaty the United States is obligated to authorize and continually supervise the activities of nongovernmental entities in outer space. The United States meets this obligation through Federal licensing regulations. Objects that go into space are licensed, registered on the U.S. registry and are governed by U.S. law.

At this time, no agency has a specific Congressional grant of on-orbit authority. The FAA has authority to license launches and reentries. It does not have authority to license a private sector object that is intended to stay in orbit for a period of time.

Some contemporary space issues such as orbital debris, space traffic management, planetary contamination by Earth-originating missions, and satellite servicing have caused some agencies to take regulatory action or make internal procedural requirements that go beyond licensing and operating satellites. For example, NASA promulgated a technical standard that seeks to limit the post-operational life of a space object to 25 years. The FCC adopted this standard as a formal rule for satellites it licenses. The FCC also requires license applicants to file a plan to avoid debris creation and deorbiting the satellite at the end of its life. Different procedures are required for satellites in low Earth orbit and those in geostationary orbit. NOAA reviews commercial remote sensing license applications for post-mission disposal on a case-by-case basis. The Planetary Protection Subcommittee of the NASA Advisory Committee has recommended reviewing commercial activities to prevent outbound contamination.

Taken together, these administrative actions demonstrate attempts at a nascent on-orbit authority. There needs to be a specific coordinated grant of onorbit authority to the agencies that are best suited to legislate and regulate an industry of this nature. Finally, as space law follows technological development, legislation and regulations must be flexible to adapt to new technologies.

IV. "What particular issues should be considered in proceeding with legislation of this kind, i.e., potential impacts on international treaties?"

The potential legal impact of this kind of legislation on international treaties is likely to be modest. The potential political impact of this kind of legislation on the international treaties is likely to be sizable. Disagreement should be expected as to the meaning of this kind legislation. Opinio juris is crucial to the development of international space law and the meaning of treaties. Without it, potential legal results cannot be realized. The legal status of some of the issues contained in the proposed Bill is unclear and the concomitant international politics are highly contentious. It is to be expected that opinio juris will be further divided on some of the issues presented in this Bill.

The international space law legal regime contains a number of well-accepted legal principles: nonappropriation of space by Nation-States; a liability regime; and, national supervision of nongovernmental entities, for example. However, what constitutes customary legal principles of international space law beyond the well-accepted principles is uncertain. Only those issues most relevant to private sector asteroid resource exploration and utilization will be addressed here.

There is a distinction between the appropriation of territory and the appropriation of natural resources. The treaty regime is clear that appropriation of territory is prohibited. The treaty regime is unclear and contradictory regarding the appropriation of natural resources. Although there are specific provisions proscribing appropriation there are also specific provisions for the "exploitation of...natural resources". There are also specific provisions that permit the placement of "personnel, space vehicles, equipment, facilities, stations and installations..." needed to extract resources. Further the appropriation of resources appears to be among the rights included in the "use" clauses of the treaties. Taken together, the plain meaning of the word "use" in all of these provisions as well as the clearest and most important treaty provisions31 indicates that the drafters and the signatories approved of the use, including extraction, of outer space resources.

What remains unclear is the ownership status of the resources when they are collected. Unlike other global commons, no agreement has been reached as to whether title to extracted space resources passes to the extracting entity. On the high seas, for example, it is long settled law that title to fish extracted from the ocean passes to the extracting entity. On the seabed "title to minerals shall pass upon recovery in accordance..." with the governing treaty. In the Antarctic mineral resource activities are to be conducted in accordance with the terms of the Antarctic Treaty System. In the absence of agreement legal opinion, opinio juris, is divided regarding the ownership status of extracted space resources. Unsurprisingly, much of it divides along lines of political opinion.

In sum, the treaty regime does seem to allow asteroid resource exploration and utilization entities to extract resources if those activities are consistent with international law and United States obligations. There is no legal clarity regarding the ownership status of the extracted resources. It is foreseeable that an entity's actions will be challenged at law and in politics.

Related to the issue of extraction is the definition of "commercial". In the United States, the term "commercial" is defined by who the actor is. "Commercial" means the "private sector". In most of the rest of the world including in western, industrialized democracies, "commercial" is defined by what the actor does. In those Nations, "commercial" means "generates revenue". In the systems that use this definition, governments can, and do, generate revenue through commercial activities. The definition of "commercial" as it applies to space has also been discussed in the United States Congress. The draft Bill uses the term "commercial entities" and "private entity" interchangeably. This Bill, were it to become law, will draw the attention of the international space community. It would be prudent to clarify that the intent of the law is to facilitate the commercial activities of the United States private sector.

As with the ownership status of extracted resources, there is no legal clarity regarding the superior status of a claim found to be "first in time". World history is filled with examples of terrestrial land claims being perfected by making the first claim to a piece of land and then productively using it. No analogous claims have ever been made in space. Therefore the status of an intentionally asserted superior right to conduct specific commercial asteroid resource utilization activities is a question of first impression.

The world's most successful space-based commercial activity to date is satellite telecommunications. Telecommunications law had to address the issue of "first in time" claims as they applied to geosynchronous orbital slots early in its history. Some Nation-States championed a slot allocation system based on "first come, first-served". Others advocated a slot allocation system based on principles of equity. Satellite telecommunications law is a complex and dynamic body of law the scope of which is beyond the invited testimony. Suffice it to say that these two positions—"first come first served" and equity—continue to compete in a complicated and highly politicized international legal regime. The competition between the positions has included producing some practical results such as distinguishing between access and appropriation as well as creating different categories of orbital allotments and assignments. Attempts may be made to apply these kinds of distinctions to asteroids.

Telecommunications law, per se, is not a precedent for asteroid resource utilization rights. However, as both telecommunications satellite activities and asteroid resource utilization activities occur in space they both have to contend with some of the same international space law principles and international politics. It is to be expected that an assertion of a superior right to conduct commercial asteroid resource utilization activities will be challenged at law and in politics.

Conclusion

H.R. 5063 acknowledges and addresses some issues that arise from the unprecedented activity of private sector asteroid resource utilization. It also acknowledges and addresses some of the United States' existing international obligations regarding activities in space. Not all relevant issues are provided in the Bill, and given the ambiguities existing in space law, it is unlikely that it possible to do so. If made into law, it should be expected that there would be both legal and political challenges to its terms. International space law contains many gaps and ambiguities. It is logical and appropriate to attempt to resolve those ambiguities in favor of the U.S. national interest. At the same time, the final results must be consistent with international law and the obligations of the United States.

I thank the committee for giving me this opportunity and thank you for your work to develop the law of space.

The following cases represent two narratives on civil law in space. The first, involves a private property claim of ownership in space and the other is the only civil case in the subject matter area of asteroids, cited in the previous testimony. In the *Nemitz* case the appeal was dismissed; however, the trial court decision, below, provides more insight into the claims of the plaintiff for infringement of his alleged property interest in the asteroid.

[Excerpt from Matthew, Feinman, "Mining the Final Frontier: Keeping Earth's Asteroid Mining Ventures from Becoming the Next Gold Rush," XIV *Journal of Technology, Law and Policy* (Spr. 2014).[30]

In 1980, Dennis Hope staked a claim on lunar property and established the Lunar Embassy in order to sell plots of land on the Moon. It was Lunar Embassy's belief, and still is, that because the United Nations, the United States Government, and the Russian government did nothing to contest the claim of the lunar property, that Hope was able to copyright his claim and sell deeds to the land. Hope claimed the OST applied only to appropriations by national governments and not the private citizens living in those countries. When making those claims, however, he neglected to realize that four years prior, in 1976; the Second Circuit upheld a UN regulation as being binding on both the member states and its inhabitants.

Twenty-one years after Dennis Hope staked his first claim in space, NASA's Near Earth Asteroid Rendezvous ("NEAR")-Shoemaker probe landed on

---

[30]At file:///C:/Users/visutton/Downloads/140-337-2-PB.pdf .

an asteroid designated 433 Eros. Upon its landing, NASA was contacted by Gregory Nemitz who claimed NASA had trespassed on his property. Nemitz maintained that "his alleged property interest in the asteroid . . . is based on his registration on the Archimedes Institute website and his filing of a Uniform Commercial Code security interest in California as both debtor and creditor with the asteroid identified as the collateral." When NASA and the U.S. State Department informed him that his claims were invalid, he filed a lawsuit in federal court to obtain recognition of his claims. Not only did the court dismiss the case, but the opinion also cited both the Moon Agreement and the OST as proof that Nemitz was unable to claim private property in space. Nemitz attempted to appeal the District Court's decision, but the Ninth Circuit affirmed the lower court's ruling.

(unreported)
2004 WL 3167042
United States District Court,
D. Nevada.

NEMITZ v. United States, NASA
No. CV–N030599–HDM (RAM).
April 26, 2004.

ORDER

MCKIBBEN, J.

Plaintiff Gregory William Nemitz ("Nemitz") filed a complaint on November 3, 2003, seeking a declaratory judgment concerning alleged private property rights on the asteroid 433, "Eros." On January 28, 2004, the Federal Defendants filed a Motion to Dismiss under Rule 12(b)(6) for failure to state a claim.

Nemitz originally alleged five causes of action: violations of the Fifth, Ninth, and Tenth Amendments to the U.S. Constitution, a breach of implied contract, and a violation of Public Law 85–568 § 102(c), (d)(9), which is codified at 42 U.S.C. 2451(c), (d)(9). Nemitz's claims center around his assertion of an ownership interest in asteroid 433, "Eros," and that the spacecraft NEAR, which NASA launched on February 17, 1996, landed on that asteroid on February 12, 2001. Nemitz alleges that this landing infringed his property rights and that he is entitled to be compensated for "parking" or "storage" fees of twenty cents per year. Nemitz sought payment from NASA, and when his claim was denied he filed this declaratory action.

In his Opposition to the United States' Motion to Dismiss, Nemitz conceded the insufficiency of his contractual claim. His remaining causes of action hinge on his alleged property interest in the asteroid, which he claims is based on his registration on the Archimedes Institute website and his filing of a Uniform Commercial Code security interest in California as both debtor and creditor with the asteroid identified as the collateral. While Article 9 of the California Commercial Code sets forth a procedure for the regulation of security interests in property, it does not create a property interest in an asteroid. The Archimedes Institute registration on which he relies disclaims any authority to confer title or rights to property on its registrants. All the website does is create a registry. There is absolutely no legal basis for asserting that such a registry creates a property interest in the asteroid. Furthermore, Nemitz states in his Opposition that he "does not seek a declaration from this Court that he has an ownership interest in Asteroid 433." Opposition, page 2, lines 19–21. Nemitz has thus failed to assert a legally protectable property interest in the asteroid.

A complaint may be dismissed as a matter of law for lack of a cognizable legal theory. *SmileCare Dental Group v. Delta Dental Plan of California, Inc.,* 88 F.3d 780 (9th Cir.1996) (citations omitted). A takings claim under the Fifth Amendment of the U.S. Constitution requires a constitutionally protected property interest. *McIntyre v. Bayer,* 339 F.3d 1097, 1099 (9th Cir.2003). Nemitz has failed to assert such an interest. Neither the Ninth nor the Tenth Amendments provides a cognizable cause of action for the denial of a property interest in outer space. Nemitz's final cause of action is based on 42 U.S.C. § 2451(c) and (d)(9), which is the "Congressional declaration of policy and purpose" for NASA. The specific provisions which Nemitz cites refer, respectively, to NASA's declared purpose to encourage "the fullest commercial use of space" and to preserve the United States' "preeminent position in aeronautics and space." Nemitz has failed to demonstrate that either statement establishes legal basis for his claim of a private property right on an asteroid.

Finally, neither the failure to the United States to ratify the Agreement Governing the Activities of States on the Moon and Other Celestial Bodies, commonly referred to as the Moon Treaty, nor the United States' ratification in 1967 of the Treaty on Principles Governing the Activities of States in the Exploration and Use of Outer Space, Including the Moon and Other Celestial Bodies, commonly referred to as the Outer Space Treaty, created any rights in Nemitz to appropriate private property rights on asteroids. Nemitz has thus failed to assert a cognizable cause of action against the Federal Defendants.

Accordingly, the Motion to Dismiss filed by the United States of America, the United States Department of State, and the National Aeronautics and Space Administration (# 11) is granted.

It is so ORDERED.

Chapter 12

Law of War and Emerging Technologies

7.3.3   Law of War

Intro to Defense Technologies and Law

The history of emerging technologies law would not be complete without considering the rapid growth in technologies that comes with war and conflict. War has played such a significant role in the development of technologies that without our history of wars throughout the centuries it is all but certain that we would not be living with the technological advances we have today. Exceptions are when the government of the United States identifies a top research priority and then ensures resources are driven to the project in order to make it succeed. Examples of this are President Kennedy's Space Program, President Reagan's Star Wars and Pres. George W. Bush's Biodefense Research Program (Centers of Excellence).

The term "military-industrial complex" has been used to describe this relationship of technology development and production reinforced by the need created by the military on the battlefield. The term is often used as a negative connotation that there is a collusion to create opportunities for industry to become wealthy on conflicts generated by the military. The vast volumes of government contracting law is intended to prevent fraud, excess and overpayments, and has been a fairly successful oversight mechanism.

This year, the marking of the 600th Anniversary of the Battle of Agincourt is a celebration for the British who mark this victory over the French. But what is most significant about this battle in the context of emerging technologies and war, is that the longbow was the emerging technology that took the enemy by surprise and is credited with making the British the dominant force on the battlefield that led to their victory and the assurance that no one would be making French the national language in England, any time soon. The longbow was able to shoot at much greater distances and a rapid volley of fire from the 8,000 archers in the battle was newly horrifying.

The United States, War and Technology
The American Civil War Era

In 1862 in the midst of the Civil War, the land grant college system was founded — a system that was to have a profound effect on the American future. It was proposed by

Representative Justin S. Morrill of Vermont and passed by Congress. When the southern states, which had always opposed the formation of the land-grant system, seceded from the Union, the Congress had the votes required to pass the legislation thus forming the first federal university system. In 1863, Congress also successfully passed legislation to establish the National Academy of Sciences, the first formalized institution in the United States, specifically for the purpose of answering questions about scientific issues for the federal government. The legislation passed at an early morning hour without discussion or opposition. The Academy was intended to answer questions about science posed by any government agency. President Lincoln was especially supportive of these developments because of the need for science-based technology to provide support for the war effort.

World War I

World War I is known as the first "scientific" war where technology was a major focus on how to win. During the war, scientific and technical development was accelerated. Trench warfare developed into chemical weapons use, and without gas masks the technology was instantly deadly for troops.

World War II

The narrative of World War II cannot be told without the advances in technology that drove its destruction. The Germans developed new small arms, the Luger, the Howitzer, the Mouzer, and they advanced their rocket technology to enable them to bomb London. The advantage gained from technology that allowed destruction at a distance was developing. The United States was in a race to have the most advanced weapons to end the war. Albert Einstein, migrated to the United States, escaping Germany and joining the teams of scientists who worked on the ultimate weapon of destruction, the atomic bomb. Ultimately ending the war, the dropping on the atomic bomb on Hiroshima, Japan, ended the war, but causing widespread destruction and costs in human lives; yet, the decision to use the destructive atomic bomb was exactly for the purpose of saving American lives that would certainly be lost if the war continued.

The development of antibiotics to treat massive numbers of wounds was accelerated from the more primitive sulfa drugs of World War I to truly astonishing successful antibiotics that saved lives. The benefit from these discoveries carried through to civilian application and most likely responsible for the increase in the average life span of the American and those who procured the new technology.

The United States flew B-17 and B-24 bombers over Germany in a bombing campaign that completed the destruction of control center for Germany.

The application of radar as a defensive technology in World War II was critical to Great Britain. Sir Robert Watson-Watt of Great Britain is credited with building the first radar set in 1935. The United States was inspired to find ways around radar and invented the stealth aircraft technology.

The Korean War (1950-1953)

The first jet war was fought over Korea in an area called "MIG Alley" between the United States and the USSR. When Communist forces invaded South Korea from the North, ground forces began to stream in to repel the invasion. The United Nations were outnumbered but air superiority shifted the power struggle. The jets operated with no Korean jets so they operated largely without any defenses, until the Russian MIGs appeared. F-86 Sabres were shipped from the U.S., only a year and a half old, all hopes were pinned on the new aerial technology.

The MIG was a new technology and flew at high speeds, but it was comparable to the F-86. This came from the common knowledge of the Messerschmitt-282 invented by the Germans during the World War II. This swept wing design led to supersonic flight. However, they used a British engine by Rolls Royce and in a gesture of diplomacy, Great Britain gave some of them to Russia. Learning that Brits were being fired at by a jet powered by their own engines was a harsh discovery.

Buzz Aldrin flew 66 missions in Korea, making him ideal for his selection to move to astronaut.

The Vietnam War (1969-1974)
[chemical defoliants between 1962 and 1971]

The M14 with its 7.62mm ammunition was the early firepower for troops in Vietnam, but the Secretary of Defense, McNamara found it too uncontrollable ad ordered M16s with 5.56mm ammunition. This new technology was not well received by the troops who considered it to be lightweight in comparison to the M14.

The the Bell UH-1 Iroquois, or "Huey" is a symbol of American technology in the Vietnam War. In addition to its versatility and rapid transport of wounded soldiers, it had close-to-the-ground fire power that provided coverage for troops.

An example of how one more step in the technology can result in battlefield superiority, is the F-105 Thunderchiefs. North Vietnam possessed a powerful anti-aircraft defense system and used radar to detect the aircraft. The F-105s were equipped with anti-radar missiles and bombs and once tagged by the enemies' radar, they were able to trace the radar back to its source and locate their target.

Some reversion to primitive Warcraft such as booby-traps and decoys were constant tools of the North Vietnamese, and were often effective and feared. However, these were not the dominant power affecting the course of the war, and technological superiority still ruled the battlefield in this War.

Desert Storm (1991)

The last great battle of the 21st Century brought with in new cutting-edge technologies for war: cruise missiles, stealth bombers and precision guided bombs. Desert Storm was the first time that the United States had engaged in war since the Vietnam War (other than a few hours in Grenada), and the new technologies that unfolded were characterized as "shock and awe" weaponry. A video image of a precision bomb going down into a building target and precisely blowing that structure, only, made it seem that technological superiority would win this war, and it did. The war lasted only three days and remains one of the significant successes of Pres. George H.W. Bush, whose approval rating soared into the high 90s percentile following the victory in Desert Storm.

The Iraq War (2003-2011)

The Iraq War was a very different type of war, with a return to primitive explosive devices, suicide bombers, including improvised explosives (IEDs) and explosively-formed projectiles (EFPs), modes of warfare that are typical in the context of vast gaps in technological sophistication, yet often effective.

The war was one that was criticized for its lack of advanced equipment, vehicles rather than lauded for its "shock and awe" types of weapons that were so memorable to the public from Desert Storm just a decade earlier. Yet, highly trained troops learned to fight in an urban warfare environment where some robotics could be used to detect booby-traps in structures, gaining a significant technological advantage.

Future Wars

The exotic technologies that are being developed for future conflicts include exoskeletons, invisibility cloaks, robots, nano-fabrics, future combined firepower 10-20 times more powerful. But the question that must be asked is whether it will take a war to bring these nascent technologies to maturity and reality?

Technologies that are developed during the course of war have written the history of technology in the world, but with that comes an escalation in killing power. That killing power and the potential effects on civilians was the impetus behind the international treaties that prohibit some of the emerging technologies that were far too devastating and cruel to be used in war. The major treaties addressing these weapons of mass destruction which were all developed from rapid advances in technologies used in wars, are the following:

Geneva Protocol

1928 (entered into force) The "Protocol for the Prohibition of the Use in War of Asphyxiating, Poisonous or other Gases, and of Bacteriological Methods of Warfare," or Geneva Protocol. The treaty prohibits the use of "asphyxiating, poisonous or other gases, and of all analogous liquids, materials or devices" and "bacteriological methods of warfare". However, it prohibits the stockpiling of chemical weapons but only prohibits the use of biological weapons, without limiting the storage, production or transport.

Biological Weapons Convention

1975 (entered into force) The "Convention on the Prohibition of the Development, Production and Stockpiling of Bacteriological (Biological) and Toxin Weapons and on their Destruction," or the short name the Biological Weapons Convention. The treaty bans an entire class of weapons for the first time, finding no acceptable reason to use these weapons.

Chemical Weapons Convention

1997 (entered into force) The "Convention on the Prohibition of the Development, Production, Stockpiling and Use of Chemical Weapons and on their Destruction

Chemical Weapons Convention," which prohibits the production, stockpiling or use of these weapons or their precursors. While there are several reservations (exceptions to the terms of the treaty made by individual nations), and the exemption of chemical weapons like crowd control tear gas, that remain legal under the treaty, it is not a ban on an entire class of weapons like the Biological Weapons Convention.

While there is no treaty banning the stockpiling or use of nuclear weapons, there are dozens of treaties that prohibit the location of nuclear weapons in geographic areas (Carribbean, Latin America, , or in environmental areas (seabed, space, etc.).

The future emerging technologies that may eventually be banned from use are certain biological or biotechnological weapons that affect humans by changing their ability to reason or to make decisions. These weapons are based on pheromones or other brain-affecting chemicals some having only temporary effects and some may have damaging or lethal effects. Similarly, nanotechnologies that can be inhaled or deliver a nano-size injection of anything, are novel technologies not yet specifically banned by any treaty.

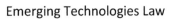

Made in the USA
Middletown, DE
08 August 2021

45289221R00110